VEGETARIAN
INSTANT POT
COOKBOOK FOR EVERYDAY

**Transform the Way You Eat with Delicious Vegetarian
Recipes for Your Instant Pot Pressure Cooker**

600
Recipes

Nartte Benjamin

Table of Content

Chapter 5 Grains Recipes...29

Chapter 6 Soup & Stew Recipes...43

Chapter 7 Chilies Recipes 65

Chapter 8 Snacks and Appetizers 74

Chapter 9 Vegetable Mains...88

Chapter 10 Side Dishes...109

Chapter 11 Pasta and Noodles 125

Chapter 12 Beans, Lentils, and Peas   137

Chapter 13 Desserts 156

Appendix 1:Measurement Conversion Chart 174
Appendix 2:Recipe Index.. 175
References..180

Introduction

Going vegetarian is a lifestyle choice many make and several maintain. It is a plant-based diet that helps your body by lowering your cholesterol, lowering your risk of chronic diseases, and lowering your overall body mass index. While this all sounds positive and healthy, I know first-hand the benefits of just how much a vegetarian diet can transform your life—my name is Nartte Benjamin, and I decided to go vegetarian 10 years ago.

It began as a New Year's resolution to stick to for a month, but it turned into an entire lifestyle overhaul. Not only did I notice my energy levels spike, but I also felt like I had more motivation to get creative with my meals and to get back into a workout routine that toned my muscles. Vegetarianism changed my life for the better. Through my love for this diet, I aim to share my wisdom and favorite Instant Pot recipes that you can create in your kitchen.

Nowadays, everyone owns an Instant Pot. It is an appliance that can do multiple tasks with the simple push of a button. No matter how busy you are or what you enjoy eating, your Instant Pot can help you create meals that are not only nutritious but also delicious. Going vegetarian requires some creativity, especially if you have been a meat-eater for a long time—there are so many ways you can supplement your diet to the point where you won't even miss meat at all.

These recipes are fi lling and satisfying. They use fresh ingredients that will make you feel good about your decision to go green. It is known that maintaining a vegetarian diet is now one of the healthiest in the world. Even those who consider themselves to be mostly carnivorous choose to eat vegetarian once in a while to balance their bodies and maintain the benefi ts of the diet.

Chapter 1: Vegetarian Diet 101

A vegetarian diet consists of eating mainly plant-based ingredients, completely abstaining from the consumption of meat and most animal by-products. Though most vegetarians are okay with eating dairy, it is preferred that the dairy is manufactured in an ethical way that is void of animal cruelty. Vegetarians choose this diet for many reasons and not all of which involve animal rights activism. Aside from its apparent benefits in that category, maintaining a lifestyle that is void of meat can provide you with positive impacts on your physical health, mental clarity, and energy levels.

Types of Vegetarian Diets

If you choose to go vegetarian, there is more than one way to accomplish this. Even within vegetarianism, there are variations of the diet that can work out to your advantage. Depending on your current lifestyle and the foods you enjoy most, you will be able to find one that suits all of your needs.

- **Lacto Vegetarian:** No red or white meat is consumed by a lacto vegetarian. They also abstain from eating fish, eggs, and other fowl. Those who follow the diet are okay with eating dairy, such as cheese, milk, and yogurt.

- **Ovo Vegetarian:** An ovo vegetarian is very similar to a lacto vegetarian. The main difference is that they do consume eggs. Some do not consider egg farming as harmful or cruel as other aspects of the dairy industry, so they feel okay about eating eggs from all animals.

- **Lacto-Ovo Vegetarian:** This is the most typical vegetarian diet you will encounter, as most individuals feel that it is the best way to eat. However, this is all up to your personal preferences. A lacto-ovo vegetarian does not consume meat, poultry, fish, fowl. However, they consume all dairy products and all eggs and egg products.

- **Pescatarian:** Some argue that being a pescatarian is not the same thing as following a vegetarian diet, but others will argue that it is in the same category. When you are a pescatarian, you choose to eat fish/seafood along with dairy and egg products. Still restricting meat and fowl, it is often seen that this is a transitional stage of vegetarianism.

- **Flexitarian:** This type of diet consists of eating mainly plant-based meals with the occasional consumption of meat. This is another diet that is seen as a transitional diet, and most would say that it is not truly vegetarian. If you are thinking of going vegetarian, adopting a flexitarian diet is still impactful because it prepares your body for making the switch to eating mostly plant-based. There are no rules when it comes to this type of diet, but it is important to listen to your body and what it needs. It is a commendable effort to eat this way because you are still eliminating your meat consumption.

Benefits of a Vegetarian Diet

Knowing about the types of vegetarian diets you can choose is important, but understanding why you might choose one is even more crucial. It is thought that up to 70% of all diseases, cancer being one of them, relate to the diet you eat (Vegetarian Times Editors, 2020). Knowing this, what you put into your body matters a lot. Through scientific research, it has been shown that a vegetarian diet wards off diseases. You will have a healthier heart, reduce your risk of cancer, and prevent any further clogging of your arteries.

With a healthy body, this also means you will be able to more easily maintain a healthy weight. Not all vegetarians maintain the lifestyle for losing or keeping their weight down, but it comes with the way you eat. Most foods nowadays are processed or filled with unnecessary fats and sugars. Going vegetarian means eating more whole foods—your newfound plant-based options will fuel you in a way unlike other foods or meat can.

Michael F. Rozien, MD, states that those who go vegetarian have the possibility of living longer. On average, maintaining a vegetarian diet can add up to 13 years to your life! This is a huge statistic that shows just how damaging the typical meat-eating diet can become. Because animal products tend to clog your arteries and slow down your immune system, you are putting yourself at risk of getting sick when you make these foods the center of your eating habits.

An additional benefit of eating vegetarian comes from the way that the diet can assist your bones. When you are eating a plant-based diet, this makes your bones much stronger. Without enough calcium, your body will begin to take from what is already there, weakening your bone density. By eating more green vegetables, tofu, and beans—vegetarian staples—you are giving your bones the chance to become less porous and strong enough to support your skeleton.

When you begin eating more vegetables, you will notice a change in the regularity of your bathroom usage. Being vegetarian does make you more regular, and this is a health benefit. Because your body is better able to process and digest the plant-based foods you eat, you will be able to use the bathroom more frequently and rid yourself of unnecessary toxins.

Vegetarian Foods and Replacements to Eat

You might wonder—what do vegetarians eat? Below is a list of some of the most commonly consumed foods that the vegetarian diet contains. Depending on what type of vegetarian diet you choose, this list can be modified. If you fear that you will not have as many options after your cut out meat, this list should ease your fears. There are so many ways that you can replace animal products in your diet that won't make you feel like you are missing out on anything you crave.

⚜ Dark leafy greens	⚜ Mushrooms (great meat substitute)	⚜ Oats	⚜ Peaches
⚜ Green vegetables	⚜ Beans	⚜ Pasta	⚜ Avocados
⚜ Potatoes/sweet potatoes	⚜ Chickpeas	⚜ Tomatoes	⚜ Tofu
⚜ Squash	⚜ Peas	⚜ Berries	⚜ Seitan (wheat gluten)
⚜ Zucchini	⚜ Grains	⚜ Apples	⚜ Tempeh (soy product)
⚜ Eggplant	⚜ Seeds	⚜ Bananas	⚜ Eggs
	⚜ Bread	⚜ Oranges	⚜ Cheese
		⚜ Pears	

This list is merely a sample of what the average vegetarian might choose to consume regularly. Given such a wide array of choices, it is easy to see that you can put together so many of these ingredients to make delicious recipes in your Instant Pot. For every craving you have, there is typically a way to get the same flavor through the way you decide to season your food.

Mushrooms, eggplant, and tofu are all great direct replacements for your favorite dishes that contain meat. One of the main reasons has to do with the texture of these ingredients—they can all be cooked in ways that make them firmer. Also, they take well to seasoning. Most of the time, it is just the taste of the seasoning that you are craving and not the actual meat itself. You will learn how to cook with these options, realizing that you still have plenty of variety with the meals you make and even the dishes you can order at restaurants.

Vegetarianism is not the limiting diet that a lot of people make it out to be. Those who believe in this idea are typically uneducated at just how many options there are that still taste delicious while being way more nutritious than the typical animal-based diet that Americans consume.

Foods to Avoid

Once you get started with your vegetarian diet, it is not only the obvious ingredients, such as meat or poultry, that you must be wary of. Certain foods that are already prepared can become risky because you don't know exactly what is in them. The following are foods that you should generally avoid because they either contain meat in them or they are cooked while using animal by-products. If you are ever unsure about anything that you do not prepare, it is always a wise idea to ask the cook.

- Refried beans (might contain lard)
- Miso soup (might contain fish broth)
- Caesar dressing (might contain anchovies)
- Gelatin (might contain animal by-product)
- Veggie pad Thai (might contain fish sauce)

These foods will not always contain animal products, but they are notorious for being non-vegetarian. If you do make a mistake by eating something that you mistook for a safe vegetarian option, understand that this is common—many people are going to make mistakes before they learn what they must avoid and why. When all else fails, ask questions about the food you are eating. It is not annoying or troublesome to know what you are putting into your body, and you should feel proud for valuing this.

9 Tips to Success on a Vegetarian Diet

Everyone wants success when they start a new diet but know that you aren't always going to reach this point overnight. Be patient with yourself as you learn these tips and tricks for becoming the best vegetarian you can be. It can take several weeks to break a habit that you might have been relying on for your entire life so far. Be patient with yourself as you explore your options and understand why eating vegetarian is the choice you want to make.

1. **Think About Protein:** It isn't hard to meet your protein needs while eating vegetarian, but you should always make it a priority. To do this, eat plenty of beans, peas, soy, and nuts. You can also get protein from sources such as eggs and dairy if you choose to eat them.

2. **Include Beans and Peas:** Eating both is a crucial part of eating a vegetarian diet. They are so beneficial to your body because they are very high in nutrients and they can be made into many familiar dishes. You can make veggie chili or hummus.

3. **Eat More Calcium:** Dairy products will provide you with excellent sources of calcium for strong bones and teeth. If you want to forego dairy, you can also get calcium by consuming tofu, select breakfast cereals, orange juice, and many dark leafy greens.

4. **Make Simple Changes:** You do not need to be strict on yourself at the very beginning of your diet. This is only going to make your cravings seem stronger and the transition feels harder. Work on modifying your diet one day at a time, even if you can only commit to eating vegetarian a few times a week to start, this is still progress being made.

5. **Modify Restaurant Meals:** Just because you decide to go vegetarian does not mean eating at restaurants is no longer an option for you. Nowadays, many restaurants are very accommodating with their meat-free options. You can also choose to modify some of your familiar favorites by asking them to cook them in a vegetarian fashion. Knowing ingredients you can substitute will help.

6. **Snack on Nuts:** When you feel like you need a substantial snack between meals, reach for some nuts. They are great for keeping you full and for providing you plenty of nutrients to get through your day. Nuts contain healthy fats that will keep you full and make you satisfied.

7. **Get Vitamin B12:** Because vitamin B12 is only found in animal products, most vegetarians take a supplement. This is simple to do, as you can take a daily capsule that will instantly provide you with the B12 you need. Make sure you are aware of this before you start your diet or your body might respond poorly to the sudden lack of B12. If you start feeling lethargic or weak, you might be experiencing a B12 deficiency.

8. **Try Veggie Versions:** There are so many options at your local grocery store for meat-free favorites. From burger patties to "chicken" nuggets, the selection is endless. While these foods might not have the most nutrition because they are usually made solely of soy, they can help you to transition into your newfound diet.

9. **Find a Pattern:** The Dietary Guidelines for Americans offers vegetarian food patterns that can help you figure out exactly what you should be eating and how much of it to consume. If you need more structure in your diet, consulting these guidelines can help you.

Chapter 2: Instant Pot for Vegetarians

Knowing you'd like to change your diet and switch to a healthier, plant-based option is a great realization to make. You can combine this effort with the use of your Instant Pot by preparing meals for yourself that are both tasty and effortless. The best part about using your Instant Pot to cook with is that it does all of the work for you. Instead of having to stand over a hot stove, you simply prepare your ingredients, place them in the pot, and then press a button—the Instant Pot will take care of the rest! You will be able to create wonderful meals for yourself that will not only taste great but will also satisfy your hunger.

Most vegetarians do not consider the use of an Instant Pot to make their meals because there is such a big association with cooking meat. The Instant Pot can cook a wide variety of dishes. From soups to cakes, your Instant Pot will do it all—once you come up with a well-balanced menu to enjoy, you can make a trip to the grocery store for all of the ingredients necessary for your week of food. Shopping this way will save you money and make your life easier because you will not be left wondering what you should eat. A big problem that new vegetarians face is not knowing what to cook, therefore, resorting to junk food that isn't nutritious.

As mentioned, meal prepping is a great option for you because it is easy and convenient. Even on your busiest days, you are giving yourself the option of having high-quality meals to choose from. This becomes especially helpful when you are trying to feed a family. When everybody gets to put in their input on what foods to make, everyone will be satisfied with the new vegetarian meal plan. For those in your family who do not want to make the switch to a 100% vegetarian diet, they will still be amazed at how great vegetarian food can taste, even craving the option from time to time.

When you meal prep with your Instant Pot, this does not mean you have to make week-long quantities of only one dish. You can make several different dishes on the same day because your Instant Pot makes the process that much easier. After prepping all of the food and cooking it up, you can then portion it into serving sizes that will give you a wide array of options to choose from. Knowing that you have these options will keep you motivated to stay with the vegetarian diet, and it won't leave you feeling limited or unsure of what you can or cannot eat.

The more that you use your Instant Pot, the more functions you will discover. Not only can you cook meals in the pot, but you can also make delicious breakfasts and even snacks. Your time spent in the kitchen will feel much more productive and fun, plus, you will feel great about using your Instant Pot to help keep you on track with your newfound vegetarian lifestyle. Even if you have tried to go veggie in the past and failed, this time is going to be different. Combining the diet plan with the Instant Pot gives you an advantage like no other—it makes the process simple for you. When you don't feel overwhelmed about what you are going to eat, you are going to enjoy the food that much more.

Instant Pot Benefits

Knowing the great benefits of eating a vegetarian diet might have you wondering what the benefits are of using an Instant Pot to cook with—there are many. Cooking is something that can feel very time-consuming, no matter how much you enjoy it. When you use an Instant Pot, you will spend a lot less time in the kitchen watching over your food as it cooks. As you explore the functions of your Instant Pot, think about how all of these benefits are going to compliment your vegetarian lifestyle, making it even easier than you imagined.

Saving Time

You have a busy life, and taking a few hours each day to prepare and cook a meal isn't realistic. Between taking care of your family, working at your job, and maintaining your household, you might not have the energy to cook. When you use your Instant Pot, you can cook your food even when you are not home. It is an efficient and great way to have a hot meal every day without the burden of spending too much time in the kitchen.

Convenience

Because you will have more free time, you will be able to spend more of it with your family and loved ones. Knowing that you do not have to be in the kitchen to constantly watch over your meal gives you the freedom to do anything you wish with your free time. You can also use this time to get in some self-care, which is equally important after a busy day.

Energy-Saving

Your Instant Pot is a single appliance that does the work of around seven different appliances. Since you do not need to use all of these appliances, you are going to save energy when you choose to cook with your Instant Pot. This will keep your utility bill down while giving you the peace of mind knowing that you will still receive the same benefits as you would if you were to use all of the pots, pans, oven, stove, or microwave.

Safety

Cooking can become dangerous if you are trying to manage too many things at once. When you put your ingredients into your Instant Pot, you do not have to worry about potentially burning yourself or your food. You won't have to keep a close watch on it, nervous that it will start a fire or overflow. As long as you follow all of the guidelines, your Instant Pot is a safer cooking option that will even be suitable for some of your other family members.

Nutrition

Cooking in an Instant Pot means you get to use a lot more whole ingredients. This is a benefit because you can keep a lot more of the nutrients in the food. By letting your food cook in its own natural juices and sauces, this means you are getting the most out of the experience. When you cook food traditionally, a lot of these vitamins are wasted by the preparation process.

Cleaning

One of the worst parts of cooking a meal is the clean-up process. When you use an Instant Pot, you only have one thing to clean. Many Instant Pot meals can be made while using liners, as well, which means you won't even have to wash dishes. Even if you do need to wash your Instant Pot, it is a lot faster and easier to clean it than it would be to clean all of the various bowls, utensils, and other appliances used in traditional cooking methods.

How to Use

Instant Pot has turned into a huge brand with many different pots to choose from. The following are a few of the most popular models, all containing different functions that can suit your lifestyle.

Instant Pot Duo & Air Fryer

This model can cook traditional pressure-cooked meals, and it also has the capability of air frying foods. Air frying is a popular cooking method nowadays because it is a healthier way to get that crisp texture you crave without using oils and other unhealthy fats to fry your food.

Instant Pot Duo

This is the best-selling model, great for individuals and families alike. It is also affordable, which becomes a factor for most when they are selecting which model suits their lifestyle best.

Instant Pot Duo Nova

With 14 food presets, this Instant Pot makes your life a lot more convenient. This is a great option for those who are beginners with the Instant Pot line, as well as those who want their food to cook quickly. It is great for first-time users because it cooks your food faster than a lot of the other Instant Pot models on the market.

Instant Pot Max

This Instant Pot not only cooks your food very quickly but gives you the option to pressure-cook and to look into canning your food. It has a large food capacity, which is great if you are making many portions or cooking for a lot of people at once. Many love the large touchscreen display that this pot comes equipped with.

Instant Pot Ultra

This is probably the most comprehensive model, a 10-in-1 pot that gives you everything you need, no matter what you wish to cook. You can prepare meals, bake cakes, and even cook eggs in this Instant Pot. This one also comes with accessories, such as a steamer rack, measuring cup, and serving spoon.

Below is a basic description of the steps necessary to in making some of the most common meals with your Instant Pot:

1. Some recipes require you to pre-cook your food before you put it in. For example, depending on how you like your eggs or your potatoes, it can help if you boil them a little before you put them in your Instant Pot. Given the recipe you follow, the instructions will let you know if there is any pre-cooking involved. Typically, your Instant Pot can cook your meals completely with minimal pre-cooking required.

2. Add some type of liquid to the pot. Whether it be water or broth, this is how you get your food to come out tender when you cook it in the Instant Pot. It is a key factor for most recipes, as the liquid is what simmers down as the pressure works to cook your food. When you are cooking raw vegetables, you might need more liquid than if you are cooking tofu, which is usually very soft already.

3. Lock your lid into place once you are ready to begin cooking. The pot clicks into place clearly, so you will be able to ensure you are doing this correctly.

4. Select your setting next. Depending on the type of Instant Pot you have, there are many presets to choose from. Most of the time, you do not need to do any of your calculations because the presets have that taken care of. If you do need to adjust the pressure or time spent cooking manually, your Instant Pot does give you this option. Following each individual recipe, you will be able to better understand how long the food will take to cook and which mode will work best. If you notice that your timer goes off and your food isn't cooked to your liking, you can always add more time, which is a plus. The more that you experiment with the pressure settings, the better you will understand what each recipe requires.

5. Before you open your lid when your food is finished cooking, it is important to determine if you need to release the pressure and let it sit for a few minutes before you fully open the lid. When you release the pressure, this allows your food to slowly keep cooking, if necessary. There are two modes you must familiarize yourself with—QPR (quick pressure release) and NPR (natural pressure release). The first one releases all the pressure quickly to stop the cooking process right away. The second is great for continuing to cook the food slowly. Foods like broccoli and salmon usually require the use of the QPR, and foods like soups and porridges need the NPR.

Vegetarian Under Pressure

Below is a time chart that will serve as your guide to cooking various foods in your Instant Pot. While these are only suggestions, you can quickly refer to this as you experiment with your Instant Pot and new vegetarian recipes.

Vegetarian Food Pressure Chart

Item	Quantity	Pressure	Time
Beans (dry)	1 Cup + 8oz water	High	20-30 Minutes + 20 Minutes NPR
Oats (dry)	1 Cup + 8oz water or milk	High	3 Minutes + 20 Minutes NPR
Rice (dry)	1 Cup + 1 Cup water	High	4-8 Minutes + NPR until liquid is gone
Carrots	1lb + 1 Cup Water	High	2 Minutes + QPR
Potatoes	1lb + 1 Cup Water under steamer basket	High	10-15 (depending on size of potatoes) + NPR 8-10 Minutes
Beets	1lb + 1 Cup Water	High	30 Minutes + QPR
Broccoli	1 Cup + ½ Cup Cold Water under steamer basket	High	1 Minute for crunchy or 2 Minutes for tender + QPR
Broccoli (steamed with no pressure)	1 Cup in a steamer basket + ¾ Cup Water	High	0 Minutes + QPR immediately
Lentils	1lb + 1 Cup Water	High	15-20 Minutes + NPR 20 Minutes
Asparagus	1lb + 1 Cup Water under steamer basket	High	1-2 Minutes + QPR

This chart will get you started by cooking many basic ingredients in a lot of vegetarian recipes. They are all diverse in the way you can prepare them, and how you season them will bring your recipes to life. Of course, each recipe can differ in cooking times, but you can see that there is a basic format for using your Instant Pot to cook these foods. Most of them are finished super quickly, showcasing the drastic difference between using an Instant Pot and cooking them conventionally.

You are going to enjoy how much free time you have as your food cooks, while also having the confidence that it is going to come out tasting delicious. While clean-up is also going to be a breeze, you will not have to dread the aftermath of making any recipe of your choosing. Before you get your Instant Pot, it is a good idea to have an idea of the kinds of foods you will enjoy eating, this way, you have an idea of what you plan on making.

Chapter 3 Basics Recipes

Simple Almond Milk

Prep time: 5 minutes | Cook time: 10 minutes | Makes 4 cups

1 cup almonds
6 cups water, divided

1. Add the almonds and 2 cups of the water to the Instant Pot.
2. Lock the lid. Select the Manual mode and set the cooking time for 10 minutes on High Pressure.
3. Once the timer goes off, perform a natural pressure release for 10 minutes, then release any remaining pressure. Carefully open the lid. Drain the almonds.
4. In a blender, combine the almonds and 4 cups of the water and blend well. Strain through a nut milk bag and store in the refrigerator.

Classic French Beurre Blanc

Prep time: 5 minutes | Cook time: 10 minutes | Makes 1 cup

2 cups dry white wine
1 tablespoon minced shallot
2 cups cold butter, cut into cubes
1 teaspoon salt

1. Press the Sauté button on the Instant Pot and heat the wine. Add the shallots to the pot and simmer for about 5 minutes. Let the wine reduce to half.
2. Whisk in the butter cubes gradually, adding a few at a time to create an emulsion.
3. Once all the butter has been whisked into the sauce, set the lid in place. Select the Manual mode and set the cooking time for 5 minutes on High Pressure. When the timer goes off, do a quick pressure release. Carefully open the lid.
4. Season with salt and serve. Serve immediately or refrigerate until ready to use.

Italian Marinara Sauce

Prep time: 10 minutes | Cook time: 13 minutes | Serves 4

2 tablespoons olive oil
1 large sweet onion, peeled and diced
1 small red bell pepper, deseeded and diced
1 large carrot, peeled and grated
4 cloves garlic, minced
1 (14.5-ounce / 411-g) can diced tomatoes in sauce
½ cup vegetable broth
1 tablespoon dried parsley
1 teaspoon dried basil
½ teaspoon dried ground fennel
¼ teaspoon salt
1 bay leaf
Pinch of dried red pepper flakes

1. Press the Sauté button on the Instant Pot and heat the oil. Add the onion, bell pepper, and carrots and sauté for 3 minutes. Stir in the garlic and sauté for an additional 30 seconds.
2. Stir the remaining ingredients into the pot.
3. Set the lid in place. Select the Manual mode and set the cooking time for 10 minutes on High Pressure. When the timer goes off, do a quick pressure release. Carefully open the lid.
4. Stir the sauce and discard the bay leaf. Use an immersion blender to purée the sauce in the pot.
5. Serve immediately. Store remaining mixture in an airtight container in the refrigerator for up to 2 to 3 days, or in the freezer for up to 1 week.

Simple Spicy Peanut Sauce

Prep time: 10 minutes | Cook time: 5 minutes | Makes 1½ cups

½ cup smooth peanut butter
2 tablespoons maple syrup
2 cloves garlic
1-inch ginger, peeled and chopped
¼ cup rice vinegar
¼ cup sesame oil
1 teaspoon cayenne pepper
1 teaspoon ground cumin
2 teaspoons dried red pepper flakes
1 cup water
Pinch of salt
Pinch of freshly ground black pepper

1. In a blender, combine all the ingredients, except for the salt and pepper, adding the water a little at a time to achieve desired consistency.
2. Pour the mixture into the Instant Pot.
3. Lock the lid. Select the Manual mode and set the cooking time for 5 minutes on High Pressure. Once the timer goes off, perform a natural pressure release for 10 minutes, then release any remaining pressure. Carefully open the lid.
4. Add salt and pepper before serving. Store the remaining mixture in an airtight container in the refrigerator for up to 2 to 3 days, or in the freezer for up to 1 week.

Spicy Red Enchilada Sauce

Prep time: 10 minutes | Cook time: 10 minutes | Makes 3 to 4 cups

6 garlic cloves, peeled
2 poblano peppers, chopped
2 tomatoes, chopped
1 or 2 canned chipotle peppers in adobo sauce
1 tablespoon adobo sauce from the can
½ red onion, chopped
½ cup vegetable stock
1 teaspoon chili powder
1 teaspoon ground cumin
1 teaspoon salt
1 teaspoon apple cider vinegar
½ teaspoon smoked paprika
8 ounces (227 g) tomato paste

1. In the Instant Pot, combine all the ingredients, except for the tomato paste. Stir well. Spoon the tomato paste on top, without mixing it in.
2. Lock the lid. Select the Manual mode and set the cooking time for 10 minutes on High Pressure. Once the timer goes off, perform a natural pressure release for 10 minutes, then release any remaining pressure. Carefully open the lid.
3. Using an immersion blender, blend the sauce until smooth.
4. Serve immediately or refrigerate until ready to use.

Butternut Squash and Basil Sauce

Prep time: 10 minutes | Cook time: 20 minutes | Makes 4 to 4½ cups

1 small butternut squash, peeled and cubed
2 medium tomatoes, quartered
2 garlic cloves, peeled
¼ to ½ cup water
4 ounces (113 g) tomato paste
1 bay leaf
1 teaspoon salt
½ teaspoon freshly ground black pepper
¼ teaspoon baking soda
Pinch of red pepper flakes
½ cup fresh sweet basil leaves, torn
1 to 2 tablespoons fresh Italian parsley leaves

1. In the Instant Pot, combine the squash, tomatoes, garlic, and water. Top with the tomato paste, bay leaf, salt, pepper, baking soda, and red pepper flakes. Do not stir.
2. Lock the lid. Select the Manual mode and set the cooking time for 20 minutes on High Pressure. Once the timer goes off, perform a natural pressure release for 10 to 15 minutes, then release any remaining pressure. Carefully open the lid.
3. Let the sauce cool for a few minutes. Discard the bay leaf and add the basil and parsley. Using an immersion blender, blend the sauce until smooth.
4. Serve immediately or refrigerate until ready to use.

White Sauce

Prep time: 5 minutes | Cook time: 8 to 9 minutes | Makes 3 cups

½ cup butter
½ cup all-purpose flour
4 cups unsweetened

soy milk, warmed
1 teaspoon salt
1 teaspoon freshly ground black pepper

1. Press the Sauté button on the Instant Pot and melt the butter. Add the flour and stir for 1 to 2 minutes to create a roux.
2. Gradually add the warmed milk to the pot, whisking until there are no lumps.
3. Lock the lid. Select the Manual mode and set the cooking time for 7 minutes on High Pressure. Once the timer goes off, perform a natural pressure release for 10 minutes, then release any remaining pressure. Carefully open the lid.
4. Season with salt and pepper. Serve immediately. Store any remaining mixture in an airtight container in the refrigerator for up to 2 days.

Red Pepper Sauce

Prep time: 5 minutes | Cook time: 7 minutes | Serves 4

2 cups roasted red peppers
2 cups vegetable broth
2 tablespoons red wine vinegar
2 tablespoons extra-

virgin olive oil
1 teaspoon garlic powder
½ cup fresh basil
Pinch of salt
Pinch of freshly ground black pepper

1. Add the red peppers, broth, vinegar, and oil to a food processor and purée until smooth. Pour the mixture into the Instant Pot.
2. Add the garlic powder to the pot and stir.
3. Lock the lid. Select the Manual mode and set the cooking time for 7 minutes on High Pressure. Once the timer goes off, perform a natural pressure release for 10 minutes, then release any remaining pressure. Carefully open the lid.
4. Add the basil, salt and pepper before serving. Store remaining mixture in an airtight container for up to 2 to 3 days in the refrigerator or 1 week in the freezer.

Sweet Grape Jelly

Prep time: 5 minutes | Cook time: 3 minutes | Makes 5 cups

5 cups grape juice
2 (1.75-ounce / 50-g) packages dry

pectin
½ cup granulated sugar

1. Press the Sauté button on the Instant Pot. Add the grape juice and pectin to the pot and stir to combine.
2. Set the lid in place. Select the Manual mode and set the cooking time for 3 minutes on High Pressure. When the timer goes off, do a quick pressure release. Carefully open the lid.
3. Let cool at room temperature 24 hours before ladling into sterilized glass containers or jars. Refrigerate for up to 5 weeks or freeze for up to 8 months.

Au Jus

Prep time: 5 minutes | Cook time: 15 to 19 minutes | Makes 1½ cups

1 tablespoon butter
1 shallot, peeled and minced
1 tablespoon all-purpose flour
2 cups vegetable broth

1 cup dry red wine
¼ teaspoon liquid smoke
1 teaspoon salt
1 teaspoon freshly ground black pepper

1. Press the Sauté button on the Instant Pot and melt the butter. Add the shallots and sauté for about 2 to 3 minutes, or until golden brown. Stir in the flour, 1 to 2 minutes to create a roux.
2. Add the broth, red wine, liquid smoke, salt, and pepper to the pot and whisk until blended.
3. Lock the lid. Select the Manual mode and set the cooking time for 7 minutes on High Pressure. Once the timer goes off, perform a natural pressure release for 10 minutes, then release any remaining pressure. Carefully open the lid.
4. Press the Sauté button on the pot and continue to simmer the au jus for about 5 to 7 minutes, or until reduced by half.
5. Serve immediately or refrigerate until ready to use.

Lemony Marinara Sauce

Prep time: 10 minutes | Cook time: 9 to 11 minutes | Serves 4

2 tablespoons olive oil
½ medium yellow onion, peeled and diced
2 cloves garlic, minced
2 (14.5-ounce / 411-g) cans diced tomatoes
½ teaspoon granulated sugar
1 tablespoon tomato paste
⅓ cup water
1 tablespoon fresh lemon juice
2 tablespoons chopped fresh basil
Pinch of salt
Pinch of freshly ground black pepper

1. Press the Sauté button on the Instant Pot and heat the oil. Add the onion and sauté for about 3 to 5 minutes, or until golden brown. Add the garlic and sauté for an additional 30 seconds.
2. Add the tomatoes, sugar, tomato paste, and water to the pot.
3. Lock the lid. Select the Manual mode and set the cooking time for 6 minutes on High Pressure. Once the timer goes off, perform a natural pressure release for 10 minutes, then release any remaining pressure. Carefully open the lid.
4. Stir in the lemon juice, basil, salt and pepper. Store in an airtight container in the refrigerator for 2 to 3 days, or in the freezer for up to 1 week.

Celery and Pepper Red Beans

Prep time: 10 minutes | Cook time: 43 to 45 minutes | Serves 8

3 tablespoons butter
1 cup diced white onion
1 cup diced green bell pepper
1 cup diced celery
2 cloves garlic, minced
2¼ cups dried red kidney beans
5 cups vegetable broth
1 teaspoon liquid smoke
½ teaspoon Worcestershire sauce
1 teaspoon hot sauce
½ teaspoon dried thyme
1 teaspoon cayenne pepper
2 bay leaves
2 teaspoons salt

1. Press the Sauté button on the Instant Pot and melt the butter. Add the onions, bell pepper, celery, and garlic. Stir-fry for 3 to 5 minutes, or until onions are translucent.
2. Stir in the remaining ingredients.
3. Lock the lid. Select the Bean/Chili mode and set the cooking time for 30 minutes on High Pressure. Once the timer goes off, perform a natural pressure release for 10 minutes, then release any remaining pressure. Carefully open the lid.
4. If a thicker consistency is desired, press the Sauté button and simmer the bean mixture for 10 minutes to thicken.
5. Remove the bay leaves before serving. Serve immediately.

Balsamic Fresh Tomato Sauce

Prep time: 5 minutes | Cook time: 20 minutes | Makes 4 cups

2 tablespoons olive oil
2 cloves garlic, minced
2½ pounds (1.1 kg) vine-ripened tomatoes, peeled, diced and juice retained
1 tablespoon balsamic vinegar
1 teaspoon dried basil
1 teaspoon dried parsley
½ teaspoon granulated sugar
Pinch of salt
Pinch of freshly ground black pepper

1. Press the Sauté button on the Instant Pot and heat the oil. Add the garlic to the pot and sauté for 30 seconds, or until fragrant.
2. Add the tomatoes to the pot along with their juice. Add the remaining ingredients to the pot.
3. Lock the lid. Select the Manual mode and set the cooking time for 10 minutes on High Pressure. Once the timer goes off, perform a natural pressure release for 15 minutes, then release any remaining pressure. Carefully open the lid.
4. Stir the sauce. If you prefer a thicker sauce, press the Sauté button and simmer uncovered for 10 minutes, or until it reaches the desired thickness.
5. Serve immediately or refrigerate until ready to use.

Super Easy Caramel Sauce

Prep time: 5 minutes | Cook time: 45 minutes | Serves 4 to 6

1 (11-ounce / 312-g) can sweetened condensed coconut milk

1 cup water
1 teaspoon coarse sea salt (optional)

1. Peel the label off the can and place the can on a trivet and into your Instant Pot. Pour in the water.
2. Lock the lid. Select the Manual mode and set the cooking time for 45 minutes on High Pressure. Once the timer goes off, perform a natural pressure release for 20 minutes, then release any remaining pressure. Carefully open the lid.
3. Remove the can and trivet. Set aside until cool enough to handle.
4. Once cooled, open the can and pour the caramel sauce into a glass jar for storage. For a salted caramel, stir in the sea salt.

Celery and Carrot Broth

Prep time: 5 minutes | Cook time: 30 minutes | Makes 4 cups

3 large stalks celery, cut in half
2 large yellow onions, peeled and halved
2 medium carrots, peeled and cut into large pieces

10 whole peppercorns
1 head garlic, cloves separated and peeled
1 bay leaf
6 cups water

1. Add all the ingredients to the Instant Pot and stir to combine.
2. Lock the lid. Select the Manual mode and set the cooking time for 30 minutes on High Pressure. Once the timer goes off, perform a natural pressure release for 20 minutes, then release any remaining pressure. Carefully open the lid.
3. Strain the stock through a fine-mesh strainer or through cheesecloth placed in a colander.
4. Store in an airtight container in the refrigerator for 2 to 3 days, or in the freezer for up to 3 months.

Vanilla-Cinnamon Applesauce

Prep time: 10 minutes | Cook time: 5 minutes | Serves 6 to 8

3 pounds (1.4 kg) apples, cored and quartered
$1/_3$ cup water
1 teaspoon ground cinnamon

1 teaspoon freshly squeezed lemon juice
1 teaspoon vanilla extract
½ teaspoon salt

1. Add all the ingredients to the Instant Pot and stir to combine.
2. Lock the lid. Select the Manual mode and set the cooking time for 5 minutes on High Pressure. Once the timer goes off, perform a natural pressure release for 10 minutes, then release any remaining pressure. Carefully open the lid.
3. Using an immersion blender, blend the applesauce until smooth.
4. Serve immediately or refrigerate until ready to use.

Homemade Vegetable Bouillon

Prep time: 5 minutes | Cook time: 10 minutes | Makes 4 cups

2 large onions, quartered
½ cup water
6 medium carrots, cut into lengths to fit the Instant Pot
4 celery stalks, cut into lengths to fit

the Instant Pot
8 sprigs fresh thyme
1 sprig fresh rosemary
1 cup nutritional yeast
Salt, to taste (optional)

1. Add the onions, water, carrots, celery, thyme and rosemary to the Instant Pot.
2. Lock the lid. Select the Manual mode and set the cooking time for 10 minutes on High Pressure. Once the timer goes off, perform a natural pressure release for 10 minutes, then release any remaining pressure. Carefully open the lid.
3. Scoop the cooked veggies and broth into a blender and add the nutritional yeast. Blend until smooth. Add salt and blend again.
4. Store in the refrigerator up to a week or put in ice-cube trays and freeze.

Fresh Garden Tomato Salsa

Prep time: 5 minutes | Cook time: 5 minutes | Makes 6 to 8 cups

8 large tomatoes, roughly chopped
6 garlic cloves, finely diced
2 jalapeño peppers, deseeded and diced
1 red bell pepper, diced
1 small red onion, diced
1 small yellow onion, diced
1 tablespoon ground cumin
3 to 4 teaspoons salt
½ teaspoon freshly ground black pepper
½ teaspoon baking soda
¼ cup tomato paste
2 tablespoons freshly squeezed lime juice
1 teaspoon chopped fresh cilantro leaves

1. In the Instant Pot, stir together the tomatoes, garlic, jalapeños, bell pepper, red onion, yellow onion, cumin, salt, pepper, and baking soda.
2. Lock the lid. Select the Manual mode and set the cooking time for 5 minutes on High Pressure. Once the timer goes off, perform a natural pressure release for 10 minutes, then release any remaining pressure. Carefully open the lid.
3. Stir in the tomato paste, lime juice and cilantro.
4. Serve chilled or at room temperature.

Andouille-Style Sausage

Prep time: 10 minutes | Cook time: 35 minutes | Makes 8 large links

1½ cups vital wheat gluten flour
¼ cup nutritional yeast
1 teaspoon garlic powder
1 teaspoon cayenne powder
1 teaspoon dried marjoram
1 teaspoon onion powder
1 teaspoon dried thyme
1 teaspoon salt
½ teaspoon ground black pepper
¼ teaspoon ground allspice
1½ cups plus 1 cup water, divided

1. Add all the ingredients, except for 1 cup water to a mixer and mix on low speed for about 5 minutes. Knead in a bread maker or by hand until the dough begins to smooth out.

2. Cut into 8 equal pieces and roll into logs. Wrap in parchment paper and add to a large foil packet.
3. Add the trivet to the Instant Pot and pour in 1 cup of the water. Place the packets on top.
4. Lock the lid. Select the Manual mode and set the cooking time for 35 minutes on High Pressure. Once the timer goes off, perform a natural pressure release for 20 minutes, then release any remaining pressure. Carefully open the lid.
5. Serve.

Baby Bella Mushroom Gravy

Prep time: 5 minutes | Cook time: 24 to 26 minutes | Serves 4 to 6

1 tablespoon olive oil
8 ounces (227 g) baby bella mushrooms, diced
½ small sweet onion, diced
2 garlic cloves, minced
2 tablespoons Worcestershire sauce
1 teaspoon Dijon mustard
1 teaspoon rubbed sage
1¼ cups vegetable stock, divided
¼ cup red wine
1 tablespoon cornstarch

1. Press the Sauté button on the Instant Pot and heat the oil. Add the mushrooms and onion. Sauté for 2 to 3 minutes, stirring frequently. Add the garlic. Cook, stirring so it doesn't burn, for 30 seconds more.
2. Add the Worcestershire sauce, mustard, sage, ¾ cup of the stock and the red wine.
3. Lock the lid. Select the Manual mode and set the cooking time for 20 minutes on High Pressure. Once the timer goes off, perform a natural pressure release for 10 minutes, then release any remaining pressure.
4. In a small bowl, whisk the remaining ½ cup of the stock and cornstarch. Carefully remove the lid and stir this slurry into the gravy.
5. Select Sauté mode again and simmer the gravy for 2 to 3 minutes, or until thickened.

Mushroom and Carrot Broth

Prep time: 10 minutes | Cook time: 20 minutes | Makes 8 cups

4 medium carrots, peeled and cut into large pieces
2 large leeks, trimmed and cut into large pieces
2 large yellow onions, peeled and quartered

1 large stalk celery, chopped
2 cups sliced button mushrooms
5 whole cloves garlic
Pinch of dried red pepper flakes
8½ cups water

1. Add all the ingredients to the Instant Pot and stir to combine.
2. Lock the lid. Select the Manual mode and set the cooking time for 20 minutes on High Pressure. Once the timer goes off, perform a natural pressure release for 15 minutes, then release any remaining pressure. Carefully open the lid.
3. Strain the broth through a fine-mesh strainer or through cheesecloth placed in a colander.
4. Store in a covered container in the refrigerator or freezer.

Instant Pot Soy Yogurt

Prep time: 5 minutes | Cook time: 8 hours | Makes 4 cups

1 (32-ounce / 907-g) container plain unsweetened soy milk

1 packet yogurt starter
1 tablespoon tapioca starch

1. Whisk together the soy milk, starter and starch in a mixing bowl. Pour the mixture into small glass jars. Sit them right on the pot bottom.
2. Set the lid in place. Select the Yogurt mode and set the cooking time for 8 hours. When the timer goes off, do a quick pressure release. Carefully open the lid.
3. Serve chilled. Store in the fridge for up to 10 days.

Cauliflower and Cashew Sour Cream

Prep time: 5 minutes | Cook time: 3 minutes | Makes 1 cup

2 cups cauliflower florets
2 cups water
3 tablespoon cashews
1 teaspoon

nutritional yeast
1 teaspoon lemon juice
½ teaspoon apple cider vinegar
Salt, to taste

1. Add the cauliflower, water and cashews to the Instant Pot.
2. Set the lid in place. Select the Manual mode and set the cooking time for 3 minutes on High Pressure. When the timer goes off, do a quick pressure release. Carefully open the lid.
3. Drain, reserving the liquid for blending.
4. In a blender, combine the cauliflower and cashews along with the nutritional yeast, lemon juice, apple cider vinegar and 1 teaspoon of the cooking liquid. Blend, scrape down the sides and add more cooking liquid if needed. Blend until smooth. Season with salt.
5. Serve immediately or refrigerate until ready to use.

Carrot and White Bean Dip

Prep time: 10 minutes | Cook time: 3 minutes | Makes 3 cups

2 cups cooked white beans
4 or 5 carrots, scrubbed or peeled and chopped
1 cup water
1 or 2 jalapeño peppers, deseeded and chopped
2 tablespoons tahini
Grated zest and juice of 1 lime
1 teaspoon smoked paprika
1 to 2 tablespoons olive oil
½ to ¾ teaspoon salt
Freshly ground black pepper, to taste

1. In the Instant Pot, combine the white beans, carrots, and water.
2. Set the lid in place. Select the Manual mode and set the cooking time for 3 minutes on High Pressure. When the timer goes off, do a quick pressure release. Carefully open the lid.
3. Drain any excess water and transfer the beans and carrots to a food processor.
4. Add the jalapeños, tahini, lime zest and juice, and paprika. Purée, adding the olive oil, 1 tablespoon at a time, to achieve the desired texture. Taste and season with the salt and pepper.
5. Serve immediately or refrigerate until ready to use.

Artichoke-Spinach Dip

Prep time: 5 minutes | Cook time: 4 minutes | Makes 2½ cups

1 cup raw cashews
1 cup unsweetened coconut milk
1 tablespoon nutritional yeast
1½ tablespoons apple cider vinegar
1 teaspoon onion powder
½ teaspoon garlic powder
½ to 1 teaspoon salt
1 (14-ounce / 397-g) can artichoke hearts in water
2 cups fresh spinach
1 cup water

1. In a blender, combine the cashews, milk, nutritional yeast, vinegar, onion powder, garlic powder, and salt. Purée until smooth and creamy, about 1 minute. Add the artichoke hearts and spinach and pulse a few times to chop up a bit. Pour the mixture into a baking pan.
2. Pour the water and insert the trivet in the Instant Pot. Put the pan on the trivet.
3. Lock the lid. Select the Manual mode and set the cooking time for 4 minutes on High Pressure. Once the timer goes off, perform a natural pressure release for 10 minutes, then release any remaining pressure. Carefully open the lid.
4. Let the baking pan cool for a few minutes before carefully lifting it out of the pot with oven mitts.
5. Transfer the dip to a bowl and serve.

Chapter 4 Breakfasts Recipes

Almond Honey Quinoa Breakfast Bowl

Prep time: 5 minutes | Cook time: 5 minutes | Serves 4

2 cups water
1 cup quinoa
1 tablespoon coconut oil
¼ teaspoon salt
1 cup almond butter
2 cups diced banana
2 tablespoons honey
¼ teaspoon ground cinnamon

1. Combine water, quinoa, oil, and salt in the pot.
2. Lock the lid. Select the Manual mode and set the cooking time for 5 minutes at High Pressure.
3. When the timer beeps, perform a quick pressure release. Carefully remove the lid.
4. Stir in the butter and divide quinoa among four bowls. Top with banana and drizzle with honey. Sprinkle with cinnamon and serve.

Mini Egg Frittatas

Prep time: 5 minutes | Cook time: 5 minutes | Serves 2

3 eggs, beaten
½ cup coconut milk
¼ cup kale
¼ cup chopped
broccoli
Salt and pepper, to taste
1 cup water

1. Stir together the beaten eggs, milk, kale, broccoli, salt, and pepper in a large bowl, then pour the mixture evenly into silicone molds.
2. Pour the water into the Instant Pot and insert a trivet. Put the silicone molds on top.
3. Lock the lid. Select the Manual mode and set the cooking time for 5 minutes at High Pressure.
4. When the timer beeps, perform a quick pressure release. Carefully remove the lid.
5. Serve warm.

Blueberry Breakfast Cobbler

Prep time: 5 minutes | Cook time: 15 minutes | Serves 4

2 apples, diced
2 peaches, diced
1 cup blueberries
4 tablespoons honey
2 tablespoons oil
½ teaspoon nutmeg
½ cup unsweetened shredded coconut
4 tablespoons sunflower seeds
Cream, for serving

1. Place the fruits into the Instant Pot. Add honey, oil, and nutmeg and mix well.
2. Secure the lid. Select the Steam mode and set the cooking time for 10 minutes at High Pressure.
3. Once cooking is complete, do a quick pressure release. Carefully open the lid.
4. Remove the cooked fruit. Add the coconut and sunflower seeds into the residual liquid. Press the Sauté button and cook for 5 minutes, stirring well.
5. Serve topped with the cream.

Swiss Chard Egg Muffins

Prep time: 5 minutes | Cook time: 8 minutes | Serves 2

1½ cups water
2 eggs
⅛ teaspoon pepper seasoning
4 tablespoons
shredded goat cheese
½ cup chopped Swiss chard
1 green onion, diced

1. Pour the water into the Instant Pot and insert a trivet.
2. Beat the eggs in a bowl and sprinkle with the pepper seasoning.
3. Divide the cheese, chard, and green onion between muffin cups. Pour the beaten eggs into each muffin cup and mix. Put the muffin cups on the trivet.
4. Secure the lid. Select the Manual mode and set the cooking time for 8 minutes at High Pressure.
5. Once cooking is complete, do a quick pressure release. Carefully open the lid.
6. Let rest for 5 minutes before serving.

Cheesy Omelet Quiche

Prep time: 5 minutes | Cook time: 30 minutes | Serves 2

1½ cups water
Cooking spray
½ cup milk
2 eggs, beaten
Salt and black pepper, to taste
1 green onion,
chopped
½ cup diced jalapeño pepper
2 tablespoons shredded Cheddar cheese

1. Pour the water into the Instant Pot and insert a trivet. Coat a baking dish with cooking spray.
2. In a bowl, whisk together the milk, eggs, salt, and black pepper. Add the green onion, jalapeño, and cheese and stir well. Pour the mixture into the prepared baking dish and cover with foil. Place the dish on the trivet.
3. Secure the lid. Select the Manual mode and set the cooking time for 30 minutes at High Pressure.
4. Once cooking is complete, do a quick pressure release. Carefully open the lid.
5. Serve warm.

Cheesy Egg Bake

Prep time: 2 minutes | Cook time: 7 minutes | Serves 4

8 eggs
Cooking spray
4 tablespoons coconut milk
Salt and pepper, to
taste
2 cups grated goat cheese
1 cup water

1. Coat a bowl with cooking spray and break the eggs into the bowl. Add milk, salt, and pepper and beat. Add the cheese and mix well.
2. Pour the water into the Instant Pot and insert a trivet. Place the bowl on the trivet.
3. Secure the lid. Select the Steam mode and set the cooking time for 7 minutes at Low Pressure.
4. Once cooking is complete, do a quick pressure release. Carefully open the lid.
5. Serve warm.

Kale and Bell pepper Egg Cups

Prep time: 5 minutes | Cook time: 6 minutes | Serves 2

4 eggs
¼ teaspoon salt
¼ cup grated goat cheese
Black pepper, to taste
½ handful kale
½ red bell pepper
1 spring onion, chopped
Cooking spray
1 cup water

1. Grease 2 custard cups with cooking spray. In a bowl, whisk the eggs, salt, cheese, and pepper. Evenly divide the kale, bell pepper, and spring onion among the custard cups. Pour the egg mixture over the veggies.
2. Pour the water into the Instant Pot and insert a trivet. Place the custard cups on the trivet.
3. Secure the lid. Select the Manual mode and set the cooking time for 6 minutes at High Pressure.
4. Once cooking is complete, do a quick pressure release. Carefully open the lid.
5. Let rest for 5 minutes before serving.

Apple Cinnamon Porridge

Prep time: 5 minutes | Cook time: 8 minutes | Serves 4

1½ cups water
1 cup quinoa, rinsed
1 apple, chopped
2 tablespoons ground cinnamon
2 tablespoons maple syrup
½ teaspoon vanilla extract
¼ to ½ teaspoon salt
½ to 1 cup coconut milk

1. Stir together the water, quinoa, apple, cinnamon, maple syrup, vanilla, and salt in the Instant Pot.
2. Lock the lid. Select the Manual mode and set the cooking time for 8 minutes at High Pressure.
3. When the timer beeps, perform a natural pressure release for 10 minutes, then release any remaining pressure. Carefully remove the lid.
4. Stir in as much milk as needed to make it creamy. Serve warm.

Greek Spinach Rice

Prep time: 10 minutes | Cook time: 8 minutes | Serves 4

2 tablespoons olive oil
2 cups chopped spring onions or green onions
3 cloves garlic, minced
1½ cups packed chopped fresh spinach
1 cup basmati rice,

rinsed and drained
¼ cup chopped fresh dill
1 tablespoon tomato paste
1 teaspoon kosher salt
1 cup water
1 tablespoon red wine vinegar

1. Set your Instant Pot to Sauté and heat the olive oil. Once the oil is hot, add the onions and garlic and cook for about 30 seconds.
2. Stir in the spinach, rice, dill, tomato paste, salt, and water.
3. Lock the lid. Select the Manual mode and set the cooking time for 4 minutes at High Pressure.
4. When the timer beeps, perform a natural pressure release for 10 minutes, then release any remaining pressure. Carefully remove the lid.
5. Stir in the vinegar and serve warm.

Creamy Peach and Pecan Oatmeal

Prep time: 5 minutes | Cook time: 7 minutes | Serves 4

1 cup old-fashioned oats
1 cup plant-based milk
1 cup water
4 ripe peaches, peeled, pitted, and diced

2 tablespoons chopped pecans
2 tablespoons packed light brown sugar
¼ teaspoon vanilla extract
Pinch of salt

1. Combine all the ingredients in the Instant Pot.
2. Secure the lid. Select the Manual mode and set the cooking time for 7 minutes at High Pressure.
3. Once cooking is complete, do a quick pressure release. Carefully open the lid.
4. Stir the oatmeal and ladle into bowls. Serve warm.

Pumpkin Spice Carrot Cake Oatmeal

Prep time: 10 minutes | Cook time: 10 minutes | Serves 8

4½ cups water
2 cups shredded carrots
1 cup steel-cut oats
1 (20-ounce/ 567-g) can crushed pineapple, undrained

1 cup raisins
1 teaspoon pumpkin pie spice
2 teaspoons ground cinnamon
Brown sugar (optional)
Cooking spray

1. Spray the bottom of the Instant Pot with cooking spray.
2. Combine the remaining ingredients except the brown sugar in the Instant Pot.
3. Secure the lid. Select the Manual mode and set the cooking time for 10 minutes at High Pressure.
4. Once cooking is complete, do a natural pressure release for 10 minutes, then release any remaining pressure. Carefully open the lid.
5. Serve sprinkled with the brown sugar, if desired.

Quick Cozy Spiced Fruit

Prep time: 5 minutes | Cook time: 1 minute | Serves 6

1 pound (454 g) frozen pineapple chunks
1 pound (454 g) sliced frozen peaches
1 cup frozen and pitted dark sweet

cherries
2 ripe pears, sliced
¼ cup pure maple syrup
1 teaspoon curry powder, plus more as needed

1. Combine all the ingredients in the Instant Pot.
2. Secure the lid. Select the Manual mode and set the cooking time for 1 minute at High Pressure.
3. Once cooking is complete, do a quick pressure release. Carefully open the lid.
4. Stir the mixture well, adding more curry powder if you like it spicy. Serve warm.

Vanilla and Brown Sugar Polenta

Prep time: 5 minutes | Cook time: 20 minutes | Serves 4

1 cup polenta
2 cups coconut milk, plus more as needed
2 cups water
½ to 1 teaspoon salt, plus more as needed

⅓ cup packed light brown sugar
1½ teaspoons vanilla extract
Fresh fruit, for topping

1. Combine the polenta, milk, water, and salt in the Instant Pot, stirring well to break up any lumps.
2. Secure the lid. Select the Porridge mode and set the cooking time for 20 minutes at High Pressure.
3. Once cooking is complete, do a natural pressure release for 15 minutes, then release any remaining pressure. Carefully open the lid.
4. Stir in the brown sugar and vanilla. Taste and add another pinch of salt, if desired, as well as more milk if you want it creamier. Serve topped with the fresh fruit.

Blueberry Baked Oatmeal with Almonds

Prep time: 5 minutes | Cook time: 25 minutes | Serves 4

1½ cups old-fashioned rolled oats
⅓ cup coconut sugar
1 tablespoon flax meal
1 teaspoon baking powder
1 teaspoon ground cinnamon
1 cup almond milk

1 teaspoon freshly grated orange zest
1 teaspoon pure vanilla extract
¼ cup applesauce
¾ cup fresh blueberries
1 cup water
⅓ cup slivered almonds, toasted

1. Stir together the oats, coconut sugar, flax meal, baking powder, and cinnamon in a medium bowl until combined.
2. Add the almond milk, orange zest, vanilla, and applesauce. Fold in the blueberries and stir to incorporate. Spoon

the oat mixture into 4 ramekins. Cover each ramekin tightly with foil.
3. Pour the water into the Instant Pot and insert a trivet. Place the ramekins on the trivet.
4. Lock the lid. Select the Manual mode and set the cooking time for 25 minutes at High Pressure.
5. When the timer beeps, perform a quick pressure release. Carefully remove the lid. Using potholders, remove the ramekins and remove the foil.
6. Serve topped with the toasted almonds.

Cinnamon Berry Toast Casserole

Prep time: 5 minutes | Cook time: 25 minutes | Serves 4 to 6

1 cup water
½ cup applesauce
¼ cup maple syrup, plus more for topping
1 teaspoon ground cinnamon
1 teaspoon vanilla extract
¼ teaspoon sea salt

5 cups cubed, stale French bread
1½ cups fresh blueberries and strawberries (halve or quarter the strawberries)
Nonstick cooking spray

1. Spray a 7-cup oven-safe glass bowl with nonstick cooking spray and set aside.
2. Pour the water into the Instant Pot and insert a trivet.
3. Whisk together the applesauce, maple syrup, cinnamon, vanilla, and sea salt in a large bowl until combined.
4. Quickly toss the bread and berries in the applesauce mixture, making sure to get even coverage.
5. Transfer the mixture to the prepared bowl and cover tightly with aluminum foil. Place the bowl on the trivet in the Instant Pot.
6. Secure the lid. Select the Manual mode and set the cooking time for 25 minutes at High Pressure.
7. Once cooking is complete, do a quick pressure release. Carefully open the lid.
8. Serve topped with a splash of maple syrup.

Holiday Morning French Toast

Prep time: 5 minutes | Cook time: 25 minutes | Serves 4 to 6

1 cup water
1 large banana, plus more for topping (optional)
¼ cup Bailey's Almande Almondmilk liqueur
¼ cup maple syrup, plus more for

serving
1 teaspoon vanilla extract
¼ teaspoon sea salt
6 cups cubed, stale French bread
Nonstick cooking spray

1. Spritz a 7-cup oven-safe glass bowl with nonstick spray and set aside.
2. Pour the water into the Instant Pot and insert a trivet.
3. Mash the banana with a fork in a large bowl. Stir in the Bailey's, maple syrup, vanilla, and sea salt, making sure the banana is completely mixed in.
4. Quickly toss the bread in the banana mixture, making sure to get even coverage.
5. Transfer to the prepared bowl, cover tightly with aluminum foil, and place the bowl on the trivet in the Instant Pot.
6. Secure the lid. Select the Manual mode and set the cooking time for 25 minutes at High Pressure.
7. Once cooking is complete, do a quick pressure release. Carefully open the lid.
8. Serve with toppings as desired.

Spinach and Cheese Strata

Prep time: 10 minutes | Cook time: 15 minutes | Serves 4

1 tablespoon vegetable oil
6 large eggs
1 cup half-and-half
1 teaspoon kosher salt
1 teaspoon black pepper
4 slices sourdough

bread, cut into cubes
3 cups chopped fresh spinach
1 cup chopped green onions
1 cup shredded Swiss cheese
1½ cups water

1. Generously grease a springform pan with vegetable oil and line the bottom with a circle of parchment paper. Set aside.
2. In a large mixing bowl, whisk together the eggs, half-and-half, salt, and pepper. Stir in the bread cubes, spinach, green onions, and Swiss cheese. Pour the mixture into the prepared pan.
3. Pour the water into the Instant Pot and insert a trivet. Place the pan with the bread mixture on the trivet.
4. Lock the lid. Select the Manual mode and set the cooking time for 15 minutes at High Pressure.
5. When the timer beeps, perform a natural pressure release for 10 minutes, then release any remaining pressure. Carefully open the lid.
6. Remove the pan from the trivet. Check the center of the strata to ensure that it is cooked through. If needed, pat the top dry with a paper towel.
7. Let rest for 5 minutes before slicing into wedges and serving.

Chocolate Instant Pot Steel-Cut Oats

Prep time: 3 minutes | Cook time: 4 minutes | Serves 4

3 cups water
1 cup steel-cut oats
3 tablespoons unsweetened cocoa powder
2 tablespoons pure maple syrup
¼ teaspoon sea salt
Toppings:

1 banana, sliced
1 cup sliced strawberries
4 tablespoons natural almond butter or peanut butter
Pure maple syrup

1. Stir together all the ingredients except toppings in the Instant Pot.
2. Secure the lid. Select the Manual mode and set the cooking time for 4 minutes at High Pressure.
3. Once cooking is complete, do a natural pressure release for 15 minutes, then release any remaining pressure. Carefully open the lid.
4. Stir the oats. They will thicken up more as they cool. Scatter the banana and strawberry slices on top. Serve with a drizzle of almond butter and a splash of maple syrup.

Blueberry Bliss Breakfast Bowls

Prep time: 2 minutes | Cook time: 10 minutes | Serves 4 to 6

2¼ cups water
1 cup millet, rinsed
2 tablespoons maple syrup
1 tablespoon freshly squeezed lemon juice
¼ teaspoon ground cinnamon
¼ teaspoon ground nutmeg
¼ to ½ teaspoon salt
1 cup coconut milk, plus more as needed
1 cup fresh blueberries
½ cup sliced toasted almonds
Zest of ½ lemon

1. In your Instant Pot, stir together the water, millet, maple syrup, lemon juice, cinnamon, nutmeg, and salt.
2. Lock the lid. Select the Manual mode and set the cooking time for 10 minutes at High Pressure.
3. When the timer beeps, perform a natural pressure release for 10 minutes, then release any remaining pressure. Carefully remove the lid.
4. Stir in the milk, adding more if you like a creamier texture.
5. Serve topped with the blueberries, toasted almonds, and lemon zest.

Tex Mex Tofu Scramble

Prep time: 5 minutes | Cook time: 10 minutes | Serves 4

1 tablespoon olive oil
3 cloves garlic, minced
1 cup chopped red bell pepper
¼ cup canned green chilies, chopped
1 teaspoon ground cumin
1 teaspoon paprika
1 teaspoon chili powder
½ teaspoon salt
½ teaspoon black pepper
1 package extra firm tofu, cubed
1 cup fresh corn kernels
1 cup diced tomatoes
¼ cup vegetable broth or water
1 avocado, sliced
¼ cup chopped fresh cilantro (optional)

1. Set your Instant Pot to Sauté and heat the olive oil.
2. Add the garlic, red bell pepper, green chilies, cumin, paprika, chili powder, salt, and black pepper, stirring well, and sauté for 5 minutes.
3. Stir in the remaining ingredients, except for the avocado and cilantro.
4. Lock the lid. Select the Manual mode and set the cooking time for 4 minutes at High Pressure.
5. When the timer beeps, perform a quick pressure release. Carefully remove the lid and stir.
6. Serve garnished with avocado slices and fresh cilantro (if desired).

Crunchy Peanut Butter Granola Bars

Prep time: 5 minutes | Cook time: 20 minutes | Serves 10

1 cup quick-cooking oats
½ cup all-natural peanut butter
$1/_3$ cup pure maple syrup
1 tablespoon extra-virgin olive oil
¼ teaspoon fine sea salt
$1/_3$ cup dried cranberries or raisins
½ cup raw pumpkin seeds
1 cup water

1. Line a 7-inch round pan with parchment paper.
2. Combine the oats, peanut butter, maple syrup, olive oil, and salt in a large bowl and stir well. Fold in the dried cranberries and pumpkin seeds, then scrape the batter into the prepared pan. Use a spatula to press the batter evenly into the bottom of the pan.
3. Pour the water into the Instant Pot and insert a trivet. Place the pan on the trivet. Cover the pan with another piece of parchment to protect the granola bars from condensation.
4. Secure the lid. Select the Manual mode and set the cooking time for 20 minutes at High Pressure.
5. Once cooking is complete, do a natural pressure release for 10 minutes, then release any remaining pressure. Carefully open the lid.
6. Remove the trivet and let the granola cool completely in the pan. Cut the cooled granola into 10 pieces and serve.

Loaded Sweet Potato Breakfast

Prep time: 2 minutes | Cook time: 12 minutes | Serves 2

1 medium sweet potato, rinsed and patted dry	2 tablespoons almond butter
1 cup water	¼ cup slivered toasted almonds
Pinch of ground cinnamon	2 tablespoons hemp seeds

1. Pierce the sweet potato all over with a fork.
2. Pour the water into the Instant Pot and insert a trivet. Place the sweet potato on the trivet.
3. Lock the lid. Select the Manual mode and set the cooking time for 12 minutes at High Pressure.
4. When the timer beeps, perform a natural pressure release for 10 minutes, then release any remaining pressure. Carefully open the lid and make sure the sweet potato is fork-tender. If not, secure the lid and cook for another 3 minutes, or until tender.
5. Remove the potato with tongs. Cut it in half lengthwise and place on two serving plates. Sprinkle with a pinch of cinnamon and drizzle with almond butter. Serve topped with the almonds and hemp seeds.

Simple Stone Fruit Compote

Prep time: 5 minutes | Cook time: 3 minutes | Makes about 2 cups

4 cups sliced stone fruit (plums, apricots, or peaches)	1 tablespoon fresh lemon juice
⅛ cup water	½ teaspoon vanilla bean paste or extract
1 tablespoon pure maple syrup, plus additional as needed	Pinch of ground cinnamon

1. Stir together all the ingredients in the Instant Pot.
2. Lock the lid. Select the Manual mode and set the cooking time for 1 minute at High Pressure.

3. When the timer beeps, perform a natural pressure release for 10 minutes, then release any remaining pressure. Carefully remove the lid.
4. Allow to simmer on Sauté for 2 minutes, stirring, or until thickened.
5. Taste and add additional maple syrup, as needed. Serve warm.

Cranberry Millet

Prep time: 5 minutes | Cook time: 10 minutes | Serves 4

1 tablespoon coconut oil	cinnamon
1 cup chopped sweet yellow onion	½ teaspoon ground sage
2 cloves garlic, minced	¼ teaspoon cayenne powder
1 teaspoon black pepper	2 cups millet
½ teaspoon salt	3 cups vegetable stock
½ teaspoon	½ cup dried cranberries

1. Set your Instant Pot to Sauté and melt the coconut oil.
2. Add the onion, garlic, pepper, salt, cinnamon, sage, and cayenne powder, stirring, and sauté for 5 minutes, or until the onions are tender.
3. Stir in the millet, vegetable stock, and dried cranberries.
4. Lock the lid. Select the Manual mode and set the cooking time for 3 minutes at High Pressure.
5. When the timer beeps, perform a natural pressure release for 10 minutes, then release any remaining pressure. Carefully remove the lid.
6. Fluff the millet before serving.

Amaranth Banana Bread

Prep time: 5 minutes | Cook time: 4 minutes | Serves 4

1 cup amaranth
2 cups sliced bananas
2 ½ cups vanilla-flavored rice milk
2 tablespoons brown sugar
½ teaspoon nutmeg
½ teaspoon cinnamon
¼ teaspoon salt
½ cup chopped walnuts

1. Combine all the ingredients, except for the walnuts, in the Instant Pot.
2. Secure the lid. Select the Manual mode and set the cooking time for 4 minutes at High Pressure.
3. Once cooking is complete, do a natural pressure release for 10 minutes, then release any remaining pressure. Carefully open the lid.
4. Stir in the walnuts before serving.

Berry Vanilla Quinoa Bowls

Prep time: 5 minutes | Cook time: 5 minutes | Serves 4

1 cup quinoa, rinsed and drained
1½ cups unsweetened almond milk, plus more for serving
½ teaspoon pure vanilla extract
Pinch of ground cinnamon
Toppings:
1 banana, sliced
1 cup berries
½ cup slivered almonds, toasted
¼ cup pure maple syrup

1. In the Instant Pot, stir together the quinoa, almond milk, vanilla, and cinnamon.
2. Lock the lid. Select the Manual mode and set the cooking time for 5 minutes at High Pressure.
3. When the timer beeps, perform a quick pressure release. Carefully remove the lid. Stir in more milk to thin into a porridge.
4. Top with banana slices and berries. Serve with a generous sprinkle of almonds and a drizzle of maple syrup.

Sweet Potato and Kale Egg Bites

Prep time: 7 minutes | Cook time: 20 minutes | Makes 7 egg bites

1 (14-ounce / 397-g) package firm tofu, lightly pressed
¼ cup coconut milk
¼ cup nutritional yeast
1 tablespoon cornstarch
½ to 1 teaspoon sea salt
½ teaspoon onion powder
½ teaspoon garlic powder
½ teaspoon ground turmeric
½ cup shredded sweet potato
Handful kale leaves, chopped small
1 cup plus 1 tablespoon water, divided
Freshly ground black pepper, to taste
Nonstick cooking spray

1. Lightly spray a silicone egg bites mold with nonstick cooking spray. Set aside.
2. Combine the tofu, milk, yeast, cornstarch, sea salt, onion powder, garlic powder, and turmeric in a food processor. Pulse until smooth.
3. Press the Sauté button to heat your Instant Pot until hot.
4. Add the sweet potato, kale, and 1 tablespoon of water. Sauté for 1 to 2 minutes. Stir the veggies into the tofu mixture and spoon the mixture into the prepared mold. Cover it tightly with aluminum foil and place on a trivet.
5. Pour the remaining 1 cup of water into the Instant Pot and insert the trivet.
6. Lock the lid. Select the Manual mode and set the cooking time for 18 minutes at High Pressure.
7. When the timer beeps, perform a natural pressure release for 10 minutes, then release any remaining pressure. Carefully remove the lid.
8. Remove the silicone mold from the Instant Pot and pull off the foil. Allow to cool for 5 minutes on the trivet. The bites will continue to firm as they cool.
9. Season to taste with pepper and serve warm.

Tropical Fruit Chutney

Prep time: 5 minutes | Cook time: 20 minutes | Serves 6

2 mangoes, chopped
1 medium-sized pear, peeled and chopped
1 papaya, chopped
1 cup apple cider vinegar
½ cup brown sugar
¼ cup golden raisins
2 tablespoons fresh

grated ginger
2 teaspoons lemon zest
½ teaspoon coriander
½ teaspoon cinnamon
¼ teaspoon cardamom

1. Stir together all the ingredients in the Instant Pot.
2. Secure the lid. Select the Manual mode and set the cooking time for 6 minutes at High Pressure.
3. Once cooking is complete, do a natural pressure release for 20 minutes, then release any remaining pressure. Carefully open the lid.
4. Press the Sauté button on the Instant Pot. Cook the chutney, stirring, for approximately 12 to 15 minutes, or until thickened. Serve warm.

Breakfast Burrito with Scrambled Tofu

Prep time: 5 minutes | Cook time: 7 minutes | Serves 2

2 cups water
2 small Yukon Gold potatoes, cut into 1-in (2.5 cm) chunks
2 tablespoons extra-virgin olive oil
10 ounces (283 g) firm organic tofu, drained and crumbled
½ teaspoon ground turmeric

2 tablespoons nutritional yeast
½ teaspoon sea salt
Pinch of freshly ground black pepper
¼ cup unsweetened plant-based milk
2 flour tortillas, warmed
½ avocado, sliced
1 cup fresh baby spinach or arugula
¼ cup salsa

1. Pour the water into the Instant Pot and insert a steamer basket. Put the potato chunks in the steamer basket.

2. Secure the lid. Select the Manual mode and set the cooking time for 2 minutes at High Pressure.
3. When the timer beeps, perform a quick pressure release. Carefully remove the lid and steamer basket. Pour the water out of the Instant Pot and wipe it dry.
4. Press the Sauté button on the Instant Pot and heat the olive oil until very hot. Add the potatoes and sauté for about 3 minutes, flipping occasionally, until crisp on the outside. Remove the potatoes from the pot and set aside on a plate.
5. Add the crumbled tofu, turmeric, nutritional yeast, salt, and pepper to the pot, and sauté for 1 to 2 minutes. For a softer scramble, you can add the milk and simmer until warm and the milk has evaporated and absorbed.
6. Assemble the burritos: Place the potatoes and tofu scramble onto the tortillas. Top with equal portions of avocado, baby spinach, and salsa. Roll into burritos and serve immediately.

Maple Cereal Bowls

Prep time: 5 minutes | Cook time: 1 minute | Serves 6

2 cups buckwheat groats, soaked for at least 20 minutes and up to overnight
3 cups water
¼ cup pure maple syrup
1 teaspoon vanilla extract

1 teaspoon ground cinnamon
¼ teaspoon fine sea salt
Almond milk, for serving
Chopped or sliced fresh fruit, for serving

1. Drain and rinse the buckwheat. In the Instant Pot, combine the buckwheat with the water, maple syrup, cinnamon, vanilla, and salt.
2. Lock the lid. Select the Manual mode and set the cooking time for 1 minute at High Pressure.
3. When the timer beeps, perform a natural pressure release for 10 minutes, then release any remaining pressure. Carefully remove the lid and stir the cooked grains.
4. Serve the buckwheat warm with almond milk and fresh fruit.

Apple Breakfast Risotto

Prep time: 10 minutes | Cook time: 12 minutes | Serves 4 to 6

2 tablespoons butter
1½ cups Arborio rice
2 apples, cored and sliced
3 cups plant-based milk
1 cup apple juice
1/3 cup brown sugar
1½ teaspoons cinnamon powder
Salt to taste
½ cup dried cherries

1. Set your Instant Pot to Sauté and melt the butter.
2. Add rice, stir and cook for 5 minutes.
3. Add the remaining ingredients, except the cherries, to the Instant Pot. Stir well.
4. Lock the lid. Select the Manual mode and set the cooking time for 6 minutes at High Pressure.
5. When the timer beeps, perform a natural pressure release for 6 minutes, then release any remaining pressure. Carefully remove the lid.
6. Stir in the cherries and close the lid. Let sit for 5 minutes. Serve warm.

Coconut Strawberry Buckwheat Breakfast Pudding

Prep time: 5 minutes | Cook time: 7 minutes | Serves 4

1 cup buckwheat groats
3 cups coconut milk
1 cup chopped fresh strawberries
½ cup unsweetened shredded coconut
1 teaspoon cinnamon
½ teaspoon almond extract
½ teaspoon pure vanilla extract
½ cup sliced almonds
½ cup cold coconut cream

1. Stir together all the ingredients, except for the almonds and coconut cream, in the Instant Pot.
2. Secure the lid. Select the Manual mode and set the cooking time for 7 minutes at High Pressure.
3. Once cooking is complete, do a natural pressure release for 20 minutes, then release any remaining pressure. Carefully open the lid.
4. Spoon the buckwheat pudding into serving dishes. Garnish with coconut cream and almonds before serving.

Nutty Raisin Oatmeal

Prep time: 10 minutes | Cook time: 5 minutes | Serves 4

¾ cup steel-cut oats
¾ cup raisins
3 cups vanilla almond milk
3 tablespoons brown sugar
4½ teaspoons butter
¾ teaspoon ground cinnamon
½ teaspoon salt
1 large apple, peeled and chopped
¼ cup chopped pecans

1. Combine all the ingredients, except for the apple and pecans, in the Instant Pot.
2. Lock the lid. Select the Manual mode and set the cooking time for 5 minutes at High Pressure.
3. When the timer beeps, perform a natural pressure release for 10 minutes, then release any remaining pressure. Carefully remove the lid.
4. Stir in the apple and let sit for 10 minutes. Spoon the oatmeal into bowls and sprinkle the pecans on top before serving.

Pear Oatmeal with Walnuts

Prep time: 5 minutes | Cook time: 7 minutes | Serves 2

1 cup old-fashioned oats
1¼ cups water
1 medium pear, peeled, cored, and cubed
¼ cup freshly squeezed orange juice
¼ cup chopped walnuts
¼ cup dried cherries
¼ teaspoon ground ginger
¼ teaspoon ground cinnamon
Pinch of salt

1. In the Instant Pot, combine the oats, water, pear, orange juice, walnuts, cherries, ginger, cinnamon, and salt.
2. Secure the lid. Select the Manual mode and set the cooking time for 7 minutes at High Pressure.
3. Once cooking is complete, do a natural pressure release for 10 minutes, then release any remaining pressure. Carefully open the lid.
4. Stir the oatmeal and spoon into two bowls. Serve warm.

Chapter 5 Grains Recipes

Wild Rice and Basmati Pilaf

Prep time: 5 minutes | Cook time: 35 minutes | Serves 6

2 tablespoon olive oil	½ teaspoon salt
2 brown onions, minced	6 sprigs fresh thyme
2 cloves garlic, minced	2 cups broth
12 ounces (340 g) mushrooms, sliced	2 cups wild rice and basmati rice mixture
	½ cup pine nuts
	½ cup minced parsley

1. Set your Instant Pot to Sauté. Add the olive oil and onions and cook for 6 minutes.
2. Add minced garlic and cook for 1 minute more. Place the remaining ingredients, except for nuts and parsley, into the Instant Pot and stir well.
3. Lock the lid. Select the Manual mode and set the cooking time for 28 minutes at High Pressure.
4. When the timer beeps, perform a natural pressure release for 15 minutes, then release any remaining pressure. Carefully remove the lid.
5. Sprinkle with the pine nuts and parsley, then serve.

Chili Polenta

Prep time: 2 minutes | Cook time: 9 minutes | Serves 6

10 cups water	3 tablespoons red paprika flakes
3 cups polenta	
3 teaspoons salt	

1. Combine the water, polenta, salt, and red paprika flakes in the Instant Pot.
2. Lock the lid. Select the Manual mode and set the cooking time for 9 minutes at High Pressure.
3. When the timer beeps, perform a natural pressure release for 15 minutes, then release any remaining pressure. Carefully remove the lid.
4. Cool for 5 minutes and serve.

Mediterranean Couscous Salad

Prep time: 20 minutes | Cook time: 2 minutes | Serves 6

Couscous:
1 cup couscous
2¾ cups water, divided

Salad:

½ cup salad greens (such as a mix of spinach, arugula, and red and green lettuce leaves)	20 minutes, then drained
4 tablespoons finely chopped carrot	½ cup shredded red cabbage, marinated in 2 tablespoons each of lemon juice and water for 20 minutes, then drained
4 tablespoons finely chopped black olives	1 teaspoon kosher salt
4 tablespoons finely chopped cucumber	1 teaspoon freshly ground black pepper
½ cup thinly sliced red onion, marinated in 2 tablespoons each of lemon juice and water for	2 tablespoons extra-virgin olive oil

1. Combine the couscous and 1¼ of cups water in a heatproof bowl.
2. Pour the remaining 1½ cups of water into the Instant Pot and insert a trivet. Place the bowl on the trivet.
3. Secure the lid. Select the Manual mode and set the cooking time for 2 minutes at High Pressure.
4. Once cooking is complete, do a natural pressure release for 5 minutes, then release any remaining pressure. Carefully open the lid.
5. Let the couscous cool for 15 minutes before fluffing with a fork.
6. Assemble the salad: Add the salad greens, carrot, olives, cucumber, onion, cabbage, salt, pepper, and olive oil to the couscous. Mix gently and serve immediately.

Easy Vegetable Biryani

Prep time: 10 minutes | Cook time: 15 minutes | Serves 6

2 tablespoons butter
3 cardamom seeds
3 whole cloves
2 dried bay leaves
1 (2-inch) cinnamon stick
1 onion, finely chopped
2 garlic cloves, finely chopped
2 teaspoons finely chopped fresh ginger
1½ cups roughly chopped fresh mint leaves
2 tomatoes, finely chopped
1½ teaspoons kosher salt
2 teaspoons ground coriander
1 teaspoon red chili powder
2 tablespoons plain Greek yogurt, plus more for serving
2 cups mixed vegetables
4 tablespoons finely chopped fresh cilantro, divided
1½ cups basmati rice
2¼ cups water

1. Set your Instant Pot to Sauté and melt the butter.
2. Add the cardamom, cloves, bay leaves, and cinnamon stick. Stir-fry for 30 seconds, then add the onion, garlic, ginger, and mint leaves. Sauté for 3 to 4 minutes until the onion is translucent.
3. Stir in the tomatoes and salt. Loosely place the lid on top and cook for 3 minutes, or until the tomatoes are softened.
4. Add the coriander, chili powder, and yogurt. Mix well and cook for 2 minutes more. Add the mixed vegetables and 2 tablespoons of cilantro, and mix well. Stir in the rice and water.
5. Secure the lid. Select the Manual mode and set the cooking time for 4 minutes at High Pressure.
6. Once cooking is complete, do a natural pressure release for 3 minutes, then release any remaining pressure. Carefully open the lid.
7. Let the rice cool for 15 minutes and remove the bay leaves. Using a fork, fluff the rice and stir in the remaining 2 tablespoons of cilantro. Serve hot with additional yogurt.

Mushrooms Farro Risotto

Prep time: 10 minutes | Cook time: 30 minutes | Serves 3

½ cup farro
2 tablespoons barley
3 cups chopped mushrooms
1 tablespoon red curry paste
1 jalapeño pepper, seeded and chopped
1 tablespoon shallot powder
2 tablespoons onion
powder
Salt and pepper, to taste
4 garlic cloves, minced
1½ cups water
2 tomatoes, diced
Chopped cilantro, for serving
Chopped scallions, for serving

1. Combine all the ingredients, except for the tomatoes, cilantro, and scallion, in the Instant Pot.
2. Secure the lid. Select the Manual mode and set the cooking time for 30 minutes at High Pressure.
3. Once cooking is complete, do a quick pressure release. Carefully open the lid.
4. Stir in the tomatoes and let sit for 2 to 3 minutes until warmed through. Sprinkle with the cilantro and scallions and serve.

Cilantro and Lime Millet Pilaf

Prep time: 5 minutes | Cook time: 10 minutes | Serves 4

1 cup chopped green onions
1 cup millet
1 teaspoon kosher salt
1 tablespoon olive
oil
1 cup water
1 cup chopped fresh cilantro or parsley
Zest and juice of 1 lime

1. In the Instant Pot, combine the green onions, millet, salt, olive oil, and water.
2. Lock the lid. Select the Manual mode and set the cooking time for 10 minutes at High Pressure.
3. When the timer beeps, perform a natural pressure release for 10 minutes, then release any remaining pressure. Carefully remove the lid.
4. Stir in the cilantro and lime zest and juice and serve.

Pea and Mint Risotto

Prep time: 5 minutes | Cook time: 20 minutes | Serves 2

2 tablespoons coconut oil	broth, divided
1 onion, peeled and diced	Salt and pepper, to taste
½ teaspoon garlic powder	½ cup fresh peas
½ cup barley	¼ teaspoon lime zest
1 cup vegetable	¼ cup chopped fresh mint leaves

1. Press the Sauté button on the Instant Pot and heat the oil.
2. Add the onion and stir-fry for 5 minutes.
3. Add garlic powder and barley and cook for 1 minute more.
4. Pour in ½ cup of vegetable broth and stir for 3 minutes until it is absorbed by barley.
5. Add the remaining ½ cup of broth, salt, and pepper.
6. Secure the lid. Select the Manual mode and set the cooking time for 10 minutes at High Pressure.
7. Once cooking is complete, do a natural pressure release for 10 minutes, then release any remaining pressure. Carefully open the lid.
8. Stir in peas, lime zest, and mint and let sit for 3 minutes until heated through. Serve immediately.

Jollof Rice

Prep time: 10 minutes | Cook time: 22 minutes | Serves 4

1 tablespoon corn oil	tomato paste
2 dried bay leaves	1½ teaspoons kosher salt
1 onion, finely chopped	1 teaspoon paprika
2 garlic cloves, finely chopped	½ teaspoon curry powder
1 teaspoon finely chopped fresh ginger	1 cup chopped carrots
1 jalapeño, seeded and finely chopped	1 cup cauliflower florets (7 or 8 florets)
2 tomatoes, coarsely chopped	1 cup short-grain white rice, rinsed
2 tablespoons	2 cups water

1. Press the Sauté button on the Instant Pot and heat the oil.
2. Once hot, add the bay leaves, onion, garlic, ginger, and jalapeños, and sauté for 5 minutes, or until the onion is translucent.
3. Stir in the tomatoes, tomato paste, and salt. Loosely place the lid on top, and cook for 3 minutes, or until the tomatoes are softened. Mix in the paprika and curry powder, then stir in the carrots and cauliflower. Add the rice and water and stir well.
4. Secure the lid. Select the Rice mode and set the cooking time for 12 minutes at Low Pressure.
5. Once cooking is complete, do a natural pressure release for 10 minutes, then release any remaining pressure. Carefully open the lid.
6. Let the rice cool for 15 minutes. Remove the bay leaves. Using a fork, gently fluff the rice and serve hot.

Creamy Mushroom Alfredo Rice

Prep time: 5 minutes | Cook time: 25 minutes | Serves 4

2 tablespoons olive oil	1½ tablespoons fresh lemon juice
¾ cup finely chopped onion	Salt and black pepper, to taste
2 garlic cloves, minced	2 ounces (57 g) creamy mushroom Alfredo sauce
1 cup rice	¼ cup coarsely chopped walnuts
2¾ cups vegetable broth	

1. Set your Instant Pot to Sauté. Add the oil, onion, and garlic to the pot and sauté for 3 minutes. Stir in the rice and broth.
2. Secure the lid. Select the Manual mode and set the cooking time for 22 minutes at High Pressure.
3. Once cooking is complete, do a natural pressure release for 10 minutes, then release any remaining pressure. Carefully open the lid.
4. Add lemon juice, salt, pepper, and sauce and stir to combine. Garnish with the chopped walnuts and serve.

Confetti Rice

Prep time: 5 minutes | Cook time: 12 minutes | Serves 4

3 tablespoons butter
1 small onion, chopped
1 cup long-grain white rice
3 cups frozen peas, thawed
1 cup vegetable broth

¼ cup lemon juice
2 cloves garlic, minced
1 tablespoon cumin powder
½ teaspoon salt
½ teaspoon black pepper

1. Set your Instant Pot to Sauté and melt the butter.
2. Add the onion and sauté for 3 minutes until soft. Add the remaining ingredients to the Instant Pot, stirring well.
3. Secure the lid. Select the Manual mode and set the cooking time for 8 minutes at High Pressure.
4. Once cooking is complete, do a quick pressure release. Carefully open the lid.
5. Fluff the rice and serve hot.

Vegetarian Thai Pineapple Fried Rice

Prep time: 10 minutes | Cook time: 10 minutes | Serves 4

1 tablespoon corn oil
3 tablespoons cashews
¼ cup finely chopped onion
¼ cup finely chopped scallions, white parts only
2 green Thai chiles, finely chopped
1 cup canned pineapple chunks
2 tablespoons roughly chopped

fresh basil leaves
½ teaspoon curry powder
¼ teaspoon ground turmeric
2 teaspoons soy sauce
1 teaspoon kosher salt
1 cup steamed short-grain white rice
1¼ cups water

1. Press the Sauté button on the Instant Pot and heat the oil.
2. Once hot, add the cashews and stir for 1 minute. Add the onion, scallions, and chiles, and sauté for 3 to 4 minutes, until the onion is translucent.

3. Mix in the pineapple, basil, curry powder, turmeric, soy sauce, and salt. Add the rice and water and stir to combine.
4. Secure the lid. Select the Manual mode and set the cooking time for 3 minutes at High Pressure.
5. Once cooking is complete, do a natural pressure release for 3 minutes, then release any remaining pressure. Carefully open the lid.
6. Let the rice rest for 15 minutes. Remove the bay leaves. Using a fork, fluff the rice and serve hot.

Cinnamon Bulgur and Lentil Pilaf

Prep time: 5 minutes | Cook time: 10 minutes | Serves 6

2 tablespoons vegetable oil
1 large onion, thinly sliced
1½ teaspoons kosher salt
½ teaspoon ground cinnamon
½ teaspoon ground allspice

1¾ cups water, divided
1 cup whole-grain red wheat bulgur
½ cup dried red lentils
¼ cup chopped fresh parsley
Toasted pine nuts (optional)

1. Press the Sauté button on the Instant Pot and heat the oil.
2. Once the oil is hot, add the onion and salt. Cook, stirring occasionally, until the onion is browned, about 5 minutes.
3. Stir in the cinnamon and allspice and cook for 30 seconds.
4. Add ¼ cup of water to deglaze the pot, scraping up the browned bits. Add the bulgur, lentils, and remaining 1½ cups of water.
5. Lock the lid. Select the Manual mode and set the cooking time for 5 minutes at High Pressure.
6. When the timer beeps, perform a natural pressure release for 10 minutes, then release any remaining pressure. Carefully remove the lid.
7. Stir gently to fluff up the bulgur. Stir in the parsley and pine nuts (if desired), then serve.

Mushroom Barley Risotto

Prep time: 10 minutes | Cook time: 40 minutes | Serves 6

3 tablespoons butter
1 onion, finely chopped
1 cup coarsely chopped shiitake mushrooms
1 cup coarsely chopped cremini mushrooms
1 cup coarsely chopped brown bella mushrooms
1 teaspoon kosher salt
1 teaspoon freshly ground black pepper
1 teaspoon Italian dried herb seasoning
1 cup pearl barley
1 (32-ounce / 907-g) container vegetable broth
½ cup shredded Parmesan cheese

1. Set your Instant Pot to Sauté and melt the butter.
2. Add the onion and cook for about 3 minutes, or until the onion is translucent. Mix in the mushrooms, salt, pepper, and Italian seasoning. Cook for 5 to 6 minutes or until the mushrooms shrink. Stir in the barley and broth.
3. Secure the lid. Select the Manual mode and set the cooking time for 30 minutes at High Pressure.
4. Once cooking is complete, do a natural pressure release for 10 minutes, then release any remaining pressure. Carefully open the lid.
5. Stir in the Parmesan cheese. Serve hot.

Polenta and Mushrooms

Prep time: 5 minutes | Cook time: 23 minutes | Serves 4

1 cup yellow cornmeal
4 cups vegetable broth
1 tablespoon butter
2 portobello mushrooms caps,
finely chopped
1 teaspoon onion powder
1 teaspoon kosher salt
1 teaspoon freshly ground black pepper

1. In a large bowl, whisk together the cornmeal and broth until there are no lumps. Set aside.
2. Set your Instant Pot to Sauté and melt the butter.

3. Add the mushrooms, onion powder, salt, and pepper, and sauté for 2 minutes. Add the cornmeal mix to the Instant Pot, stirring well.
4. Lock the lid. Select the Porridge mode and set the cooking time for 20 minutes at High Pressure.
5. When the timer beeps, perform a natural pressure release for 10 minutes, then release any remaining pressure. Carefully remove the lid.
6. Stir the polenta and serve hot.

Za'atar-Spiced Bulgur Wheat Salad

Prep time: 10 minutes | Cook time: 2 minutes | Serves 6

Bulgur Wheat:
1 cup bulgur wheat
2¼ cups water, divided

Salad:
¼ cup finely chopped cucumber
¼ cup finely chopped fresh parsley
2 tablespoons finely chopped fresh mint
2 tablespoons extra-virgin olive oil
2 tablespoons
freshly squeezed lemon juice
5 cherry tomatoes, finely chopped
1 teaspoon kosher salt
½ teaspoon freshly ground black pepper
1 teaspoon za'atar spice blend

1. Combine the bulgur wheat and 1¼ cups of water in a heatproof bowl.
2. Pour the remaining 1 cup of water into the Instant Pot and insert a trivet. Place the bowl on the trivet.
3. Secure the lid. Select the Manual mode and set the cooking time for 2 minutes at High Pressure.
4. Once cooking is complete, do a natural pressure release for 5 minutes, then release any remaining pressure. Carefully open the lid.
5. Let the bulgur wheat cool for 20 minutes before fluffing it with a fork.
6. Assemble the salad: Add the cucumber, parsley, mint, olive oil, lemon juice, tomatoes, salt, pepper, and za'atar seasoning to the bulgur wheat. Mix gently and serve immediately.

Citrus-Sweet Basmati Rice

Prep time: 3 minutes | Cook time: 4 minutes | Serves 4 to 6

2 cups water
2 cups basmati rice, rinsed and drained
1 teaspoon salt, plus more as needed
½ teaspoon garlic powder

¼ cup Cara Cara Orange–Vanilla white balsamic vinegar
¼ cup chopped fresh parsley
Salt, to taste

1. Combine the water, rice, salt, and garlic powder in the Instant Pot.
2. Secure the lid. Select the Manual mode and set the cooking time for 4 minutes at High Pressure.
3. Once cooking is complete, do a natural pressure release for 5 minutes, then release any remaining pressure. Carefully open the lid.
4. Fluff the rice and stir in the vinegar and parsley. Taste and add more salt, as needed.

Indian Cumin Rice

Prep time: 4 minutes | Cook time: 8 minutes | Serves 4 to 6

1 tablespoon olive oil
2 teaspoons cumin seeds
½ teaspoon ground cardamom

2 cups basmati rice, rinsed well, drained, and dried
2½ cups water
1 teaspoon salt

1. Set your Instant Pot to Sauté and heat the olive oil until shimmering.
2. Add the cumin seeds and cardamom and cook for about 1 minute until fragrant, stirring frequently.
3. Stir in the rice, water, and salt.
4. Secure the lid. Select the Manual mode and set the cooking time for 6 minutes at High Pressure.
5. Once cooking is complete, do a natural pressure release for 10 minutes, then release any remaining pressure. Carefully open the lid.
6. Fluff the rice and serve warm.

Curry Vegetable Rice

Prep time: 15 minutes | Cook time: 23 minutes | Serves 4 to 6

1 tablespoon olive oil
1 clove garlic, minced
¼ cup chopped shallots
2 cups water
1½ cups basmati rice, rinsed

1 cup frozen peas
½ cup chopped carrots
2 teaspoons curry powder
Salt and ground black pepper to taste

1. Set your Instant Pot to Sauté and heat the olive oil until it shimmers.
2. Sauté the garlic and shallots until fragrant, about 2 minutes.
3. Add the remaining ingredients to the Instant Pot and stir to mix well.
4. Lock the lid. Select the Rice mode and set the cooking time for 20 minutes at High Pressure.
5. When the timer beeps, perform a natural pressure release for 10 minutes, then release any remaining pressure. Carefully remove the lid.
6. Fluff the rice with the rice spatula or fork and serve.

Creamy Jasmine Rice

Prep time: 5 minutes | Cook time: 4 minutes | Serves 4 to 6

2 cups jasmine rice, rinsed and drained
½ cup water
1 (14-ounce / 397-

g) can coconut milk
¼ teaspoon sea salt, plus more as needed

1. Combine the rice, water, coconut milk, and salt in the Instant Pot.
2. Secure the lid. Select the Manual mode and set the cooking time for 4 minutes at High Pressure.
3. Once cooking is complete, do a natural pressure release for 10 minutes, then release any remaining pressure. Carefully open the lid.
4. Fluff the rice and taste and season with more salt, as needed.

Spanish Rice

Prep time: 3 minutes | Cook time: 15 minutes | Serves 4 to 6

2 tablespoons butter
2 cups long grain rice
8 ounces (227 g) tomato sauce
1½ cups water
1 teaspoon cumin

1 teaspoon chili powder
½ teaspoon onion powder
½ teaspoon garlic powder
½ teaspoon salt

1. Set your Instant Pot to Sauté and melt the butter.
2. Add the rice and sauté for 4 minutes, stirring occasionally.
3. Add the remaining ingredients to the Instant Pot and stir well.
4. Secure the lid. Select the Manual mode and set the cooking time for 10 minutes at High Pressure.
5. Once cooking is complete, do a natural pressure release for 10 minutes, then release any remaining pressure. Carefully open the lid.
6. Fluff the rice with the rice spatula or fork, then serve.

Red Onion-Feta Couscous Pilaf

Prep time: 5 minutes | Cook time: 5 minutes | Serves 4

2 tablespoons vegetable oil
1 teaspoon cumin seeds
1 teaspoon ground turmeric
1 cup frozen peas and carrots
1 cup Israeli couscous
½ cup diced yellow onion

1 teaspoon kosher salt
1 teaspoon garam masala
1 cup water
½ cup chopped red onion
½ cup crumbled feta cheese
Black pepper, to taste

1. Press the Sauté button on the Instant Pot and heat the oil.
2. Once the oil is hot, stir in the cumin seeds and turmeric, allowing them to sizzle for 10 seconds. Turn off the Instant Pot.

3. Add the peas and carrots, couscous, yellow onion, salt, garam masala, and water. Stir to combine.
4. Lock the lid. Select the Manual mode and set the cooking time for 3 minutes at High Pressure.
5. When the timer beeps, perform a natural pressure release for 5 minutes, then release any remaining pressure. Carefully remove the lid.
6. Stir in the red onion and feta cheese. Season to taste with black pepper and serve.

Mujadara (Lebanese Lentils and Rice)

Prep time: 5 minutes | Cook time: 15 minutes | Serves 6

⅓ cup dried brown lentils
2 tablespoons vegetable oil
1 large yellow onion, sliced
1 teaspoon kosher salt, or more to

taste
1 cup basmati rice, rinsed and drained
½ teaspoon ground cumin
½ teaspoon ground coriander
2 cups water

1. Place the lentils in a small bowl. Cover with hot water and soak for 15 to 20 minutes, then drain.
2. Press the Sauté button on the Instant Pot and heat the oil.
3. Add the onion and season with a little salt and cook, stirring, until the onions begin to crisp around the edges but are not burned, 5 to 10 minutes. Remove half the onions from the pot and reserve as a garnish.
4. Add the soaked lentils, rice, cumin, coriander, salt, and water, stirring well.
5. Lock the lid. Select the Manual mode and set the cooking time for 6 minutes at High Pressure.
6. When the timer beeps, perform a natural pressure release for 10 minutes, then release any remaining pressure. Carefully remove the lid.
7. Transfer to a serving dish. Sprinkle with the reserved cooked onions and serve.

Vegetable Fried Millet

Prep time: 10 minutes | Cook time: 25 minutes | Serves 4

1 teaspoon vegetable oil
½ cup thinly sliced oyster mushrooms
1 cup finely chopped leeks
2 garlic cloves, minced
½ cup green lentils, rinsed
1 cup millet, soaked and drained
½ cup sliced bok choy
1 cup chopped asparagus
1 cup chopped snow peas
2¼ cups vegetable stock
Salt and black pepper, to taste
A drizzle of lemon juice
¼ cup mixed chives and parsley, finely chopped

1. Press the Sauté button on the Instant Pot and heat the oil.
2. Cook the mushrooms, leeks, and garlic for 3 minutes. Add lentils and millet, stir, and cook for 4 minutes.
3. Stir in the bok choy, asparagus, snow peas, and vegetable stock.
4. Secure the lid. Select the Manual mode and set the cooking time for 10 minutes at High Pressure.
5. Once cooking is complete, do a quick pressure release. Carefully open the lid.
6. Season to taste with salt and pepper. Serve sprinkled with the lemon juice, chives, and parsley.

Quinoa Salad with Apples and Pecans

Prep time: 7 minutes | Cook time: 8 minutes | Serves 4 to 6

1 cup quinoa, rinsed
1 cup water
¼ teaspoon salt, plus more as needed
2 apples, unpeeled and cut into large dices
2 tablespoons freshly squeezed lemon juice
1 tablespoon white
rice vinegar
2 celery stalks, halved lengthwise and chopped
½ bunch scallions, green and light green parts, sliced
¾ to 1 cup dried cranberries, white raisins, and regular raisins
2 tablespoons avocado oil
½ to 1 teaspoon chili powder, plus more as needed
Pinch freshly ground
black pepper
½ to 1 cup chopped pecans
½ cup chopped fresh cilantro

1. Combine the quinoa, water, and salt in the Instant Pot.
2. Secure the lid. Select the Manual mode and set the cooking time for 8 minutes at High Pressure.
3. Once cooking is complete, do a natural pressure release for 10 minutes, then release any remaining pressure. Carefully open the lid.
4. Transfer the quinoa to a large salad bowl. Refrigerate for 5 minutes to cool.
5. Mix the apples, lemon juice, and vinegar in a small resealable container. Cover and shake lightly to coat the apples, then refrigerate.
6. Remove the cooled quinoa and stir in the celery, scallions, cranberry-raisin mix, oil, and chili powder. Taste and season with more salt and pepper, as needed. Add the apples and lemon-vinegar juice into the salad and stir well.
7. Serve topped with the pecans and cilantro.

Quinoa Pilaf with Cranberries and Almonds

Prep time: 2 minutes | Cook time: 10 minutes | Serves 2 to 4

1 cup quinoa, rinsed
2 cups water
1 cup dried cranberries
½ cup slivered almonds
¼ cup salted sunflower seeds

1. Combine the water and quinoa in the Instant Pot.
2. Lock the lid. Select the Manual mode and set the cooking time for 10 minutes at High Pressure.
3. Once cooking is complete, do a quick pressure release. Carefully open the lid.
4. Add the cranberries, almonds, and sunflower seeds and gently mix until well incorporated. Serve warm.

Curried Sorghum

Prep time: 10 minutes | Cook time: 20 minutes | Serves 4

1 cup sorghum
3 cups water
Salt, to taste
1 cup milk
2 teaspoons sugar
3 tablespoons rice wine vinegar
1 tablespoon curry

powder
½ teaspoon chili powder
2 cups carrots
¼ cup finely chopped green onion
½ cup golden raisins

1. Combine the sorghum, water, and salt in the Instant Pot.
2. Secure the lid. Select the Manual mode and set the cooking time for 20 minutes at High Pressure.
3. Once cooking is complete, do a quick pressure release. Carefully open the lid.
4. In a medium bowl, add the milk, sugar, vinegar, salt, curry powder, and chili powder and whisk well.
5. Drain the sorghum and transfer to a large bowl. Add the milk mixture, carrots, green onion, and raisins. Stir to combine and serve.

Cinnamon Brown Rice

Prep time: 5 minutes | Cook time: 25 minutes | Serves 4

1 tablespoon olive oil
3 cloves garlic, crushed and minced
½ cup chopped sweet yellow onion
½ teaspoon cumin
½ teaspoon nutmeg
½ teaspoon

cinnamon
½ teaspoon sweet paprika
½ teaspoon sea salt
1½ cups brown rice
2½ cups vegetable broth
½ cup chopped fresh parsley

1. Set your Instant Pot to Sauté and heat the olive oil.
2. Add the garlic, onion, cumin, nutmeg, cinnamon, sweet paprika, and sea salt and sauté for 2 to 3 minutes, stirring frequently, or until the onions are softened.
3. Add the rice and vegetable broth to the Instant Pot.

4. Secure the lid. Select the Manual mode and set the cooking time for 20 minutes at High Pressure.
5. Once cooking is complete, do a quick pressure release. Carefully open the lid.
6. Fluff the rice with a fork and stir in the fresh parsley before serving.

Vegatable Rice Pilaf

Prep time: 10 minutes | Cook time: 8 minutes | Serves 4 to 6

1 tablespoon olive oil, or avocado oil
½ sweet onion, chopped
1 celery stalk, sliced
1 carrot, halved lengthwise and sliced
1 cup broccoli florets
½ cup sliced white mushrooms
2 garlic cloves,

minced
1 cup vegetable stock
1 cup basmati rice, rinsed and drained
Salt and freshly ground black pepper, to taste
½ cup frozen peas
½ cup sliced almonds

1. Set your Instant Pot to Sauté and heat the olive oil until it shimmers.
2. Add the onion, celery, carrot, broccoli, and mushrooms and sauté for 2 to 3 minutes, stirring frequently. Add the garlic and turn off the Instant Pot. Sauté for 30 seconds, stirring frequently.
3. Stir in the stock and rice and season with salt and pepper to taste.
4. Secure the lid. Select the Manual mode and set the cooking time for 3 minutes at High Pressure.
5. Once cooking is complete, do a natural pressure release for 15 minutes, then release any remaining pressure. Carefully open the lid.
6. Stir in the frozen peas, rest the lid back on (no need to lock it), and let sit for 3 to 4 minutes until warmed through. Serve sprinkled with the almonds.

Garlic and Butter Brown Rice

Prep time: 5 minutes | Cook time: 32 minutes | Serves 4 to 6

2 tablespoons olive oil
1 small sweet onion, diced
6 to 8 garlic cloves, minced
2½ cups vegetable stock
2 cups long-grain brown rice, rinsed and drained

1 teaspoon salt, plus more as needed
Pinch freshly ground black pepper, plus more as needed
1 teaspoon freshly squeezed lemon juice
1 tablespoon butter
Fresh parsley, for garnish

1. Set your Instant Pot to Sauté and heat the olive oil until shimmering.
2. Add the onion and sauté for 2 to 3 minutes until tender.
3. Stir in the garlic and cook for about 1 minute. Add the stock, rice, salt, and pepper, stirring well.
4. Secure the lid. Select the Manual mode and set the cooking time for 27 minutes at High Pressure.
5. Once cooking is complete, do a natural pressure release for 10 minutes, then release any remaining pressure. Carefully open the lid.
6. Drizzle with the lemon juice and stir in the butter. Taste and add more salt and pepper, as needed. Serve garnished with the parsley.

Yellow Potato and Basmati Rice Pilaf

Prep time: 5 minutes | Cook time: 12 minutes | Serves 3

1½ tablespoons olive oil
½ large onion, diced small
1 large garlic clove, finely diced
3 medium-sized potatoes, diced
1½ tablespoons

chopped cilantro stalks
½ teaspoon turmeric powder
1 cup basmati rice, rinsed
1 cup water
Salt, to taste
1 teaspoon butter

1. Set your Instant Pot to Sauté and heat the olive oil.
2. Add all the vegetables to the Instant Pot and sauté for 5 minutes, stirring occasionally.
3. Stir in all the remaining ingredients except the butter.
4. Secure the lid. Select the Manual mode and set the cooking time for 7 minutes at High Pressure.
5. Once cooking is complete, do a natural pressure release for 7 minutes, then release any remaining pressure. Carefully open the lid.
6. Add the butter and stir until melted. Serve warm.

Creamy Pumpkin Risotto

Prep time: 5 minutes | Cook time: 15 minutes | Serves 4 to 6

2 ounces (57 g) extra-virgin olive oil
2 cloves garlic, minced
1 small yellow onion, chopped
4 cups vegetable stock
2 cups Arborio rice
¾ cup pumpkin purée

1 teaspoon chopped thyme
½ teaspoon nutmeg
½ teaspoon cinnamon
½ teaspoon grated ginger
½ cup coconut cream
Salt, to taste

1. Set your Instant Pot to Sauté and heat the olive oil.
2. Add the garlic and onion, stirring, and sauté for 1 to 2 minutes until fragrant.
3. Add the remaining ingredients except the coconut cream and salt to the Instant Pot and stir to combine.
4. Lock the lid. Select the Manual mode and set the cooking time for 10 minutes at High Pressure.
5. When the timer beeps, perform a quick pressure release. Carefully remove the lid.
6. Stir in the coconut cream and season to taste with salt. Serve warm.

Greek-Style Quinoa

Prep time: 10 minutes | Cook time: 13 minutes | Serves 4

1 tablespoon olive oil
3 cloves garlic, minced
1 cup chopped red onion
½ cup quinoa
2 cups chopped tomatoes
2 cups spinach, torn
2 cups chopped zucchini
2 cups vegetable broth
½ cup chopped black olives
½ cup pine nuts

1. Set your Instant Pot to Sauté and heat the olive oil.
2. Add the garlic and onion and sauté for approximately 5 minutes, stirring frequently.
3. Add the remaining ingredients, except for the pine nuts, to the Instant Pot and stir to combine.
4. Secure the lid. Select the Manual mode and set the cooking time for 8 minutes at High Pressure.
5. Once cooking is complete, do a natural pressure release for 10 minutes, then release any remaining pressure. Carefully open the lid.
6. Fluff the quinoa and stir in the pine nuts, then serve.

Leek and Mushroom Risotto

Prep time: 7 minutes | Cook time: 13 minutes | Serves 4 to 6

4 tablespoons butter, divided
1 leek, white and lightest green parts only, halved and sliced, rinsed well
12 ounces (340 g) baby bella mushrooms, sliced
2 garlic cloves, minced
1 cup Arborio rice,
rinsed and drained
2¾ cups vegetable stock
½ teaspoon salt, plus more as needed
1 teaspoon dried thyme
Juice of ½ lemon
Freshly ground black pepper, to taste
Chopped fresh parsley, for garnish

1. Set your Instant Pot to Sauté and heat 2 tablespoons of butter until melted.

2. Add the leek and mushrooms and sauté for about 2 minutes, stirring frequently. Add the garlic and cook for about 30 seconds.
3. Add the rice and toast it for 1 minute. Turn off the Instant Pot.
4. Stir in the stock, thyme, and salt.
5. Secure the lid. Select the Manual mode and set the cooking time for 8 minutes at High Pressure.
6. Once cooking is complete, do a quick pressure release. Carefully open the lid.
7. Stir in the remaining 2 tablespoons of butter and lemon juice. Taste and season with more salt and pepper, as needed. Serve garnished with fresh parsley.

Simple Fried Rice

Prep time: 5 minutes | Cook time: 10 minutes | Serves 4 to 6

1 tablespoon sesame oil
1 small onion, diced
1¾ cups jasmine rice, rinsed and drained
1¾ cups water
¼ cup soy sauce
¾ teaspoon ground ginger
¾ teaspoon garlic powder
1½ to 2 cups frozen mixed vegetable (peas, carrots, corn)

1. Set your Instant Pot to Sauté and heat the sesame oil until it shimmers.
2. Add the onion and cook for 1 minute, stirring frequently.
3. Turn off the Instant Pot and add the rice, water, soy sauce, ginger, and garlic powder.
4. Secure the lid. Select the Manual mode and set the cooking time for 5 minutes at High Pressure.
5. Once cooking is complete, do a natural pressure release for 10 minutes, then release any remaining pressure. Carefully open the lid.
6. Stir in the frozen vegetables, rest the lid back on (no need to lock it), and let sit for 3 to 4 minutes until warmed through. Serve immediately.

Corn and Pea Rice

Prep time: 5 minutes | Cook time: 8 minutes | Serves 3

1½ tablespoons olive oil
½ large onion, diced small
1 cup basmati rice, rinsed
½ cup frozen sweet corn kernels
½ cup frozen garden peas
¾ cup water
1½ tablespoons chopped cilantro stalks
1 large garlic clove, finely diced
½ teaspoon turmeric powder
Salt, to taste

1. Press the Sauté button on the Instant Pot. Add the olive oil and onion and sauté for 5 minutes, stirring frequently.
2. Add all the remaining ingredients to the Instant Pot and stir.
3. Secure the lid. Select the Manual mode and set the cooking time for 3 minutes at High Pressure.
4. Once cooking is complete, do a natural pressure release for 7 minutes, then release any remaining pressure. Carefully open the lid.
5. Fluff the rice and serve warm.

Quinoa and Spinach

Prep time: 5 minutes | Cook time: 2 minutes | Serves 4

1½ cups quinoa, rinsed
1½ cups water
4 cups spinach
1 bell pepper,
chopped
3 stalks of celery, chopped
¼ teaspoon salt

1. Combine all ingredients in the Instant Pot.
2. Secure the lid. Select the Manual mode and set the cooking time for 2 minutes at High Pressure.
3. Once cooking is complete, do a natural pressure release for 10 minutes, then release any remaining pressure. Carefully open the lid.
4. Fluff the quinoa and serve.

Farro Salad with Cherries

Prep time: 5 minutes | Cook time: 40 minutes | Serves 4 to 6

3 cups water
1 cup whole grain farro, rinsed
1 tablespoon extra-virgin olive oil
1 tablespoon apple cider vinegar
2 cups cherries, cut
into halves
¼ cup chopped green onions
1 teaspoon lemon juice
Salt, to taste
10 mint leaves, chopped

1. Combine the water and farro in the Instant Pot.
2. Lock the lid. Select the Manual mode and set the cooking time for 40 minutes at High Pressure.
3. When the timer beeps, perform a quick pressure release. Carefully remove the lid.
4. Drain the farro and transfer to a bowl. Stir in the olive oil, vinegar, cherries, green onions, lemon juice, salt, and mint. Serve immediately.

Apple and Celery Barley Salad

Prep time: 10 minutes | Cook time: 20 minutes | Serves 2 to 4

2½ cups water
1 cup pearl barley, rinsed
Salt and white pepper, to taste
1 green apple,
chopped
¼ cup chopped celery
¾ cup jarred spinach pesto

1. Combine the water, barley, salt, and white pepper in the Instant Pot.
2. Lock the lid. Select the Manual mode and set the cooking time for 20 minutes at High Pressure.
3. When the timer beeps, perform a quick pressure release. Carefully remove the lid.
4. Drain the barley and transfer to a bowl. Add the chopped apple, celery, and spinach pesto, tossing to coat, and serve.

Easy Pearl Barley

Prep time: 2 minutes | Cook time: 25 minutes | Serves 4

3 cups water
1½ cups pearl barley, rinsed

Salt, to taste
Peanut butter, to taste (optional)

1. Combine the water, barley, and salt in the Instant Pot.
2. Lock the lid. Select the Manual mode and set the cooking time for 25 minutes at High Pressure.
3. Once cooking is complete, do a natural pressure release for 15 minutes, then release any remaining pressure. Carefully open the lid.
4. Add the peanut butter to taste, if desired. Serve hot.

Tomato Polenta with Basil

Prep time: 10 minutes | Cook time: 10 minutes | Serves 6 to 8

2 tablespoons olive oil
2 cloves garlic, chopped
½ cup diced onion
1/3 cup finely chopped sun-dried tomatoes
3 tablespoons minced fresh basil
2 tablespoons

minced fresh parsley
2 teaspoons minced fresh oregano
1 teaspoon minced fresh rosemary
1 bay leaf
1 teaspoon kosher salt
4 cups vegetable stock
1 cup polenta

1. Set your Instant Pot to Sauté and heat the olive oil.
2. Add the garlic and onion and sauté for about 3 minutes until fragrant.
3. Add the tomatoes, basil, parsley, oregano, rosemary, bay leaf, salt, and stock, stirring well. Top the mixture with polenta.
4. Lock the lid. Select the Manual mode and set the cooking time for 5 minutes at High Pressure.
5. When the timer beeps, perform a natural pressure release for 10 minutes, then release any remaining pressure. Carefully remove the lid.
6. Serve warm.

Carrot and Corn Congee

Prep time: 5 minutes | Cook time: 30 minutes | Serves 4

Congee:

6 cups water
1 cup grated carrot
1 cup corn kernels
½ cup minced celery
1/3 cup moong dal
1/3 cup brown rice
1/3 cup millet
1 tablespoon soy sauce

2 teaspoons grated ginger
½ teaspoon ground turmeric
½ teaspoon ground ginger
½ teaspoon salt
¼ teaspoon black pepper

Topping (Optional):

Chopped cilantro
Chopped scallions

Sesame oil

1. Combine all the congee ingredients in the Instant Pot.
2. Secure the lid. Select the Porridge mode and set the cooking time for 30 minutes at High Pressure.
3. Once cooking is complete, do a natural pressure release for 10 minutes, then release any remaining pressure. Carefully open the lid.
4. Serve with bowls of your choice of toppings, if desired.

Toasted Almond Risotto

Prep time: 10 minutes | Cook time: 5 minutes | Serves 3

2 cups vanilla almond milk
½ cup Arborio (short-grain Italian) rice
2 tablespoons agave

syrup
1 teaspoon vanilla extract
¼ cup toasted almond flakes, for garnish

1. Combine all ingredients except the almond flakes in the Instant Pot.
2. Lock the lid. Select the Manual mode and set the cooking time for 5 minutes at High Pressure.
3. When the timer beeps, perform a natural pressure release for 20 minutes, then release any remaining pressure. Carefully remove the lid.
4. Serve garnished with the almond flakes.

Fig Millet

Prep time: 5 minutes | Cook time: 10 minutes | Serves 4 to 6

2 cups water
1¾ cups millet
1 cup almond milk
1/3 cup chopped

dried figs
2 tablespoons
coconut oil

1. Combine all ingredients in the Instant Pot.
2. Secure the lid. Select the Soup mode and set the cooking time for 10 minutes at High Pressure.
3. Once cooking is complete, do a natural pressure release for 10 minutes, then release any remaining pressure. Carefully open the lid.
4. Fluff the millet with a fork and serve warm.

Spinach and Tomato Couscous

Prep time: 10 minutes | Cook time: 8 minutes | Serves 4

2 tablespoons butter
1 cup couscous
1¼ cups water
½ cup chopped

spinach
1½ tomatoes,
chopped

1. Set your Instant Pot to Sauté and melt the butter.
2. Add the couscous and cook for 1 minute.
3. Pour in the water and stir well.
4. Lock the lid. Select the Manual mode and set the cooking time for 5 minutes at High Pressure.
5. When the timer beeps, perform a quick pressure release. Carefully remove the lid.
6. Transfer the couscous to a large bowl. Add the spinach and tomatoes, stir, and serve.

Butternut Squash Risotto with Sage

Prep time: 10 minutes | Cook time: 12 minutes | Serves 3

1 tablespoon olive oil
2 garlic cloves
1 sprig sage, leaves removed
½ (2 pounds / 907 g) butternut squash, diced

1 cup Arborio (short-grain Italian) rice
2 cups water
2 tablespoons white wine
1 teaspoon sea salt
½ teaspoon freshly ground nutmeg

1. Press the Sauté button on the Instant Pot. Add the olive oil, garlic, and sage and cook for 2 minutes.
2. Add the diced butternut squash and stir-fry for 5 minutes until just tender.
3. Add all the remaining ingredients to the Instant Pot and stir.
4. Secure the lid. Select the Manual mode and set the cooking time for 5 minutes at High Pressure.
5. Once cooking is complete, do a natural pressure release for 20 minutes, then release any remaining pressure. Carefully open the lid.
6. Stir the risotto and serve hot.

Israeli Couscous with Veggies

Prep time: 15 minutes | Cook time: 5 minutes | Serves 4 to 6

1 tablespoon olive oil
½ large onion, chopped
2 bay leaves
1 large red bell pepper, chopped
1 cup grated carrot
1¾ cups Israeli couscous
1¾ cups water
½ teaspoon garam masala
2 teaspoons salt, or more to taste
1 tablespoon lemon juice
Chopped cilantro, for garnish

1. Set your Instant Pot to Sauté and heat the olive oil.
2. Add the onion and bay leaves and sauté for 2 minutes.
3. Stir in the bell pepper and carrot and sauté for another 1 minute.
4. Add the couscous, water, garam masala, and salt. Stir to combine well.
5. Lock the lid. Select the Manual mode and set the cooking time for 2 minutes at High Pressure.
6. When the timer beeps, perform a natural pressure release for 10 minutes, then release any remaining pressure. Carefully remove the lid.
7. Fluff the couscous and stir in the lemon juice. Taste and season with more salt, if needed. Garnish with the chopped cilantro and serve hot.

Chapter 6 Soup & Stew Recipes

Broccoli-Cheddar Soup

Prep time: 10 minutes | Cook time: 10 minutes | Serves 6

1 tablespoon salted butter
1 yellow onion, finely chopped
1 garlic clove, finely chopped
½ cup grated carrot
2½ cups broccoli florets
2 cups vegetable broth
1 cup plus 3 tablespoons water, divided
1 cup heavy whipping cream
1 tablespoon cream cheese
1 cup shredded Cheddar cheese
1 tablespoon all-purpose flour

1. Set your Instant Pot to Sauté and melt the butter.
2. Add the onion and garlic and cook until the onion is translucent, about 5 minutes. Add the carrot, broccoli, broth, and 1 cup of water.
3. Secure the lid. Select the Manual mode and set the cooking time for 5 minutes at High Pressure.
4. Once cooking is complete, do a natural pressure release for 5 minutes, then release any remaining pressure. Carefully open the lid.
5. Using a potato masher, break up the broccoli into smaller chunks. Select Sauté, and add the cream, cream cheese, and cheese. Stir for about 3 minutes, until the cheese melts.
6. In a small bowl, whisk the flour with the remaining 3 tablespoons of water until smooth. Add this slurry to the soup and stir for 2 minutes.
7. Cover the pot with the lid and leave the Instant Pot for at least 15 minutes before serving.

Chestnut Soup

Prep time: 10 minutes | Cook time: 20 minutes | Serves 4

½ pound (227 g) fresh chestnuts
4 tablespoons butter
1 spring sage
1 onion, minced
1 stalk celery, minced
¼ teaspoon white

pepper
1 potato, minced
2 cups vegetable broth
2 tablespoons rum
¼ teaspoon nutmeg
2 tablespoons cream

1. Purée the fresh chestnuts in a blender. Set aside.
2. Place the butter, sage, onion, celery, and white pepper in the Instant Pot and sauté for 4 minutes. Add potato, broth, and puréed chestnuts, stirring well.
3. Secure the lid. Select the Soup mode and set the cooking time for 15 minutes at High Pressure.
4. Once cooking is complete, do a natural pressure release for 10 minutes, then release any remaining pressure. Carefully open the lid.
5. Stir in the rum, nutmeg, and cream. Using an immersion blender, purée the soup until a smooth consistency is achieved. Serve.

Butternut Squash Coconut Milk Soup

Prep time: 10 minutes | Cook time: 25 minutes | Serves 8

1 tablespoon extra-virgin olive oil
½ cup finely chopped onion
2 garlic cloves, finely chopped
2 pounds (907 g) butternut squash, peeled and cut into 1-inch chunks

3 teaspoons dried oregano
3 teaspoons kosher salt
1 (32-ounce / 907-g) container vegetable broth
1 (14-ounce / 397-g) can full-fat coconut milk

1. Set your Instant Pot to Sauté and heat the olive oil.
2. Once hot, add the onion and garlic, and sauté until the onion is translucent, about 5 minutes.
3. Stir in the butternut squash, oregano, and salt. Pour in the broth.
4. Secure the lid. Select the Manual mode and set the cooking time for 15 minutes at High Pressure.
5. Once cooking is complete, do a natural pressure release for 8 minutes, then release any remaining pressure. Carefully open the lid.
6. Using an immersion blender, purée the soup. Select Sauté and stir in the coconut milk. Simmer the soup for 5 minutes. Serve hot.

Carrot and Split Pea Soup

Prep time: 5 minutes | Cook time: 23 minutes | Serves 4 to 6

1 tablespoon roasted walnut oil
1 celery stalk, diced
2 carrots, diced
1 teaspoon smoked paprika
1 teaspoon dried thyme
1 bay leaf
½ to 1 teaspoon

salt, plus more as needed
2 garlic cloves, minced
2½ cups vegetable stock
1 cup green split peas
Freshly ground black pepper, to taste

1. Set your Instant Pot to Sauté and heat the walnut oil until shimmering.
2. Add the celery, carrots, paprika, thyme, bay leaf, and salt. Sauté for 2 to 3 minutes, stirring frequently, until fragrant.
3. Turn off the Instant Pot and stir in the garlic. Cook for 30 seconds more.
4. Pour in the stock and peas and stir to combine.
5. Secure the lid. Select the Manual mode and set the cooking time for 18 minutes at High Pressure.
6. Once cooking is complete, do a natural pressure release for 15 minutes, then release any remaining pressure. Carefully open the lid.
7. Remove and discard the bay leaf. Taste and season with more salt and pepper, as needed. Serve warm.

Tarragon Corn Soup

Prep time: 5 minutes | Cook time: 15 minutes | Serves 4

2 tablespoons butter
2 finely sliced garlic cloves
2 bay leaves
6 corn with cobs, cut in halves
4 sprigs tarragon
2 cups water
Salt and black pepper, to taste
1 tablespoon minced chives

1. Set your Instant Pot to Sauté and melt the butter.
2. Add the garlic and sauté for 4 minutes, stirring occasionally.
3. Add the bay leaves, corn with cobs, and tarragon sprigs, then add the water to cover the ingredients.
4. Secure the lid. Select the Soup mode and set the cooking time for 10 minutes at High Pressure.
5. Once cooking is complete, do a quick pressure release. Carefully open the lid.
6. Discard bay leaves and tarragon sprigs. Season to taste with salt and black pepper and let simmer for 3 minutes. Sprinkle with the chives and serve.

Tuscan Kale and Potato Soup

Prep time: 10 minutes | Cook time: 40 minutes | Serves 6

2 tablespoons extra-virgin olive oil
1 yellow onion, finely chopped
4 garlic cloves, finely chopped
½ teaspoon fennel seeds
10 ounces (283 g) baby kale, roughly chopped
3 teaspoons kosher salt
2 teaspoons freshly ground black pepper
1½ teaspoons dried
rosemary
1 teaspoon dried oregano
1 teaspoon dried basil
1½ pounds (680 g) potatoes, peeled and cubed
1 medium carrot, cut into 1-inch chunks
2 celery stalks, cut into 1-inch chunks
1 (32-ounce / 907-g) container vegetable broth

1. Set your Instant Pot to Sauté and heat the olive oil.

2. Once hot, add the onion, garlic, and fennel seeds, and cook until the onion is translucent, about 5 minutes.
3. Add the kale, salt, pepper, rosemary, oregano, and basil. Sauté until the kale wilts, about 5 minutes. Add the potatoes, carrot, celery, and broth, and mix well.
4. Secure the lid. Select the Manual mode and set the cooking time for 30 minutes at High Pressure.
5. Once cooking is complete, do a natural pressure release for 10 minutes, then release any remaining pressure. Carefully open the lid.
6. Using a potato masher, roughly mash the potatoes. This helps to thicken the soup. Mix thoroughly and serve hot.

Creamy Mushroom and Carrot Soup

Prep time: 10 minutes | Cook time: 15 minutes | Serves 4

1 tablespoon extra-virgin olive oil
10 ounces (283 g) cremini mushrooms, finely sliced
2 carrots, diced
2 tablespoons butter
2 stalks celery, diced
3 garlic cloves, minced
½ teaspoon dried
thyme
1 onion, diced
1 bay leaf
½ cup half-and-half
Salt and black pepper, to taste
1 sprig of rosemary
2 tablespoons minced parsley leaves

1. Press the Sauté button on the Instant Pot and heat the oil until hot.
2. Add the mushrooms, carrots, butter, celery, garlic, thyme, and onion and sauté for 4 minutes. Add the bay leaf.
3. Secure the lid. Select the Soup mode and set the cooking time for 10 minutes at High Pressure.
4. Once cooking is complete, do a natural pressure release for 10 minutes, then release any remaining pressure. Carefully open the lid.
5. Stir in the half and half. Season with salt and black pepper to taste. Garnish with rosemary and parsley before serving.

Lemon Rice Soup

Prep time: 10 minutes | Cook time: 22 minutes | Serves 6

2 tablespoons olive oil
3 teaspoons minced garlic
1 cup chopped celery
1 cup sliced onion
¾ cup long-grain rice
1 cup chopped carrots
6 cups vegetable broth
Salt and pepper, to taste
2 tablespoons all-purpose flour
¾ cup freshly squeezed lemon juice

1. Place the olive oil, garlic, celery, and onion in the Instant Pot and press the Sauté button. Sauté for 4 minutes and add the remaining ingredients except flour and lemon juice to the Instant Pot.
2. Lock the lid. Select the Manual mode and set the cooking time for 12 minutes at High Pressure.
3. When the timer beeps, perform a natural pressure release for 10 minutes, then release any remaining pressure. Carefully remove the lid.
4. Stir in the flour and lemon juice. Select Sauté and simmer for 5 minutes. Season to taste with salt and pepper. Serve hot.

Cozy Veggie and Wild Rice Soup

Prep time: 10 minutes | Cook time: 40 minutes | Serves 4 to 6

8 tablespoons butter, divided
5 celery stalks, sliced
5 carrots, sliced, with thicker end cut into half-moons
8 ounces (227 g) baby bella mushrooms, sliced
4 garlic cloves, minced
1 small sweet onion, diced
2 bay leaves
½ teaspoon paprika
½ teaspoon dried thyme
½ teaspoon salt, plus more as needed
4 cups vegetable stock
1 cup wild rice
½ cup all-purpose flour
1 cup coconut milk
Freshly ground black pepper, to taste

1. Press the Sauté button on the Instant Pot and heat 2 tablespoons of butter to melt.
2. Add the celery, carrots, mushrooms, garlic, onion, bay leaves, paprika, thyme, and salt, stirring well. Cook for 2 to 3 minutes, just until fragrant. Turn off the Instant Pot.
3. Add the stock and wild rice and stir to combine.
4. Secure the lid. Select the Manual mode and set the cooking time for 35 minutes at High Pressure.
5. Meanwhile, melt the remaining 6 tablespoons of butter in a small pan over medium-low heat. Whisk in the flour and cook for 3 to 4 minutes. Whisk in the milk, getting rid of any lumps to finish the roux. Set aside.
6. Once cooking is complete, do a quick pressure release. Carefully open the lid.
7. Remove and discard the bay leaves. Press the Sauté button again and stir in the roux until warmed through and thickened.
8. Taste and season with more salt and pepper, as needed. Serve warm.

Creamy Pumpkin Soup

Prep time: 5 minutes | Cook time: 20 minutes | Serves 4

2 cups water
1 tablespoon wheat flour
2 cups coconut cream
3 cups chopped pumpkin
1 teaspoon salt
1 teaspoon paprika
¼ teaspoon ground cardamom
½ teaspoon turmeric

1. In a bowl, stir together water and wheat flour until smooth. Pour the mixture into the Instant Pot.
2. Add coconut cream, chopped pumpkin, salt, paprika, ground cardamom, and turmeric. Stir to combine.
3. Secure the lid. Select the Manual mode and set the cooking time for 20 minutes at High Pressure.
4. Once cooking is complete, do a quick pressure release. Carefully open the lid.
5. Using an immersion blender, purée the soup. Ladle into bowls and serve.

Turmeric Vegetable Soup

Prep time: 10 minutes | Cook time: 10 minutes | Serves 2

½ cup coconut milk
1 teaspoon grated ginger
1 teaspoon turmeric
1 teaspoon minced garlic
1 teaspoon salt
1 teaspoon chili flakes
½ teaspoon ground black pepper
2 potatoes, chopped
½ carrot, grated
1 onion, grated
1 ounce (28 g) celery stalk, minced
1 cup water

1. Heat the coconut milk on Sauté mode for 3 minutes.
2. Add grated ginger, turmeric, garlic, salt, chili flakes, and ground black pepper and stir well.
3. Sauté the liquid until you get light spice smell, then add the potato, carrot, onion, and celery stalk. Pour in the water.
4. Secure the lid. Select the Soup mode and set the cooking time for 5 minutes at High Pressure.
5. Once cooking is complete, do a natural pressure release for 5 minutes, then release any remaining pressure. Carefully open the lid.
6. Using an immersion blender, purée the soup until smooth. Serve hot.

Curried Butternut Squash and Apple Soup

Prep time: 15 minutes | Cook time: 15 minutes | Serves 6

2 teaspoons vegetable oil
1 onion, minced
3 cups peeled and cubed butternut squash
1 teaspoon finely grated fresh ginger
1 apple, peeled and cubed
2 to 3 teaspoons curry powder
¼ teaspoon ground turmeric
1 teaspoon cayenne pepper
4 cups vegetable broth
Salt and ground black pepper, to taste
1 tablespoon fresh lemon juice
2½ tablespoons minced fresh cilantro

1. Press the Sauté button on the Instant Pot and heat the oil.
2. Add the onion and cook for 3 minutes.
3. Add the butternut squash and sauté for 4 to 5 minutes. Add ginger, apple and spices and cook for 1 to 2 minutes. Pour in the broth.
4. Secure the lid. Select the Manual mode and set the cooking time for 5 minutes at High Pressure.
5. Once cooking is complete, do a natural pressure release for 5 minutes, then release any remaining pressure. Carefully open the lid.
6. Select Sauté and season to taste with salt and black pepper. Continue to cook for 2 to 3 minutes.
7. Stir in the lemon juice. Garnish with the cilantro and serve.

Fresh Tomato Gazpacho

Prep time: 5 minutes | Cook time: 3 minutes | Serves 4

1½ cups water
4 large tomatoes, slit on the top in a cross shape
4 fresh basil leaves, finely chopped
1 teaspoon kosher salt
1 teaspoon sugar
½ teaspoon ground cumin
½ teaspoon paprika
½ teaspoon freshly squeezed lemon juice
1 English cucumber, peeled, seeded, and cut into bite-size chunks

1. Pour the water into the Instant Pot, then add the tomatoes.
2. Secure the lid. Select the Manual mode and set the cooking time for 3 minutes at High Pressure.
3. Once cooking is complete, do a quick pressure release. Carefully open the lid.
4. Drain the tomatoes and let cool for 5 minutes. Peel the tomato skin and discard.
5. In a blender, combine the tomatoes, basil, salt, sugar, cumin, paprika, and lemon juice, and purée until smooth (or your preferred consistency). Add the cucumber, and pulse the mixture for a chunky gazpacho. Chill for at least for 1 hour before serving.

Paprika Carrot Soup

Prep time: 10 minutes | Cook time: 4 minutes | Serves 2 to 3

7 carrots, chopped
1¼ cups vegetable stock
1 (1-inch) piece fresh ginger, peeled and chopped
½ sweet onion, chopped
½ teaspoon sweet paprika
½ teaspoon salt, plus more as needed
Freshly ground black pepper, to taste
Fresh herbs, for garnish (optional)

1. In the Instant Pot, combine the carrots, stock, ginger, onion, paprika, and salt. Season to taste with pepper.
2. Secure the lid. Select the Manual mode and set the cooking time for 4 minutes at High Pressure.
3. Once cooking is complete, do a natural pressure release for 5 minutes, then release any remaining pressure. Carefully open the lid.
4. Using an immersion blender, blend the soup until completely smooth. Taste and season with more salt and pepper, as needed. If desired, serve garnished with fresh herbs.

Cream of Asparagus Soup

Prep time: 15 minutes | Cook time: 16 minutes | Serves 6

1 tablespoon salted butter
½ cup finely chopped onion
3 garlic cloves, finely chopped
1½ pounds (680 g) asparagus, woody stems trimmed and cut into 1-inch
pieces
2 teaspoons kosher salt
1 teaspoon freshly ground black pepper
1½ cups vegetable broth
1 cup heavy whipping cream

1. Set your Instant Pot to Sauté and melt the butter.
2. Add the onion and garlic and cook until the onion is translucent, about 5 minutes.
3. Add the asparagus, salt, pepper, and broth. Continue cooking, stirring frequently, for 6 to 7 minutes or until the asparagus is soft.
4. Secure the lid. Select the Manual mode and set the cooking time for 4 minutes at High Pressure.
5. Once cooking is complete, do a natural pressure release for 10 minutes, then release any remaining pressure. Carefully open the lid.
6. Using an immersion blender, purée the soup. Add the cream, and mix thoroughly. Cover with the lid and leave the Instant Pot for at least 15 minutes. Serve hot.

Easy Creamy Tomato Basil Soup

Prep time: 5 minutes | Cook time: 10 minutes | Serves 4 to 6

2 tablespoons butter
1 small sweet onion, chopped
2 garlic cloves, minced
1 celery stalk, chopped
1 large carrot, chopped
3 cups vegetable stock
3 pounds (1.4 kg)
tomatoes, quartered
¼ cup nutritional yeast
¼ cup chopped fresh basil, plus more for garnish
Salt, to taste
Freshly ground black pepper, to taste
½ to 1 cup coconut milk

1. Set your Instant Pot to Sauté and melt the butter.
2. Add the onion and garlic and sauté for 3 to 4 minutes, stirring frequently. Add the celery and carrot and cook for another 1 to 2 minutes, stirring frequently. Pour in the stock.
3. Add the tomatoes, yeast, ¼ cup of basil, and a pinch of salt. Stir well.
4. Secure the lid. Select the Manual mode and set the cooking time for 5 minutes at High Pressure.
5. Once cooking is complete, do a natural pressure release for 8 minutes, then release any remaining pressure. Carefully open the lid.
6. Using an immersion blender, blend the soup to your preferred consistency. Whisk in the milk. Taste and season with more salt and pepper, if desired. Garnish with the fresh basil and serve.

Vegetarian Pho (Vietnamese Noodle Soup)

Prep time: 15 minutes | Cook time: 50 minutes | Serves 6

1 tablespoon corn oil
1 bunch scallions, white parts only, coarsely chopped
2 garlic cloves, finely chopped
5 white mushrooms, halved
2 teaspoons finely chopped fresh ginger
1 tablespoon thinly sliced lemongrass
1 (1-inch) cinnamon stick
1 dried bay leaf
3 star anise pods
3 cardamom seeds
3 whole cloves
1 tablespoon coriander seeds

1 teaspoon fennel seeds
1 tablespoon sugar
2 teaspoons kosher salt
1 teaspoon soy sauce, plus additional as needed
4 cups water
6 ounces (170 g) rice noodles, cooked
4 ounces (113 g) extra-firm tofu, cubed
Sprouts, for garnish
Fresh basil leaves, for garnish
Jalapeños, seeded and cut into rounds, for garnish
Sriracha, for garnish

1. Press the Sauté button on the Instant Pot and heat the oil.
2. Once hot, add the scallions, garlic, mushrooms, and ginger, and sauté for 2 minutes or until the mushrooms shrink. Add the lemongrass, cinnamon, bay leaf, star anise, cardamom, cloves, coriander seeds, fennel seeds, sugar, salt, and soy sauce, and mix well. Add the water and mix again.
3. Secure the lid. Select the Manual mode and set the cooking time for 40 minutes at High Pressure.
4. Once cooking is complete, do a natural pressure release for 10 minutes, then release any remaining pressure. Carefully open the lid.
5. Assemble the Pho: Using a fine-mesh strainer, strain the broth, discarding the vegetables and spices.
6. Divide the cooked noodles among bowls. Add broth to each bowl, and top each with tofu cubes, sprouts, and basil. Drizzle with additional soy sauce. Garnish with the jalapeños and Sriracha and serve hot.

Seitan and Rutabaga Stew

Prep time: 10 minutes | Cook time: 15 minutes | Serves 4 to 6

1 pound (454 g) seitan, patted dry
¼ teaspoon fine sea salt
½ teaspoon freshly ground black pepper
1 tablespoon avocado oil
1 yellow onion, diced
4 cloves garlic, minced
½ cup red wine
1 teaspoon fresh thyme leaves
1 teaspoon chopped fresh sage leaves
1 teaspoon chopped fresh rosemary

1 cup vegetable broth
2 teaspoons Dijon mustard
1 (1-pound / 454-g) large rutabaga, peeled and cut into 1-inch pieces
4 medium carrots (about 8 ounces / 227 g in total), peeled and sliced into 1-inch rounds
3 waxy potatoes (about 1 pound / 454 g in total), cut into 1-inch pieces
1 tablespoon tomato paste

1. Sprinkle the seitan with the salt and pepper.
2. Select the Sauté setting on the Instant Pot, add the oil, and heat for 2 minutes.
3. Add the seitan and sear for 4 minutes until golden brown. Flip and sear for 3 minutes more. Transfer the seitan to a dish and set aside.
4. Add the onion and garlic to the pot and sauté for 4 minutes until the onion softens.
5. Stir in the wine. Let the wine simmer until it has mostly evaporated, about 4 minutes.
6. Add the thyme, sage, and rosemary, and sauté for 1 minute more. Add the broth and mustard and stir to dissolve.
7. Bring the mixture up to a simmer, then stir in the seitan, rutabaga, carrots, and potatoes. Add the tomato paste on top. Do not stir.
8. Secure the lid. Select the Meat/Stew setting and set the cooking time for 4 minutes at High Pressure.
9. When timer beeps, perform a quick pressure release. Open the pot and gently stir the stew to incorporate the tomato paste and make sure everything is coated with the cooking liquid.
10. Ladle the stew into bowls and serve hot.

Corn and Potato Chowder

Prep time: 10 minutes | Cook time: 12 minutes | Serves 6

4 potatoes, peeled and cubed (about 1½ pounds / 680 g)
Kernels from 2 ears of corn (approximately 1½ cups)
2 teaspoons dried thyme
2 teaspoons freshly ground black pepper
2 teaspoons kosher salt
1 teaspoon onion powder
3½ cups water

1. In the Instant Pot, combine the potatoes, corn, thyme, pepper, salt, onion powder, and water.
2. Secure the lid. Select the Manual mode and set the cooking time for 12 minutes at High Pressure.
3. Once cooking is complete, do a natural pressure release for 10 minutes, then release any remaining pressure. Carefully open the lid.
4. Stir the soup. Using an immersion blender, purée the soup. Serve hot.

Tibetan Vegetable Noodle Soup

Prep time: 10 minutes | Cook time: 8 minutes | Serves 6

5 ounces (142 g) wheat noodles
1 cup water
2 tablespoons corn oil
2 shallots, finely chopped
2 garlic cloves, finely chopped
1 bunch scallions, finely chopped, white and green parts separated
½ cup shredded green cabbage
½ cup grated carrot
½ cup finely chopped mushrooms
1 teaspoon curry powder
2 teaspoons soy sauce
1 teaspoon Sriracha
2 teaspoons sugar
1 teaspoon kosher salt
1 (32-ounce / 907-g) container vegetable broth

1. In a medium bowl, soak the noodles in the water for 5 minutes. Drain and set aside.
2. Press the Sauté button on the Instant Pot and heat the oil.
3. Once hot, add the shallots, garlic, and white parts of the scallions, and cook for 2 minutes. Add the cabbage, carrot, mushrooms, curry powder, soy sauce, Sriracha, sugar, and salt. Mix well and cook for 3 to 4 minutes. Add the noodles and vegetable broth.
4. Secure the lid. Select the Manual mode and set the cooking time for 3 minutes at High Pressure.
5. Once cooking is complete, do a natural pressure release for 5 minutes, then release any remaining pressure. Carefully open the lid.
6. Stir the soup well and serve hot.

Middle Eastern Lentil Soup

Prep time: 10 minutes | Cook time: 10 minutes | Serves 4

2½ cups water, divided
½ cup red lentils, rinsed and drained
2 garlic cloves, finely chopped
½ cup finely chopped onion
1 teaspoon freshly ground black pepper
½ teaspoon ground turmeric
½ teaspoon ground cumin
1 teaspoon kosher salt
¼ cup chopped fresh parsley
2 tablespoons freshly squeezed lemon juice

1. Pour 1½ cups water into the Instant Pot, and add the lentils, garlic, and onion.
2. Secure the lid. Select the Manual mode and set the cooking time for 10 minutes at High Pressure.
3. Once cooking is complete, do a natural pressure release for 10 minutes, then release any remaining pressure. Carefully open the lid.
4. Using a potato masher, thoroughly mash the lentils.
5. Select Sauté, and add the pepper, turmeric, cumin, salt, and parsley. Mix well and stir in the remaining 1 cup of water. Simmer for 10 minutes. Turn off the Instant Pot and stir in the lemon juice. Serve hot.

Curried Carrot and Ginger Soup

Prep time: 10 minutes | Cook time: 18 minutes | Serves 4

2 teaspoons corn oil
2 teaspoons finely chopped fresh ginger
5 large carrots, cut into bite-size pieces
1 teaspoon curry powder
2 tablespoons red lentils, rinsed
2 teaspoons kosher salt
2½ cups water

1. Press the Sauté button on the Instant Pot and heat the oil.
2. Once hot, add the ginger and carrots, and sauté for about 2 minutes, until the carrots start to soften. Stir in the curry powder, lentils, salt, and water.
3. Secure the lid. Select the Manual mode and set the cooking time for 15 minutes at High Pressure.
4. Once cooking is complete, do a natural pressure release for 5 minutes, then release any remaining pressure. Carefully open the lid.
5. Using an immersion blender, purée the soup. Mix thoroughly, and serve hot.

Vegetable Noodle Soup

Prep time: 10 minutes | Cook time: 4 minutes | Serves 4 to 6

4 carrots, chopped into bite-sized pieces
4 celery stalks, chopped into bite-sized pieces
2 sweet potatoes, peeled and chopped into bite-sized pieces
1 sweet onion, chopped into bite-sized pieces
1 tomato, diced
4 cups vegetable stock, plus more as needed
1 to 1½ cups water, plus more as needed
1 cup broccoli florets
1 cup dried pasta
2 garlic cloves, minced
1 bay leaf
1 teaspoon dried basil
1 teaspoon dried oregano
1 teaspoon dried thyme
1 to 2 teaspoons salt
Pinch freshly ground black pepper
Chopped fresh parsley, for garnish (optional)
Lemon zest, for garnish (optional)

1. Combine all the ingredients except the parsley and lemon zest in the Instant Pot, making sure all the good stuff is submerged (add more water or stock, if needed).
2. Secure the lid. Select the Manual mode and set the cooking time for 4 minutes at High Pressure.
3. Once cooking is complete, do a natural pressure release for 5 minutes, then release any remaining pressure. Carefully open the lid and stir.
4. Remove and discard the bay leaf and serve garnished as desired.

Spinach and Butternut Squash Soup

Prep time: 10 minutes | Cook time: 13 minutes | Serves 4

1 tablespoon coconut oil
2 cloves garlic, minced
1 cup chopped red onion
4 cups chopped fresh spinach
1 teaspoon dried thyme
½ teaspoon nutmeg
½ teaspoon salt
1 teaspoon coarse ground black pepper
10 cups butternut squash, peeled and cubed
4 cups vegetable stock
1 cup plain soy yogurt
¼ cup toasted pumpkin seeds (optional)

1. Set your Instant Pot to Sauté and melt the coconut oil.
2. Add the garlic, red onion, spinach, thyme, nutmeg, salt, and black pepper. Sauté for 5 minutes, stirring frequently.
3. Stir in the butternut squash and vegetable stock.
4. Secure the lid. Select the Manual mode and set the cooking time for 8 minutes at High Pressure.
5. Once cooking is complete, do a quick pressure release. Carefully open the lid.
6. Whisk in the soy yogurt. Using an immersion blender, blend the soup until creamy.
7. Serve garnished with the toasted pumpkin seeds, if desired.

Sweet Potato and Chipotle Chowder

Prep time: 3 minutes | Cook time: 2 minutes | Serves 4 to 6

1¼ cups vegetable stock
1 (14-ounce / 397-g) can coconut milk
2 large sweet potatoes, peeled and diced large
2 to 4 canned chipotle peppers in adobo sauce, diced
1 small onion, diced
1 red bell pepper, diced
1 teaspoon ground cumin
½ to 1 teaspoon salt
1½ cups frozen sweet corn
Adobo sauce from the canned peppers, to taste

1. In a medium bowl, whisk together the stock and coconut milk until combined. Pour into the Instant Pot and add the sweet potatoes, chipotles, onion, bell pepper, cumin, and salt.
2. Secure the lid. Select the Manual mode and set the cooking time for 2 minutes at High Pressure.
3. Once cooking is complete, do a natural pressure release for 5 minutes, then release any remaining pressure. Carefully open the lid.
4. Stir in the frozen corn and adobo sauce, if you want more heat. Allow to sit for 1 to 2 minutes before serving.

Leek and Potato Soup

Prep time: 5 minutes | Cook time: 10 minutes | Serves 4

3 tablespoons butter
2 large leeks, white and very light green parts only, cleaned well and chopped
2 garlic cloves, minced
4 cups vegetable stock
1 pound (454
g) Yukon Gold potatoes, cubed
1 bay leaf
½ teaspoon salt, plus more as needed
1/3 cup extra-virgin olive oil
2/3 cup soy milk
Freshly ground white pepper, to taste

1. Set your Instant Pot to Sauté and melt the butter.
2. Add the leeks and sauté for about 2 to 3 minutes until tender, stirring occasionally.

3. Add the garlic and cook for 30 to 45 seconds more, stirring frequently, until fragrant.
4. Pour in the stock and add the potatoes, bay leaf, and salt. Stir to mix well.
5. Secure the lid. Select the Manual mode and set the cooking time for 5 minutes at High Pressure.
6. Once cooking is complete, do a natural pressure release for 15 minutes, then release any remaining pressure.
7. In a blender, combine the olive oil and soy milk. Blend until completely mixed. This is an easy dairy-free substitute for heavy cream.
8. Carefully open the lid, remove and discard the bay leaf. Whisk in the "cream." Using an immersion blender, purée the soup until smooth.
9. Taste and season with more salt and pepper, as needed. Serve immediately.

Butternut Squash and Cauliflower Soup

Prep time: 5 minutes | Cook time: 25 minutes | Serves 3

2 teaspoons olive oil
1 garlic clove, minced
½ medium onion, diced
1 cup vegetable broth
½ pound (227 g) frozen cauliflower
½ pound (227 g) frozen, cubed, butternut squash
½ teaspoon paprika
¼ teaspoon dried thyme
2 pinches of sea salt
½ cup coconut milk

1. Set your Instant Pot to Sauté and heat the olive oil.
2. Add the garlic and onion and cook for 2 minutes.
3. Add the broth, cauliflower, butternut, and all the spices to the Instant Pot, stirring well.
4. Secure the lid. Select the Manual mode and set the cooking time for 5 minutes at High Pressure.
5. Once cooking is complete, do a quick pressure release. Carefully open the lid.
6. Add the milk to the soup and blend with an immersion blender until creamy.
7. Serve hot.

Corn Vegetable Soup

Prep time: 10 minutes | Cook time: 10 minutes | Serves 4

5 cups vegetable broth
2½ cups corn kernels
1 cup minced cabbage
1 cup minced carrot
1 tablespoon soy sauce
2 teaspoons sesame

oil
2 teaspoons minced garlic
2 teaspoons grated ginger
1½ teaspoons ground cumin
Ground pepper, to taste

1. Combine all the ingredients except the pepper in the Instant Pot.
2. Secure the lid. Select the Manual mode and set the cooking time for 10 minutes at High Pressure.
3. Once cooking is complete, do a natural pressure release for 10 minutes, then release any remaining pressure. Carefully open the lid.
4. Purée the soup with an immersion blender until smooth. Season to taste with pepper and serve immediately.

French Onion Soup

Prep time: 10 minutes | Cook time: 30 minutes | Serves 6

¼ cup olive oil
5 Vidalia onions, thinly sliced
2 tablespoons soy sauce
½ teaspoon baking soda
½ cup red zinfandel

wine
1 tablespoon chopped fresh thyme
8 cups vegetable stock
1 cup shredded cashew cheese

1. Set your Instant Pot to Sauté and heat the olive oil.
2. Add the onions and soy sauce and sauté for 3 minutes.
3. Add the baking soda and stir. Continue cooking, stirring frequently, for another 3 minutes.
4. Secure the lid. Select the Manual mode and set the cooking time for 20 minutes at High Pressure.

5. Once cooking is complete, do a quick pressure release. Carefully open the lid.
6. Set your Instant Pot to Sauté again and add the fresh thyme and red zinfandel wine. Cook for 5 to 7 minutes, stirring frequently, or until the wine has mostly reduced. Pour in the vegetable stock.
7. Secure the lid. Select the Manual mode and set the cooking time for 5 minutes at High Pressure.
8. Once cooking is complete, do a quick pressure release. Carefully open the lid.
9. Ladle the soup into bowls and serve topped with shredded cashew cheese.

Mushroom and Tofu Soup

Prep time: 9 minutes | Cook time: 10 minutes | Serves 4 to 6

2 tablespoons butter
1 small sweet onion, chopped
1½ pounds (680 g) white button mushrooms, sliced
2 teaspoons dried thyme
2 garlic cloves,

minced
1 teaspoon sea salt
1¾ cups vegetable stock
½ cup silken tofu
Chopped fresh thyme, for garnish (optional)

1. Set your Instant Pot to Sauté and melt the butter.
2. Add the onion and sauté for 1 to 2 minutes until tender.
3. Add the mushrooms, garlic, dried thyme, and salt. Cook for another 2 minutes and then turn off the Instant Pot. Pour in the stock.
4. Secure the lid. Select the Manual mode and set the cooking time for 6 minutes at High Pressure.
5. Meanwhile, put the tofu into a food processor or blender and process until smooth. Set aside.
6. Once cooking is complete, do a natural pressure release for 10 minutes, then release any remaining pressure. Carefully open the lid.
7. Using an immersion blender, blend the soup until completely creamy. Stir in the tofu and serve garnished with fresh thyme, if desired.

Smoky Tomato White Bean Soup

Prep time: 3 minutes | Cook time: 32 minutes | Serves 4 to 6

1 cup dried great northern white beans, rinsed
¼ cup raw millet
1 cup vegetable stock
1 small to medium tomato, diced
3½ to 4 cups water, plus more as needed

1 (14-ounce / 397-g) can coconut milk
1 to 1½ teaspoons smoked paprika, plus more as needed
1 teaspoon salt, plus more as needed
1 cup frozen sweet corn

1. Combine all the ingredients except the corn in the Instant Pot.
2. Secure the lid. Select the Manual mode and set the cooking time for 32 minutes at High Pressure.
3. Once cooking is complete, do a natural pressure release for 10 minutes, then release any remaining pressure. Carefully open the lid.
4. Stir in the corn. Taste and adjust the seasonings, as needed. Serve hot.

Classic Minestrone Soup

Prep time: 5 minutes | Cook time: 10 minutes | Serves 4 to 6

2 tablespoons olive oil
2 celery stalks, sliced
1 sweet onion, diced
1 large carrot, sliced, with thicker end cut into half-moons
2 garlic cloves, minced
1 teaspoon dried basil
1 teaspoon dried oregano
1 bay leaf
½ to 1 teaspoon salt, plus more as

needed
1 zucchini, roughly diced
1 (16-ounce / 454-g) can kidney beans, drained and rinsed
1 (28-ounce / 794-g) can diced tomatoes
6 cups vegetable stock
1 cup small dried pasta
2 to 3 cups fresh baby spinach
Freshly ground black pepper, to taste

1. Set your Instant Pot to Sauté and heat the olive oil.
2. Add the celery, onion, and carrot and sauté for 2 to 3 minutes, stirring frequently.
3. Stir in the garlic and cook for another 1 minute, stirring frequently.
4. Turn off the Instant Pot and add the basil, oregano, bay leaf, and salt. Stir and allow to sit for 30 seconds to 1 minute.
5. Add the zucchini, kidney beans, tomatoes, stock, and pasta, stirring well.
6. Secure the lid. Select the Manual mode and set the cooking time for 4 minutes at High Pressure.
7. Once cooking is complete, do a quick pressure release. Carefully open the lid.
8. Remove and discard the bay leaf. Stir in the spinach and let sit for 2 minutes until wilted. Taste and season with more salt and pepper, as needed. Serve hot.

Thai Red Curry Zucchini Soup

Prep time: 10 minutes | Cook time: 1 minute | Serves 2

1½ cups water
¾ cup coconut milk
1½ teaspoons red curry paste
1 teaspoon lemon zest
1 medium zucchini, spiralized (about 3

cups)
½ cup chopped red pepper
½ cup thin carrot coins
2 tablespoons nutritional yeast
Salt, to taste

For Serving (Optional):
Lime wedges   Chopped cilantro

1. Combine the water, coconut milk, red curry paste, lemon zest, zucchini, red pepper, and carrot coins in the Instant Pot.
2. Secure the lid. Select the Manual mode and set the cooking time for 1 minute at Low Pressure.
3. Once cooking is complete, do a quick pressure release. Carefully open the lid.
4. Stir in the nutritional yeast and season with salt to taste. Serve garnished with the lime wedges and cilantro, if desired.

Barley and Parsnip Stew

Prep time: 15 minutes | Cook time: 20 minutes | Serves 4

1 cup pearl barley
2 parsnips, peeled and chopped
2 cups chopped peeled sweet potato
1 large yellow onion, chopped
1 (28-ounce / 794-g) can diced tomatoes, with

juices
1 teaspoon dried basil
1 teaspoon dried oregano
4 cups water
Salt and freshly ground black pepper, to taste

1. In the Instant Pot, combine the barley, parsnips, sweet potato, onion, tomatoes with juice, basil, oregano, and water.
2. Close the lid, then select Manual mode and set cooking time for 20 minutes on High Pressure.
3. Once the cook time is complete, quick release the pressure. Open the lid. Season with salt and pepper.
4. Serve immediately.

Smoked Paprika Lentil Soup

Prep time: 10 minutes | Cook time: 15 minutes | Serves 10

2 tablespoons olive oil
6 garlic cloves, minced
2 celery stalks
2 onions, chopped finely
2 cups green lentils, rinsed
2 cups red lentils, rinsed

1½ pounds (680 g) potatoes
4 carrots, sliced
1½ bunches rainbow chard
4 teaspoons cumin
3 teaspoons smoked paprika
2 teaspoons salt
Pepper, to taste
10 cups water

1. Press the Sauté button on the Instant Pot and heat the olive oil.
2. Add garlic, celery, and onions and sauté for 4 minutes. Add the remaining ingredients to the Instant Pot, stirring well.
3. Lock the lid. Select the Manual mode and set the cooking time for 9 minutes at High Pressure.

4. When the timer beeps, perform a natural pressure release for 10 minutes, then release any remaining pressure. Carefully remove the lid. Serve warm.

White Beans and Greens Soup

Prep time: 5 minutes | Cook time: 20 minutes | Serves 6

1 tablespoon vegetable oil
4 large cloves garlic, minced
2 cups diced carrots
1 cup diced onion
1 cup diced celery
2 cups sliced cremini, shiitake, maitake, or baby bella mushrooms
2 tablespoons dried herbes de Provence
1 bay leaf
1 teaspoon red pepper flakes
½ teaspoon freshly ground black pepper,

plus additional for serving
5 cups vegetable broth
2 cups water
¼ cup tomato paste
1½ cups dried cannellini beans, soaked for 12 hours or overnight, rinsed
8 cups loosely packed greens
Juice of 1 large lemon (about 3 tablespoons)
1 to 1½ teaspoons salt (optional)

1. Press the Sauté button on the Instant Pot and heat the oil.
2. Add the garlic, carrots, onion, and celery and sauté for 3 minutes.
3. Add the mushrooms and seasonings and sauté for 3 to 5 minutes more. Add the vegetable broth, water, and tomato paste. Stir well.
4. Stir in the beans and greens.
5. Secure the lid. Select the Manual mode and set the cooking time for 8 minutes at High Pressure.
6. Once cooking is complete, do a natural pressure release for 10 minutes, then release any remaining pressure. Carefully open the lid.
7. Stir in the lemon juice and taste before adding salt. Remove the bay leaf and serve with additional black pepper.

Detox Turmeric Veggie Soup

Prep time: 15 minutes | Cook time: 20 minutes | Serves 8

4 cups cubed butternut squash
2 medium sweet potatoes, peeled and cut into pieces
2 cups carrots, peeled and cut into chunks
1 medium onion
2 teaspoons minced garlic
1 teaspoon grated fresh ginger
2 teaspoons turmeric powder
1 teaspoon garam masala
1 teaspoon mild curry powder
¼ teaspoon cayenne pepper
1 teaspoon sea salt
3½ cups vegetable broth
14 ounces (397 g) coconut milk

1. Place all the ingredients in the Instant Pot and stir well.
2. Secure the lid. Select the Manual mode and set the cooking time for 20 minutes at High Pressure.
3. Once cooking is complete, do a quick pressure release. Carefully open the lid.
4. Purée the soup with an immersion blender and serve hot.

Lentil Soup with Garam Masala

Prep time: 5 minutes | Cook time: 15 minutes | Serves 6

1 tablespoon vegetable oil
2 tablespoons finely diced shallot
1 cup diced carrots
1 cup diced celery
½ teaspoon garam masala
½ teaspoon ground cinnamon
½ teaspoon cumin
1 bay leaf
1¾ cups dried brown or green lentils, rinsed and drained
2 cups vegetable broth
3 cups water
¼ to ½ teaspoon sea salt (optional)
Freshly ground black pepper, to taste

1. Set your Instant Pot to Sauté and heat the oil.
2. Add the shallot, carrots, and celery and sauté for 3 to 5 minutes, until the shallot and celery are tender, stirring occasionally.
3. Add the garam masala, cinnamon, cumin, bay leaf, and lentils and stir well. Pour in the vegetable broth and water and stir to mix well.
4. Secure the lid. Select the Manual mode and set the cooking time for 8 minutes at High Pressure.
5. Once cooking is complete, do a natural pressure release for 10 minutes, then release any remaining pressure. Carefully open the lid.
6. Remove the bay leaf and sprinkle with salt (if desired). Season to taste with black pepper and serve.

Creamy Tofu Vegetable Soup

Prep time: 5 minutes | Cook time: 10 minutes | Serves 8

2 to 3 tablespoons butter
3 cloves garlic, minced
1 (14-ounce / 397-g) package soft tofu
1 cup almond milk
2 tablespoons lemon juice
1 teaspoon dried dill
½ teaspoon salt
4 cups diced potatoes
2 cups sliced mushrooms
2 cups sliced onion, cut into half-moons
1 cup chopped celery
1 cup chopped carrot
4 cups vegetable broth
Ground black pepper, to taste

1. Set your Instant Pot to Sauté and melt the butter.
2. Add the garlic and sauté for 1 minute.
3. Pulse the tofu, almond milk, lemon juice, salt, and dill in a food processor until creamy.
4. Add the potatoes, mushrooms, onion, carrots, and celery to the Instant Pot, stirring well. Pour the tofu mixture into the pot and stir in the vegetable broth.
5. Secure the lid. Select the Manual mode and set the cooking time for 5 minutes at High Pressure.
6. Once cooking is complete, do a quick pressure release. Carefully open the lid.
7. Season to taste with black pepper and serve.

Easy Swiss Chard Stem Soup

Prep time: 3 minutes | Cook time: 4 minutes | Serves 6

8 cups diced Swiss Chard stems
3 leeks, chopped
1 potato, peeled and diced
1 celeriac, peeled and diced
1½ cups vegetable stock
1 cup coconut milk
Salt and pepper, to taste

1. Combine all the ingredients in the Instant Pot.
2. Lock the lid. Select the Manual mode and set the cooking time for 4 minutes at High Pressure.
3. When the timer beeps, perform a natural pressure release for 8 minutes, then release any remaining pressure. Carefully remove the lid. Serve warm.

Super Flageolet Bean and Millet Stew

Prep time: 10 minutes | Cook time: 20 minutes | Serves 6

1 teaspoon olive oil
¼ cup sliced shallot
1 apple, diced
½ cup diced parsnip
1 golden beet, diced
1½ cups dried flageolet beans, soaked in water overnight, rinsed and drained
½ cup millet
1 (14-ounce / 398-g) can diced tomatoes
1 bay leaf
1 teaspoon whole fennel seed, crumbled
1 teaspoon dried thyme
1 teaspoon dried sweet basil
2½ cups vegetable broth
2½ cups water
1 to 2 tablespoons lemon juice
¼ teaspoon black pepper

1. In the Instant Pot, heat the oil on Sauté mode.
2. Add the shallot and sauté for 1 minute to soften a bit.
3. Add the apple, parsnip, and beet and sauté for 4 minutes.
4. Add the beans, millet, diced tomatoes, bay leaf, fennel, thyme, and basil. Stir to combine.

5. Cover the vegetables and beans with broth and water by 3 inches.
6. Secure the lid. Select Manual mode and set cooking time for 10 minutes on High Pressure.
7. When timer beeps, use a natural pressure release for 15 minutes, then release any remaining pressure.
8. Remove the lid and stir in the lemon juice. Remove the bay leaf before serving. Add ground pepper and serve.

Ethiopian-Inspired Spinach and Lentil Soup

Prep time: 5 minutes | Cook time: 65 minutes | Serves 6

2 tablespoons butter
1 tablespoon olive oil
1 onion, finely chopped
2 teaspoons ground coriander
1 teaspoon garlic powder
½ teaspoon turmeric powder
½ teaspoon cinnamon powder
¼ teaspoon clove powder
¼ teaspoon cardamom powder
¼ teaspoon cayenne pepper
¼ teaspoon grated nutmeg
2 cups lentils, soaked overnight and rinsed
8 cups water
Salt and pepper, to taste
2 cups chopped spinach leaves
4 tablespoons lemon juice

1. Set your Instant Pot to Sauté and heat the butter and olive oil.
2. Add the onion, garlic powder, coriander, cinnamon, turmeric, clove, cayenne pepper, cardamom, and nutmeg and cook for about 2 minutes until fragrant, stirring frequently.
3. Stir in the lentils and water. Season to taste with salt and pepper.
4. Secure the lid. Select the Manual mode and set the cooking time for 60 minutes at High Pressure.
5. Once cooking is complete, do a quick pressure release. Carefully open the lid.
6. Set your Instant Pot to Sauté again and add the spinach leaves and lemon juice. Stir and let simmer for a few minutes until the leaves are wilted. Serve warm.

Classic Borscht (Beet Soup)

Prep time: 15 minutes | Cook time: 15 minutes | Serves 7

4 tablespoons olive oil
2 medium white onions, chopped
2 large grated carrots
4 medium beets
4 large white potatoes, peeled and diced
½ medium white cabbage, thinly sliced
8 medium cloves

garlic, diced
10 cups water
4 cups vegetable stock
½ cup dried porcini mushrooms
4 tablespoons apple cider vinegar
3 tablespoons tomato paste
2 teaspoons salt
1 teaspoon pepper
Fresh parsley, for garnish

1. Press the Sauté button on the Instant Pot and add the oil and onions. Cook for 3 minutes, stirring frequently.
2. Add the carrots, beets, potatoes, and cabbage, and sauté for 1 minute.
3. Add the remaining ingredients except the parsley to the Instant Pot and stir well.
4. Secure the lid. Select the Manual mode and set the cooking time for 10 minutes at High Pressure.
5. Once cooking is complete, do a natural pressure release for 10 minutes, then release any remaining pressure. Carefully open the lid.
6. Garnish with the parsley and serve.

Potato, Cabbage, and Carrot Soup

Prep time: 15 minutes | Cook time: 15 minutes | Serves 6

1 tablespoon olive oil
2 cups minced onion
1½ teaspoons minced garlic
1½ teaspoons caraway seeds
1 teaspoon smoked or plain paprika
8 cups water
1 cup vegetable stock

4 cups cubed potatoes
4 cups chopped cabbage
2 cups sliced carrots
1½ teaspoons dried dill
½ cup nutritional yeast
Salt and pepper, to taste

1. Set your Instant Pot to Sauté and heat the olive oil.
2. Add the onion and sauté for 5 minutes until translucent.
3. Add the garlic, caraway seeds, and paprika and sauté for 2 minutes more.
4. Stir in the remaining ingredients, except for the nutritional yeast, salt, and pepper.
5. Secure the lid. Select the Manual mode and set the cooking time for 5 minutes at High Pressure.
6. Once cooking is complete, do a natural pressure release for 10 minutes, then release any remaining pressure. Carefully open the lid.
7. Add the nutritional yeast and stir to combine. Season to taste with salt and pepper.

Spinach Enchilada Soup

Prep time: 10 minutes | Cook time: 15 minutes | Serves 4

1 tablespoon olive oil
½ cup diced red onion
2 cloves garlic, minced
1 medium-sized poblano pepper, seeded and chopped
1 tablespoon minced jalapeño pepper
2 cups fresh spinach, torn
1 teaspoon ground cumin

½ teaspoon salt
½ teaspoon black pepper
4 cups vegetable stock
1 (15-ounce / 425-g) can black beans, drained and rinsed
1 cup chopped tomatoes
1 cup golden hominy
¾ cup enchilada sauce
¼ cup chopped fresh cilantro

1. Set your Instant Pot to Sauté and heat the olive oil.
2. Add the red onion, garlic, poblano pepper, jalapeño pepper, spinach, cumin, salt, and black pepper, stirring well, and sauté for 5 minutes.
3. Add the remaining ingredients, except for the cilantro, to the Instant Pot.
4. Secure the lid. Select the Manual mode and set the cooking time for 10 minutes at High Pressure.
5. Once cooking is complete, do a quick pressure release. Carefully open the lid.
6. Garnish with the fresh cilantro and serve.

Creamy Potato and Broccoli Soup

Prep time: 5 minutes | Cook time: 10 minutes | Serves 6

1 tablespoon vegetable oil
1 onion, chopped
3 cloves garlic, diced
1 cup vegetable broth
1 cup unsweetened almond milk
1 cup water
1 Yukon Gold potato,
cut into chunks
1 large broccoli head, cut into florets
2 tablespoons soy sauce
3 teaspoons nutritional yeasts
Salt and pepper, to taste

1. Press the Sauté button on the Instant Pot and heat the oil.
2. Sauté the onion and garlic until fragrant, about 2 minutes.
3. Add the remaining ingredients to the Instant Pot and stir well.
4. Secure the lid. Select the Manual mode and set the cooking time for 7 minutes at High Pressure.
5. Once cooking is complete, do a natural pressure release for 10 minutes, then release any remaining pressure. Carefully open the lid.
6. Serve hot.

White Bean and Swiss Chard Stew

Prep time: 6 minutes | Cook time: 10 minutes | Serves 4 to 6

1 tablespoon olive oil
2 carrots, sliced, with thicker end cut into half-moons
1 celery stalk, sliced
½ onion, cut into large dices
2 or 3 garlic cloves, minced
3 tomatoes, chopped
¼ to ½ teaspoon red pepper flakes
½ teaspoon dried oregano
½ teaspoon dried rosemary
½ teaspoon salt, plus more as needed
¼ teaspoon dried basil
Pinch freshly ground black pepper, plus more as needed
2 cups cooked great northern beans
1 small bunch Swiss chard leaves, chopped
Nutritional yeast, for sprinkling (optional)

1. Set your Instant Pot to Sauté and heat the olive oil until it shimmers.
2. Add the carrots, celery, and onion. Sauté for 2 to 3 minutes, stirring occasionally. Add the garlic and cook for 30 seconds more. Turn off the Instant Pot.
3. Stir in the tomatoes, red pepper flakes, oregano, rosemary, salt, basil, black pepper, and beans.
4. Secure the lid. Select the Manual mode and set the cooking time for 4 minutes at High Pressure.
5. Once cooking is complete, do a quick pressure release. Carefully open the lid.
6. Stir in the Swiss chard and let sit for 2 to 3 minutes until wilted. Taste and season with salt and pepper, as needed. Sprinkle the nutritional yeast over individual servings, if desired.

Mung Bean and Collard Stew

Prep time: 15 minutes | Cook time: 15 minutes | Serves 4

1 teaspoon vegetable oil
½ cup chopped carrot
1 cup cubed sweet potatoes
2 cloves garlic, minced
1 cup diced onion
½ cup chopped celery
3 cups loosely packed collard green
strips
¼ teaspoon turmeric
¼ teaspoon paprika
1 teaspoon ground ginger
2 cups curry broth
1 cup water
1 cup dried mung beans
2 tablespoons lemon juice
½ teaspoon sea salt

1. In the Instant Pot, heat the oil on medium heat, add the carrot, potatoes, garlic, onion, and celery and sauté for 5 minutes.
2. Add the collard greens, turmeric, paprika, ginger, curry broth, water, and mung beans. Stir to combine.
3. Secure the lid. Select Manual mode and set cooking time for 8 minutes on High Pressure.
4. When timer beeps, use a natural pressure release for 15 minutes, then release any remaining pressure. Open the lid.
5. Stir in the lemon juice and add salt before serving.

Artichoke and Chickpea Soup

Prep time: 5 minutes | Cook time: 6 minutes | Serves 4

1 large potato, diced
3 cloves garlic, minced
½ package extra-firm tofu, pressed, drained, and diced
1 (14-ounce / 397-g) can artichoke hearts, drained
1 (14-ounce / 397-g) can chickpeas, rinsed and drained

5 cups vegetable broth
1 tomato, diced
2 stalks celery, chopped
1 teaspoon turmeric
1 teaspoon paprika
¼ teaspoon ground black pepper
¼ cup capers, for garnish

1. Combine all the ingredients except the black pepper and capers in the Instant Pot.
2. Secure the lid. Select the Manual mode and set the cooking time for 6 minutes at High Pressure.
3. Once cooking is complete, do a quick pressure release. Carefully open the lid and stir in the black pepper.
4. Garnish with the capers and serve hot.

African Yam and Peanut Stew

Prep time: 20 minutes | Cook time: 60 minutes | Serves 4

3 yams, chopped
1 white onion, roughly chopped
1 teaspoon minced ginger root
1 teaspoon garlic, diced
1 tablespoon almond butter
1 teaspoon cilantro
1 teaspoon oregano
1 teaspoon cayenne pepper
1 teaspoon onion

powder
1 teaspoon ground black pepper
1 teaspoon cumin
¼ cup peanuts, chopped
1 bell pepper, chopped
1 cup collard greens, chopped
3 tablespoons peanut butter
½ cup almond milk
2 cups water

1. Select the Instant Pot to Sauté mode. Add the yams, onion, minced ginger root, and diced garlic with almond butter for 5 minutes. Stir constantly.

2. Meanwhile, mix up together the cilantro, oregano, cayenne pepper, onion powder, ground black pepper, and cumin in a small bowl.
3. Add the mixture in the Instant Pot, then add the peanuts, bell pepper, collard, and peanut butter. Add almond milk and water.
4. Close the lid. Set Meat/Stew mode and set cooking time for 50 minutes on High Pressure.
5. When timer beeps, use a quick pressure release. Open the lid.
6. Let the stew sit for at least 15 minutes before serving.

Miso Soup with Tofu and Kale

Prep time: 5 minutes | Cook time: 10 minutes | Serves 6

1 to 2 teaspoons vegetable oil
4 cloves garlic, cut in half
1 small sweet onion, quartered
2 medium carrots, cut into 2- to 3-inch pieces
4 cups low-sodium

vegetable broth
1 (12-ounce / 340-g) package silken (light firm) tofu
1 bunch kale (off the stem), plus a few leaves for garnish
¼ cup yellow miso
Ground black pepper, to taste

1. Press the Sauté button on the Instant Pot and heat the oil.
2. Add the garlic, onion, and carrots and sauté for 5 minutes, stirring occasionally.
3. Add the vegetable broth and tofu. Crumble the tofu into pieces with a spoon. Add the kale and stir to incorporate.
4. Secure the lid. Select the Manual mode and set the cooking time for 4 minutes at High Pressure.
5. Once cooking is complete, do a natural pressure release for 10 minutes, then release any remaining pressure. Carefully open the lid.
6. Stir in the miso and blend the soup with an immersion blender until smooth.
7. Season to taste with black pepper and serve garnished with extra kale.

Refried Tempeh and Pinto Bean Stew

Prep time: 10 minutes | Cook time: 15 minutes | Serves 6

1 teaspoon olive oil
1 small onion, cut into half-moon slices
2 large cloves garlic, minced
1½ cups vegetable broth, divided
1 (8-ounce, 227-g) package tempeh, quartered
1 (15-ounce / 425-g) can pinto beans, rinsed and drained, divided

1 small jalapeño, deseeded and finely diced
4 ounces (113 g) canned chopped green chiles
1 (14-ounce / 398-g) can fire-roasted diced tomatoes
1½ cups water
½ teaspoon chipotle or Ancho chile pepper
½ teaspoon salt

1. Heat the olive oil in the Instant Pot on the Sauté function.
2. Add the onion and garlic, and sauté for about 3 minutes.
3. Add the quartered tempeh and ½ cup of the broth to the pot. Sauté and crumble the tempeh with a spoon for 5 minutes.
4. Meanwhile, in a small bowl, add ½ cup of the pinto beans and the diced jalapeño. Mash with a potato masher.
5. Continue to stir and sauté and crumble the tempeh until it resembles small white beans.
6. Transfer the mashed beans to the pot and, using the potato masher, mash into the tempeh.
7. Add the remaining whole beans, green chilies, tomatoes, water, and vegetable broth to the pot, combining well.
8. Cover the pot, select the Manual function, set the timer for 5 minutes at Low Pressure.
9. When timer beeps, use a natural pressure release for 15 minutes, then release any remaining pressure.
10. Open the lid and serve immediately.

Super West African Chickpea Stew

Prep time: 5 minutes | Cook time: 7 minutes | Serves 6

1½ tablespoons refined coconut oil
1 large yellow onion, diced
6 garlic cloves, minced
2-inch piece fresh ginger, grated or minced
1 Scotch bonnet pepper, deseeded and minced
1 teaspoon ground coriander
1 teaspoon ground turmeric
¼ teaspoon ground cinnamon
½ teaspoon dried thyme
1½ teaspoons ground cumin
½ teaspoon freshly cracked black pepper
¼ teaspoon ground cloves
2 cups vegetable

broth
1 pound (454 g) sweet potatoes, peeled and cut into ¾-inch cubes
1½ teaspoons kosher salt
½ cup peanut butter
1 (15-ounce / 425-g) can chickpeas, drained and rinsed
1 (28-ounce / 794-g) can crushed tomatoes
3 tablespoons tomato paste
4 cups kale, stems and midribs removed and sliced into strips
½ cup fresh cilantro, roughly chopped
1 tablespoon fresh lime juice
1/3 cup roasted peanuts, roughly chopped

1. Select the Sauté setting on the Instant Pot and let the pot heat for a few minutes before adding the oil.
2. Once the oil is hot, add the onion. Cook until the onion is softened, about 3 to 4 minutes.
3. Add the garlic, ginger, and chile pepper and cook for 1 minute, tossing frequently.
4. Add the coriander, turmeric, cinnamon, thyme, cumin, black pepper, and cloves. Stir the spices into the vegetables and cook until the mixture is fragrant, about 30 seconds.
5. Pour in the vegetable broth to deglaze the pan, using a wooden spoon to scrape up any browned bits on the bottom of the pot.

6. Add the sweet potatoes, salt, peanut butter, and chickpeas. Stir to combine.
7. Pour the crushed tomatoes and tomato paste on top, but do not stir, allowing the tomatoes and paste to sit on top.
8. Secure the lid. Select the Manual mode and set the cook time to 5 minutes on High Pressure.
9. When timer beeps, allow a natural pressure release for 5 minutes, then release any remaining pressure.
10. Open the pot and stir in the kale. Select the Sauté setting and cook until wilted and cooked through, about 2 minutes. Stir in the cilantro and lime juice.
11. Transfer the stew to bowls and garnish with the roasted peanuts. Serve immediately.

Mushroom, and Red Lentil Miso Stew

Prep time: 5 minutes | Cook time: 6 to 7 minutes | Serves 4

8 ounces (227 g) shiitake mushrooms, sliced (about 2½ cups)	fresh ginger, peeled and minced
1 red onion, thinly sliced	1 cup dried red lentils
1 to 2 teaspoons toasted sesame oil	4 cups water, plus more as needed
Salt, to taste	2 to 3 tablespoons miso paste
1 (1-inch) piece	Freshly ground black pepper, to taste

1. Set the Instant Pot to Sauté mode. Add the mushrooms, red onion, sesame oil, and salt. Cook for 6 to 7 minutes, stirring occasionally, until the vegetables are softened. Add the ginger in the last minute.
2. Add the lentils and water to the pot. Close the lid, then select Manual mode and set cooking time for 3 minutes on High pressure.
3. Once the cook time is complete, quick release the pressure. Open the lid. Let cool for a few minutes.
4. Meanwhile, in a small bowl, stir together the miso and an equal amount of cool water to dissolve, then add it to the pot and stir through. Season with pepper.
5. Serve immediately.

Ikarian Longevity Veggie Stew

Prep time: 10 minutes | Cook time: 12 minutes | Serves 6

1 tablespoon olive oil	chopped fresh oregano
1 yellow onion, chopped	1 teaspoon sea salt
2 carrots, diced	1½ cups dry black-eyed peas, soaked in water overnight
4 cloves garlic, minced	⅛ cup fresh lemon juice
2 stalks celery, diced	3 cups chopped kale leaves, stems removed
3 cups vegetable broth	
1½ cups fresh chopped tomatoes, with juices	Freshly ground black pepper, to taste
1 tablespoon	

1. Select Sauté mode, and heat the oil in the Instant Pot until hot.
2. Add the onion and sauté until softened and golden, 3 to 5 minutes.
3. Add the carrots, garlic, and celery, and sauté for 1 minute more.
4. Add the broth to deglaze the pan, scraping up any bits on the bottom of the pot.
5. Add the tomatoes, oregano, salt, and soaked black-eyed peas, and stir to combine.
6. Lock the lid. Select Manual mode and set the cook time for 6 minutes on High Pressure.
7. Once the cook time is complete, allow the pressure to release naturally for 5 minutes, then quick release any remaining pressure.
8. Carefully remove the lid. Stir in the lemon juice and kale and cook for 2 more minutes on Sauté mode until the kale is wilted.
9. Season with pepper. Serve immediately.

Double Beans and Barley Stew

Prep time: 5 minutes | Cook time: 25 minutes | Serves 6

1 teaspoon olive oil
2 stalks celery, diced
¼ cup sliced shallot
1 teaspoon deseeded and minced fresh jalapeño
1 cup chopped green beans
1 cup dried navy beans
½ cup sliced baby bella mushrooms
1 tomato, diced
1 bay leaf
1 teaspoon herbes de Provence
1 teaspoon dried thyme
1 teaspoon ground black pepper
4 cups vegetable broth
3 cups water
¾ cup dried pearl barley, rinsed and drained
Juice of 1 lemon
¼ teaspoon ground cardamom
½ to 1 teaspoon sea salt

1. In the Instant Pot, heat the oil on Sauté mode.
2. Add the celery, shallot, and jalapeño and sauté for 3 minutes, until the celery is soft.
3. Add the green beans, navy beans, mushrooms, tomato, bay leaf, herbs, thyme, black pepper, broth, water, and barley. Stir to combine.
4. Secure the lid. Select Manual mode and set cooking time for 20 minutes on High Pressure.
5. When timer beeps, use a natural release for 15 minutes, then release any remaining pressure.
6. Remove the lid and stir in the lemon juice, cardamom, and salt. Remove the bay leaf before serving.

Coconut Curry Lentil and Kale Soup

Prep time: 10 minutes | Cook time: 15 minutes | Serves 4

1 tablespoon coconut oil
2 cloves garlic, minced
1 tablespoon fresh grated ginger
1 cup sliced sweet yellow onion
2 cups chopped kale
2 tablespoons red curry paste
2 cups vegetable broth
2 cups unsweetened coconut milk
1½ cup red lentils, rinsed and drained
½ cup chopped cashews
1 tablespoon chopped fresh lemongrass (optional)

1. Set your Instant Pot to Sauté and melt the coconut oil.
2. Add the garlic, ginger, onion and kale. Sauté for 3 minutes, stirring occasionally.
3. Stir in the red curry paste and sauté for 1 to 2 minutes more.
4. Add the vegetable broth, coconut milk, and lentils and stir well.
5. Secure the lid. Select the Manual mode and set the cooking time for 10 minutes at High Pressure.
6. Once cooking is complete, do a quick pressure release. Carefully open the lid.
7. Ladle the soup into serving bowls. Serve garnished with the cashews and lemongrass (if desired).

Hearty Vegetable Wild Rice Soup

Prep time: 25 minutes | Cook time: 10 minutes | Serves 12

6 cups reduced-sodium vegetable broth
2 (14½-ounce / 411-g) cans fire-roasted diced tomatoes, undrained
1¾ cups sliced baby portobello mushrooms
1 cup uncooked wild rice
2 medium carrots, chopped
2 celery ribs, sliced
2 garlic cloves, minced

1 medium onion, chopped
1 medium sweet potato, peeled and cubed
1 medium parsnip, peeled and chopped
1 medium green pepper, chopped
¾ teaspoon salt
¼ teaspoon pepper
2 bay leaves
2 fresh thyme sprigs, plus additional for serving (optional)

1. Combine all the ingredients in the Instant Pot.
2. Secure the lid. Select the Manual mode and set the cooking time for 20 minutes at High Pressure.
3. Once cooking is complete, do a natural pressure release for 10 minutes, then release any remaining pressure. Carefully open the lid.
4. Discard the bay leaves and thyme sprigs before serving. Serve with additional thyme, if desired.

Quinoa Vegetable Stew

Prep time: 10 minutes | Cook time: 15 minutes | Serves 4

2 teaspoons corn oil
1 yellow onion, minced
3 Roma tomatoes, minced
¼ cup frozen corn kernels, thawed to room temperature
1 zucchini, cut into 1-inch chunks
½ cup chopped red bell pepper
1½ cups broccoli florets
¼ cup diced carrot

½ cup quinoa, rinsed
1 teaspoon ground coriander
½ teaspoon paprika
½ teaspoon ground cumin
1 (32-ounce / 907-g) container vegetable broth
2 teaspoons kosher salt
4 tablespoons minced fresh cilantro, divided

1. Press the Sauté button on the Instant Pot and heat the oil. Once hot, add the onion and sauté 5 minutes, stirring occasionally.
2. Add the tomatoes, corn, zucchini, bell pepper, broccoli, and carrot and mix well. Stir in the quinoa, coriander, paprika, cumin, broth, salt, and 2 tablespoons of cilantro.
3. Secure the lid. Select the Manual mode and set the cooking time for 8 minutes at High Pressure.
4. Once cooking is complete, do a natural pressure release for 5 minutes, then release any remaining pressure. Carefully open the lid.
5. Stir in the remaining 2 tablespoons of cilantro and serve hot.

Sweet Potato and Black Bean Stew

Prep time: 5 minutes | Cook time: 30 minutes | Serves 6

2 tablespoons avocado oil
4 cups vegetable broth
½ cup chopped onion
4 cloves garlic, minced
2 carrots, chopped
1 large sweet potato, diced into equal, bite-size pieces
2 small tomatoes, diced
3 stalks celery, chopped
½ teaspoon ground cinnamon
1 teaspoon garam masala
1 cup dried black beans, rinsed and drained
2 bay leaves
½ teaspoon sea salt
¼ teaspoon black pepper

1. In the Instant Pot, heat the oil on Sauté mode.
2. Add the onion and garlic and sauté for 2 minutes until the onion is soft.
3. Add the carrots and sweet potato and sauté for another 3 minutes.
4. Add the tomatoes, celery, cinnamon, and garam masala and stir to coat all the vegetables with the spices.
5. Add the black beans, bay leaves, and vegetable broth. Stir to combine.
6. Secure the lid. Select Manual mode and set cooking time for 24 minutes.
7. When timer beeps, use a natural pressure release for 15 minutes, then release any remaining pressure.
8. Remove the lid, remove the bay leaves, stir in the salt and pepper, and serve.

Chapter 7 Chilies Recipes

Instant Pot Ratatouille

Prep time: 5 minutes | Cook time: 17 minutes | Serves 8

2 tablespoons extra-virgin olive oil
3 garlic cloves, finely chopped
1 medium onion, cut into ¼-inch slices
2 small zucchini, cut into ¼-inch slices
1 small eggplant, cut into ¼-inch slices
1 small butternut squash, peeled and cut into ¼-inch slices
1 yellow bell pepper, cut into ¼-inch slices
3 teaspoons dried thyme
10 fresh basil leaves, finely chopped
2 teaspoons kosher salt
1 teaspoon freshly ground black pepper
3 medium tomatoes, cut into ¼-inch slices
3 cups vegetable broth

1. Set your Instant Pot to Sauté and heat the olive oil until it shimmers.
2. Add the garlic and onion and sauté for about 5 minutes.
3. Add the zucchini, eggplant, butternut squash, bell pepper, thyme, basil leaves, salt, and black pepper. Sauté for an additional 4 minutes. Transfer the vegetables to a tray and set aside to cool.
4. Arrange the sautéed vegetables and tomato slices in a pattern in a ceramic dish.
5. Place the dish in the Instant Pot and pour the broth over the vegetables.
6. Secure the lid. Select the Manual mode and set the cooking time for 10 minutes at High Pressure.
7. Once cooking is complete, do a quick pressure release. Carefully open the lid.
8. Allow to cool for 5 minutes before serving.

Hearty Taco Chili

Prep time: 10 minutes | Cook time: 16 minutes | Serves 6 to 8

2 tablespoons olive oil
1 (8-ounce / 227-g) package unflavored tempeh, cut into large dices
1 teaspoon smoked paprika
1 small onion, diced
1 jalapeño pepper, diced
1 green bell pepper, diced
1 to 2 tablespoons water
1 (15-ounce / 425-g) can diced tomatoes with green chilies, drained
1 (16-ounce / 454-g) can chili beans, undrained
1 (15-ounce / 425-g) can black beans, rinsed and drained
1 teaspoon ground cumin
1 teaspoon salt
½ teaspoon garlic powder
½ teaspoon chili powder, plus more as needed
Chopped scallion, green and light green parts, for garnish
Tortilla chips, for serving

1. Set your Instant Pot to Sauté and heat the olive oil until it shimmers.
2. Add the tempeh and paprika and sauté for 6 to 7 minutes, stirring frequently.
3. Add the onion, jalapeño, and bell pepper and sauté for 2 to 3 minutes more, or until softened. Add 1 to 2 tablespoons of water to the pot to prevent sticking. Turn off the Instant Pot.
4. Stir in the tomatoes with green chilies, chili beans, black beans, cumin, salt, garlic powder, and chili powder.
5. Secure the lid. Select the Manual mode and set the cooking time for 5 minutes at High Pressure.
6. Once cooking is complete, do a natural pressure release for 10 minutes, then release any remaining pressure. Carefully open the lid.
7. If the chili is too thin, set your Instant Pot to Sauté again and cook until the desired consistency is reached.
8. Garnish with the scallion and serve with the tortilla chips.

Ritzy Summer Chili

Prep time: 10 minutes | Cook time: 15 minutes | Serves 6

2 tablespoons olive oil
1 poblano chile or green bell pepper, deseeded and diced
1 jalapeño chile, deseeded and diced
1 celery stalk, diced
2 cloves garlic, minced
1 yellow onion, diced
½ teaspoon fine sea salt, plus more as needed
2 tablespoons chili powder
1 teaspoon dried oregano
½ teaspoon ground cumin
¼ teaspoon cayenne pepper
2 zucchini, diced
1 (15-ounce / 425-g) can peruano beans, rinsed and drained
1 (12-ounce / 340-g) bag frozen corn
1 cup vegetable broth
1 (14.5-ounce / 411-g) can diced fire-roasted tomatoes
¼ cup chopped fresh cilantro
2 green onions, white and tender green parts, thinly sliced

1. Select the Sauté setting on the Instant Pot, add the oil, and heat for 1 minute.
2. Add the poblano and jalapeño chiles, celery, garlic, onion, and salt, and sauté for about 5 minutes, until the vegetables soften.
3. Add the chili powder, oregano, cumin, and cayenne and sauté for about 1 minute more.
4. Add the zucchini, beans, corn, and broth and stir to combine. Pour the tomatoes and their liquid over the top. Do not stir.
5. Secure the lid. Select Manual mode and set the cooking time for 5 minutes at High Pressure.
6. When timer beeps, perform a quick pressure release. Open the pot, give a stir.
7. Ladle the chili into bowls and sprinkle with cilantro and green onions. Serve hot.

Black Bean, Pumpkin, and Kale Chili

Prep time: 10 minutes | Cook time: 12 minutes | Serves 4

¾ cup dried black beans, soaked in water overnight, rinsed and drained
2 cups chopped pumpkin
1 (28-ounce / 794-g) can crushed tomatoes
2 tablespoons chili powder
1 teaspoon onion powder
3 cups water
½ teaspoon garlic powder
2 cups finely shredded kale
½ teaspoon salt

1. Combine the black beans, pumpkin, tomatoes, chili powder, onion powder, water, and garlic powder.
2. Close the lid, then select Manual mode and set cooking time for 10 minutes on High Pressure.
3. Once the cook time is complete, let the pressure release naturally for about 20 minutes, then release any remaining pressure. Open the lid.
4. Stir in the kale to wilt on Sauté mode for 2 minutes more. Season with salt. Serve warm.

Butternut Squash and Kale Chili

Prep time: 10 minutes | Cook time: 20 minutes | Serves 6

1 teaspoon vegetable oil
2 cloves garlic, minced
½ cup diced onion
¼ cup diced green bell pepper
3 cups diced butternut squash (½-inch cubes)
1 teaspoon chili powder
1½ teaspoons cumin
1 tablespoon Sriracha sauce
1 cup dried brown lentils, rinsed and drained
2 tomatoes, diced
3 cups vegetable broth
4 cups loosely packed kale, cut or torn into bite-size pieces
1 tablespoon lemon juice
Salt and ground black pepper, to taste

1. In the Instant Pot, heat the oil on Sauté mode.
2. Add the garlic, onion, and bell pepper and sauté for 2 minutes, until the onion softens.
3. Add the squash, chili powder, cumin, and Sriracha and sauté for 4 minutes. Stir in the lentils and tomatoes.
4. Add the vegetable broth to cover by 1 inch. Add the kale and stir to combine.
5. Cover the lid. Select Manual mode and set cooking time for 10 minutes on High Pressure.
6. When timer beeps, use a natural pressure release for 15 minutes, then release any remaining pressure.
7. Remove the lid. Stir in the lemon juice. Add salt and ground black pepper and serve.

Salsa Verde Cannellini Bean Chili

Prep time: 10 minutes | Cook time: 10 minutes | Serves 4 to 6

1 tablespoon olive oil
1 yellow onion, diced
1 green bell pepper, deseeded and diced
1 jalapeño pepper, deseeded and diced
1 clove garlic, grated
2 (15.5-ounce / 439-g) cans cannellini beans, drained and rinsed
1 cup salsa verde
1 teaspoon ground cumin
1 teaspoon ground coriander
¼ teaspoon cayenne pepper
4 cups vegetable stock
Salt and freshly ground black pepper, to taste
4 ounces (113 g) plant-based cheese, softened

1. Press Sauté button on the Instant Pot and allow the pot to heat for 2 minutes.
2. Add the oil, onion, bell pepper and jalapeño to the pot. Sauté for 3 minutes. Stir in the garlic.
3. Add the beans, salsa verde, cumin, coriander, cayenne, stock, and salt and black pepper, to taste. Stir to combine.
4. Secure the lid. Press Manual button and set cooking time for 5 minutes on High Pressure.
5. When timer beeps, quick release the pressure. Remove the lid and mix in the plant-based cheese.
6. Serve immediately.

Cannellini Bean Kuru Fasulye

Prep time: 15 minutes | Cook time: 20 minutes | Serves 4

1 onion, diced
1 bell pepper, chopped
1 teaspoon coconut oil
2 tablespoons tomato paste
1 cup cannellini beans

1 teaspoon chili flakes
1 teaspoon ground black pepper
6 cups water
1 teaspoon salt
1 teaspoon cayenne red pepper

1. Cook diced onion and bell pepper with coconut oil in the Instant Pot on Sauté mode for 3 minutes.
2. Add tomato paste and cannellini beans.
3. Mix the ingredients and add chili flakes, ground black pepper, water, salt, and red pepper.
4. Close the lid. Set Manual mode set cooking time for 15 minutes on High Pressure.
5. When timer beeps, use a natural pressure release for 15 minutes, then release any remaining pressure. Open the lid.
6. Serve immediately.

Székely Chickpea Goulash

Prep time: 5 minutes | Cook time: 20 minutes | Serves 6

1 cup dried chickpeas, soaked in water overnight, rinsed and drained
1 teaspoon olive oil
2 cloves garlic, minced
½ cup half-moon slices yellow onion
1½ cups chopped carrots
2 tablespoons paprika, plus more for garnish

1 teaspoon freshly ground black pepper, plus more for serving
1 cup tomato sauce
1 bay leaf
2 cups vegetable broth
1½ cups water
1 teaspoon sea salt
2 pounds (907 g) sauerkraut, drained
½ cup coconut cream

1. In the Instant Pot, heat the olive oil on Sauté mode.

2. Add the garlic, onion, and carrots and sauté for 3 minutes, until the onion softens.
3. Stir in the paprika and black pepper. Add the chickpeas, tomato sauce, bay leaf, vegetable broth, and water to cover by ½ inch.
4. Secure the lid. Select Manual mode and set cooking time for 13 to 15 minutes on High Pressure.
5. When timer beeps, use a natural pressure release for 15 minutes, then release any remaining pressure.
6. Remove the cover and stir in the salt. Remove and discard the bay leaf.
7. Stir in the sauerkraut and coconut cream and simmer until heated through. Garnish with more paprika and freshly ground black pepper. Serve immediately.

Feijoada

Prep time: 10 minutes | Cook time: 35 minutes | Serves 6 to 8

1 large onion, diced
3 or 4 garlic cloves, minced
1 tablespoon olive oil
2 cups dried black beans
1 tablespoon ground cumin

1 tablespoon smoked paprika
4 cups water
1 tablespoon dried oregano
Salt, to taste
¼ cup fresh cilantro, chopped

1. Set the Instant Pot to Sauté mode. Add the onion, garlic, and olive oil. Cook for about 5 minutes, stirring occasionally, until the onion is softened.
2. Add the black beans, cumin, paprika, water, and oregano, stirring to combine.
3. Close the lid, then select Manual mode and set cooking time for 30 minutes.
4. When the cook time is complete, let the pressure release naturally for about 30 minutes, then release any remaining pressure. Open the lid.
5. Season with salt. Stir in the cilantro before serving.

Hearty Black-Eyed Pea and Collard Chili

Prep time: 10 minutes | Cook time: 20 minutes | Serves 4

1 teaspoon olive oil
½ cup diced red onion
3 cloves garlic, minced
2 cups chopped carrot
2 cups chopped celery
4 large collard green leaves, halved, center ribs removed, cut into ¼-inch wide strips
½ teaspoon ground coriander
1 teaspoon ground cinnamon
1 tablespoon dried oregano
2 tablespoons chili powder
1 teaspoon ground cumin
1 teaspoon deseeded and diced fresh jalapeño
2 cups dried black-eyed peas, rinsed and drained
1 (28-ounce / 794-g) can diced tomatoes
1 (8-ounce / 227-g) can tomato sauce
2 bay leaves
2 cups vegetable broth
1 cup water
¼ teaspoon sea salt

1. In the Instant Pot heat the oil on Sauté mode.
2. Add the onion and garlic and sauté for about 2 minutes until the onion begins to soften.
3. Add the carrots and celery and continue to sauté for another 3 to 5 minutes.
4. Add the collard greens, coriander, cinnamon, oregano, chili powder, cumin, and jalapeño and sauté for a minute.
5. Add the black-eyed peas, diced tomatoes, tomato sauce, bay leaves, broth, and water. Stir to combine.
6. Secure the lid. Select Manual mode and set cooking time for 10 minutes on High Pressure.
7. When timer beeps, use a natural pressure release for 15 minutes, then release any remaining pressure.
8. Remove the cover. Add salt to taste. Remove the bay leaves before serving.

Rich Brown Lentil and Millet Chili

Prep time: 10 minutes | Cook time: 20 minutes | Serves 6

2 tablespoons olive oil
1 cup finely diced yellow onion
2 cloves garlic, minced
1 seeded and finely diced fresh jalapeño
½ teaspoon ground cinnamon
1 teaspoon chili powder
1 teaspoon ground cumin
1 cup dried brown lentils, rinsed and drained
1 cup millet, rinsed and drained
½ cup diced summer squash
4 cups diced fresh tomatoes
2 cups bite-size pieces kale
1 bay leaf
2 cups vegetable broth
4 cups water
Juice of 1 lemon
1 tablespoon chopped fresh sweet basil
½ teaspoon sea salt

1. Heat the olive oil in the Instant Pot. Add the onion and cook for 3 to 4 minutes, stirring occasionally, until softened.
2. Add the garlic, stir, then add the jalapeño, cinnamon, chili powder, and cumin and sauté for a few minutes more, until the jalapeño softens.
3. Add the lentils, millet, squash, tomatoes, kale, bay leaf, broth, and water and stir to combine.
4. Cover the lid. Select Manual mode and set cooking time for 8 minutes on High Pressure.
5. When timer beeps, use a natural pressure release for 15 minutes, then release any remaining pressure.
6. Carefully remove the lid. Select Sauté mode and bring to a simmer, then add the lemon juice, basil, and salt.
7. Stir and let simmer for a few minutes more. Serve immediately.

Adzuki Bean and Cabbage Chili

Prep time: 10 minutes | Cook time: 10 minutes | Serves 6

1½ cups dried adzuki beans, soaked in water overnight, rinsed and drained
1 tablespoon sesame oil
1 cup diced onion
3 cloves garlic, minced
1 cup chopped carrots
1 (14-ounce / 398-g) can fire-roasted diced tomatoes
2 tablespoons tomato paste
1 teaspoon dulse flakes
4 cups vegetable broth
1 tablespoon yuzu pepper sauce
1 tablespoon soy sauce
1 teaspoon sea salt
2 cups sliced cabbage

1. In the Instant Pot, heat the oil on Sauté mode.
2. Add the onion, garlic, and carrots and sauté for 3 minutes, until the onion is soft.
3. Add the beans, tomatoes, tomato paste, dulse, broth, pepper sauce, soy sauce, sea salt, and cabbage. Stir to combine.
4. Secure the lid. Select Manual mode and set cooking time for 7 minutes on High Pressure.
5. When timer beeps, use a natural pressure release for 15 minutes, then release any remaining pressure.
6. Open the lid and serve immediately.

Sumptuous Spring Veggie Chili

Prep time: 3 minutes | Cook time: 9 minutes | Serves 4

1 (8-ounce / 227-g) can cannellini beans, rinsed
2 radishes, trimmed, sliced
1 cup sliced carrots
1 cup fennel bulb, sliced
¼ cup onion, chopped
2 tablespoon shallots, chopped
¼ cup chopped celery
2 cloves garlic, chopped
1 cup tomato paste
1 teaspoon chipotle powder
½ cup vegetable broth
½ teaspoon cumin
1 teaspoon dried oregano
Pinch of rosemary
Pinch of cayenne
Salt and ground black pepper, to taste
1 medium zucchini, cubed
½ cup corn kernels
2 cherry tomatoes, quartered

1. Combine all ingredients, into the Instant pot, except the zucchinis, corn, and cherry tomatoes.
2. Lock the lid and select Manual mode. Set cooking time for 8 minutes on High Pressure.
3. When timer beeps, use a natural pressure release for 5 minutes, then release any remaining pressure. Open the lid.
4. Stir in the zucchinis, corn, and tomatoes. Lock the lid and set cooking time for 1 minute on High Pressure on Manual mode.
5. When timer beeps, perform a quick pressure release and open the lid.
6. Serve warm.

Split Pea and Barley Potato Stew

Prep time: 10 minutes | Cook time: 15 minutes | Serves 6

½ cup chopped celery

2 cups chopped carrots

3 cups diced russet potatoes (about 3 large potatoes)

1½ cups half-moon slices onions

3 large cloves garlic, minced

1 teaspoon avocado oil

¾ cup dried split peas, rinsed and drained

¼ cup dried pearled barley

1 cup sliced baby bella mushrooms

½ teaspoon dried fennel seed

¼ teaspoon dried anise seed

1 teaspoon ground ginger

¾ teaspoon dried dill weed

1 bay leaf

2 tablespoons tomato paste

4 cups water

1 teaspoon sea salt, to taste

½ teaspoon ground black pepper

1. Combine the celery, carrots, potatoes, onions, and garlic in the Instant Pot. Drizzle the avocado oil over the vegetables and sauté for 5 minutes on Sauté mode.
2. Add the split peas, barley, mushrooms, fennel, anise, ginger, dill, bay leaf, tomato paste, and water. Stir to mix well.
3. Cover the pot, select Manual mode, and set the timer for 7 minutes on High Pressure.
4. When timer beeps, use a natural pressure release for 15 minutes, then release any remaining pressure.
5. Remove the lid, stir in salt and pepper, and serve.

Corn and Kidney Bean Chili

Prep time: 5 minutes | Cook time: 10 minutes | Serves 4

1 teaspoon olive oil

½ cup diced carrot

1 cup diced onion

3 cloves garlic, minced

½ cup chopped celery

1 (14.5-ounce / 411-g) can whole kernel corn, drained

1 cup diced green bell pepper

1 cup diced red bell pepper

1 teaspoon chili powder

½ teaspoon ground cumin

1 (28-ounce / 794-g) can diced tomatoes

2 tablespoons tomato paste

2 cups vegetable broth

1 fresh jalapeño, deseeded and finely diced

½ teaspoon cayenne pepper

1 teaspoon red pepper flakes

1 cup water

1½ cups red kidney beans, rinsed and drained

1. In the Instant Pot, heat the oil on Sauté mode.
2. Add the carrot, onion, garlic, and celery and sauté for 3 minutes.
3. Add the corn, bell peppers, chili powder, cumin, diced tomatoes, tomato paste, broth, jalapeño, cayenne, red pepper flakes, water, and beans.
4. Secure the lid. Select Manual mode and set cooking time for 6 minutes at Low Pressure.
5. When timer beeps, use a natural pressure release for 15 minutes, then release any remaining pressure. Open the lid.
6. Serve immediately.

Red Lentil and Kale Dhal

Prep time: 15 minutes | Cook time: 20 minutes | Serves 4

1 tablespoon avocado oil
1 teaspoon mustard seeds
1 tablespoon turmeric powder
1 tablespoon cumin seeds
½ teaspoon cayenne powder
3 garlic cloves, minced
1 onion, thinly sliced
1 tablespoon grated ginger
1½ cups red lentils, washed, drained
2 cups chopped tomatoes
3 cups vegetable broth
1 teaspoon sugar
2 cups chopped kale
2 tablespoons chopped cilantro
Salt and ground black pepper, to taste

1. Set the Instant Pot to Sauté mode, heat the oil and sauté mustard seeds, turmeric, cumin seeds, and cayenne powder, for 1 minute or until fragrant.
2. Stir in garlic, onion, and ginger. Cook for 2 minutes and mix in lentils, tomatoes, and sugar.
3. Seal the lid, select Manual mode, and set cooking time for 10 minutes on High Pressure.
4. When timer beeps, do a natural pressure release for 10 minutes, then release any remaining pressure.
5. Unlock the lid, stir in kale and half of cilantro, and sprinkle with salt and black pepper. Select Sauté and allow kale to wilt, 3 to 4 minutes.
6. Spoon dhal into bowls and serve hot.

Ritzy Winter Chili

Prep time: 10 minutes | Cook time: 15 minutes | Serves 4 to 6

3 tablespoons olive oil
2 cloves garlic, minced
2 leeks, white and tender green parts, halved lengthwise and thinly sliced
2 jalapeño chiles, deseeded and diced
1 teaspoon fine sea salt
1 canned chipotle chile in adobo sauce, minced
3 tablespoons chili powder
1 cup vegetable broth
2 carrots, peeled and diced
1 (15-ounce / 425-g) can black beans, rinsed and drained
1 (1-pound / 454-g) delicata squash, deseeded and diced
1 (14.5-ounce / 411-g) can diced fire-roasted tomatoes
Chopped fresh cilantro, for serving

1. Select the Sauté setting on the Instant Pot, add the oil and garlic, and heat for 2 minutes, until the garlic is bubbling.
2. Add the leeks, jalapeños, and salt and sauté for 5 minutes, until the leeks are wilted.
3. Add the chipotle chile and chili powder and sauté for 1 minute more. Stir in the broth.
4. Add the carrots, beans and the squash. Pour the tomatoes and their liquid over the top. Do not stir.
5. Secure the lid. Select Manual mode and set the cooking time for 5 minutes at High Pressure.
6. When timer beeps, perform a quick pressure release. Open the pot, give a stir.
7. Ladle the chili into bowls and sprinkle with cilantro. Serve hot.

Rich Acorn Squash Chili

Prep time: 15 minutes | Cook time: 16 minutes | Serves 6

1 tablespoon olive oil
½ cup chopped onion
1 cup sliced carrots
1 large celery stalks, chopped
2 cloves garlic, minced
1½ cups cubed acorn squash
10 ounces (283 g) can red kidney beans, drained
10 ounces (283 g) can cannellini beans, drained

2 (10-ounce / 283-g) can crushed tomatoes
¾ cup corn kernels
1 teaspoon Tabasco sauce
1 teaspoon mesquite powder
1 teaspoon chili flakes
1 teaspoon dried oregano
1 teaspoon ground cumin
1 teaspoon smoked paprika

1. Heat the oil in the Instant pot on Sauté mode.
2. Add the onion and carrots. Sauté for 3 minutes or until soft.
3. Add the celery and sauté for 2 minutes. Add the garlic and sauté for 1 minute.
4. Add the remaining ingredients and lock the lid.
5. Select Manual mode and set cooking time for 10 minutes on High Pressure.
6. When timer beeps, use a natural pressure release for 5 minutes, then release any remaining pressure. Open the lid.
7. Serve warm.

Ritzy Beans and Quinoa Chili

Prep time: 10 minutes | Cook time: 7 minutes | Serves 6

1 tablespoon olive oil
1 large yellow onion, diced
3 cloves garlic, minced
1 green bell pepper, deseeded and diced
1 cup peeled and diced sweet potato cubes (about 1 inch)
1 (15-ounce / 425-g) can black beans, drained and rinsed
1 (15-ounce / 425-g) can kidney beans, drained and rinsed
½ cup uncooked quinoa, rinsed and drained

1 (4-ounce / 113-g) can diced green chiles
1 (26-ounce / 737-g) box chopped or diced tomatoes
1½ tablespoons chili powder
1 tablespoon ground cumin
½ teaspoon smoked paprika
½ teaspoon sea salt
2 cups vegetable broth
Fresh cilantro leaves, for garnish
1 avocado, sliced, for garnish

1. Select Sauté mode, and heat the oil in the Instant Pot until hot.
2. Add the onion and sauté for 1 minute. Add the garlic, bell pepper, and sweet potatoes, and sauté 1 minute more.
3. Add the black beans, kidney beans, quinoa, chiles, tomatoes, chili powder, cumin, paprika, salt, and broth, and stir.
4. Lock the lid. Select Manual mode and set the cook time for 5 minutes on High Pressure.
5. Once the cook time is complete, quick release the pressure and carefully remove the lid.
6. Serve warm, garnished with cilantro and avocado.

Chapter 8 Snacks and Appetizers

Spiced Instant Pot Nuts

Prep time: 5 minutes | Cook time: 20 minutes | Serves 4

1 tablespoon butter
1 cup almonds
1 cup pecans
1 cup raisins
1 cup cashews
1½ teaspoons chilli powder
½ teaspoon brown sugar
½ teaspoon cumin powder
½ teaspoon garlic powder
½ teaspoon black pepper
¼ teaspoon cayenne pepper
Salt, to taste

1. Combine the butter, almonds, pecans, raisins and cashews in the Instant Pot. Season with all the spices and stir.
2. Lock the lid. Select the Manual mode and set the cooking time for 20 minutes on High Pressure. Once the timer goes off, perform a natural pressure release for 15 minutes, then release any remaining pressure. Carefully open the lid.
3. Serve immediately.

Vinegary and Spicy Roasted Olives

Prep time: 5 minutes | Cook time: 6 minutes | Serves 6

2 cups green and black olives, mixed
2 garlic cloves, minced
1 tablespoon olive oil
2 tablespoons
vinegar
½ inch turmeric, finely grated
1 fresh red chilli, thinly sliced
2 sprigs rosemary
2 tangerines

1. Add all the ingredients, except for the tangerines, to the Instant Pot and stir to combine. Squeeze the tangerines over the mixture.
2. Lock the lid. Select the Manual mode and set the cooking time for 6 minutes on High Pressure. Once the timer goes off, perform a natural pressure release for 10 minutes, then release any remaining pressure. Carefully open the lid.
3. Serve immediately.

Easy Queso Blanco Dip

Prep time: 5 minutes | Cook time: 5 to 7 minutes | Serves 10

8 ounces (227 g) shredded Oaxaca cheese
½ (8-ounce / 227-g) package Neufchatel cheese
4 ounces (113 g) heavy cream
1 can minced green chili
1 tablespoon minced pickled jalapeño pepper
1½ teaspoons pickled jalapeño pepper juice

1. Set the Instant Pot on the Slow Cook mode and set temperature to High.
2. Add the Oaxaca cheese, Neufchatel cheese and heavy cream to the pot and stir until melted.
3. Reduce temperature to Low and cook for 5 to 7 minutes.
4. Stir in the green chili, jalapeño pepper and pickling juice.
5. Mix well before serving.

Garlicky Potatoes

Prep time: 5 minutes | Cook time: 4 minutes | Serves 4

4 medium russet yellow potatoes, cut into 8 to 12 chunks
6 cloves garlic, peeled and cut into half
1 cup vegetable broth
½ a cup soy milk
¼ cup minced parsley
Salt, to taste

1. Add the potato chunks, garlic and broth into the Instant Pot.
2. Lock the lid. Select the Manual mode and set the cooking time for 4 minutes on High Pressure. Once the timer goes off, perform a natural pressure release for 10 minutes, then release any remaining pressure. Carefully open the lid.
3. Using a potato masher, mash the potatoes and add the soy milk, parsley and salt.
4. Stir well to combine and serve.

BBQ Whole Butternut Squash

Prep time: 5 minutes | Cook time: 6 minutes | Serves 4

1 whole butternut squash
¼ teaspoon smoked paprika
Salt and black
pepper, to taste
1 tablespoon butter
1 tablespoon BBQ sauce

1. Season the butternut squash with the paprika, salt and pepper.
2. Add the butter and the seasoned butternut squash to the Instant Pot.
3. Lock the lid. Select the Manual mode and set the cooking time for 6 minutes on High Pressure. Once the timer goes off, perform a natural pressure release for 10 minutes, then release any remaining pressure. Carefully open the lid.
4. Top with the BBQ sauce and serve.

Pear and Apple Crisp

Prep time: 5 minutes | Cook time: 5 minutes | Serves 4

3 tablespoons butter, melted
1 teaspoon ground cinnamon
½ cup packed brown sugar
½ cup all-purpose flour
½ cup old-fashioned
rolled oats
½ teaspoon freshly grated nutmeg
2 apples, peeled and sliced
2 pears, peeled and sliced
½ cup water

1. Take a bowl and mix together the brown sugar, butter, oats, flour, cinnamon, and nutmeg.
2. Evenly layer the apples and pears in the inner pot. Then evenly spread the oat mixture on top of the fruit and pour the water on top of the oat mixture.
3. Set the lid in place. Select the Manual mode and set the cooking time for 5 minutes on High Pressure. When the timer goes off, do a quick pressure release. Carefully open the lid.
4. Stir the crisp. Select the Sauté mode and cook until it bubbles.
5. Serve warm.

Easy Banana Chips

Prep time: 5 minutes | Cook time: 25 minutes | Serves 3

3 bananas, cut into ⅛-inch slices
3 tablespoons nutmeg
2 tablespoons lemon juice
1 cup water

1. Stir together all the ingredients, except for the water, in a bowl.
2. Evenly spread a layer of banana slices on a baking sheet.
3. Place the trivet in the Instant Pot and transfer the baking sheet on it.
4. Lock the lid. Select the Manual mode and set the cooking time for 25 minutes on High Pressure. Once the timer goes off, perform a natural pressure release for 15 minutes, then release any remaining pressure. Carefully open the lid.
5. Serve immediately.

Vanilla Rice Pudding

Prep time: 5 minutes | Cook time: 20 minutes | Serves 4

2 cups whole milk
1¼ cups water
1 teaspoon cinnamon
½ teaspoon grated nutmeg
Pinch of salt
1 cup long-grain
rice, rinsed and drained
1 teaspoon vanilla extract
1 can (14-ounce / 397-g) condensed milk

1. Add the whole milk, water, cinnamon, nutmeg and salt into the Instant Pot.
2. Add rice and stir to combine.
3. Lock the lid. Select the Porridge mode and set the cooking time for 20 minutes on High Pressure. Once the timer goes off, perform a natural pressure release for 10 minutes, then release any remaining pressure. Carefully open the lid.
4. Add the vanilla extract and condensed milk. Stir well until creamy and serve.

Sweet Grilled Peaches

Prep time: 5 minutes | Cook time: 7 minutes | Serves 6

5 medium peaches, pitted
2 tablespoons olive oil
½ teaspoon brown sugar
½ teaspoon ground cinnamon
¼ teaspoon ground cloves
¼ teaspoon salt
1 cup water

1. Brush the cut side of the peaches with the olive oil. Sprinkle the peaches with the remaining ingredients, except for the water.
2. Pour the water and insert the trivet in the Instant Pot. Put the peaches on the trivet.
3. Lock the lid. Select the Manual mode and set the cooking time for 7 minutes on High Pressure. Once the timer goes off, perform a natural pressure release for 10 minutes, then release any remaining pressure. Carefully open the lid.
4. Serve immediately.

Spinach and Paneer Sauce

Prep time: 10 minutes | Cook time: 13 minutes | Serves 4

15 cashews
4 tablespoons almond milk
2 tablespoons coconut oil
1 or 2 teaspoons minced hot green chilies
1 teaspoon cumin
1 teaspoon minced garlic
1 teaspoon ginger
1 onion, chopped
1 pound (454 g) spinach, chopped
1½ cup water, divided
Salt, to taste
2 cups cubed paneer
1 teaspoon garam masala

1. In a blender, combine the cashews and almond milk. Pulse until smooth.
2. Press the Sauté button on the Instant Pot and heat the oil. Add the green chilies, cumin, garlic and ginger to the pot and sauté for 1 minute.
3. Add the onion and continue to sauté for 2 minutes. Stir in the spinach, salt and 1 cup of the water.

4. Set the lid in place. Select the Manual mode and set the cooking time for 10 minutes on High Pressure. When the timer goes off, do a quick pressure release. Carefully open the lid.
5. Pour in ½ cup of the water. Using an immersion blender, blend the mixture until it becomes a smooth paste.
6. Toss in the cashew paste, paneer and garam masala. Stir gently before serving.

Thyme Carrots

Prep time: 5 minutes | Cook time: 2 minutes | Serves 2

4 carrots, peeled and cut into sticks
1½ teaspoon fresh thyme
2 tablespoons butter
½ cup water
Salt, to taste

1. Press the Sauté button on the Instant Pot and melt the butter. Add the carrots, thyme, salt, and water to the pot.
2. Set the lid in place. Select the Manual mode and set the cooking time for 2 minutes on High Pressure. When the timer goes off, do a quick pressure release. Carefully open the lid.
3. Serve hot.

Spiced Pecans

Prep time: 5 minutes | Cook time: 20 minutes | Serves 4

½ pound (227 g) pecan halves
1 tablespoon olive oil
½ tablespoon chilli powder
1 teaspoon dried
oregano
1 teaspoon dried thyme
¼ teaspoon garlic powder
¼ teaspoon cayenne pepper

1. Add all the ingredients to the Instant Pot and stir to combine.
2. Lock the lid. Select the Manual mode and set the cooking time for 20 minutes on Low Pressure. Once the timer goes off, perform a natural pressure release for 15 minutes, then release any remaining pressure. Carefully open the lid.
3. Serve immediately.

Vinegary Pearl Onion

Prep time: 5 minutes | Cook time: 5 minutes | Serves 4

1 pound (454 g) pearl onions, peeled	4 tablespoons balsamic vinegar
Pinch of salt and black pepper	1 tablespoon coconut flour
½ cup water	1 tablespoon stevia
1 bay leaf	

1. In the pot, mix the pearl onions with salt, pepper, water, and bay leaf.
2. Set the lid in place. Select the Manual mode and set the cooking time for 5 minutes on Low Pressure. When the timer goes off, do a quick pressure release. Carefully open the lid.
3. Meanwhile, in a pan, add the vinegar, stevia, and flour. Mix and bring to a simmer. Remove from the heat. Pour over the pearl onions. Mix and serve.

Citrus Barley and Buckwheat Salad

Prep time: 10 minutes | Cook time: 35 minutes | Serves 4

1 cup wheat berries	crushed and minced
1 cup pearl barley	¼ cup pine nuts
3 cups vegetable broth	1 cup finely chopped kale
¼ cup minced shallots	1 cup chopped tomatoes
¼ cup olive oil	½ teaspoon salt
¼ cup lemon juice	½ teaspoon black pepper
2 cloves garlic,	

1. In the Instant Pot, combine the wheat berries, pearl barley, vegetable broth and shallots. Mix well.
2. Lock the lid. Select the Manual mode and set the cooking time for 35 minutes on High Pressure. Once the timer goes off, perform a natural pressure release for 20 minutes, then release any remaining pressure. Carefully open the lid.
3. Meanwhile, combine the olive oil, lemon juice and garlic in a bowl. Whisk until well combined.

4. Remove the grains from the cooker and transfer them to a large bowl. Allow them to sit out long enough to cool slightly.
5. Add the dressing, pine nuts, kale and tomatoes to the grains and stir.
6. Season with salt and black pepper, as desired.
7. Serve warm or cover and chill until ready to serve.

Celery Wheat Berry Salad

Prep time: 15 minutes | Cook time: 40 minutes | Serves 12

1½ tablespoons vegetable oil	2 medium stalks celery, finely diced
6¾ cups water	1 medium zucchini, peeled, grated and drained
1½ cups wheat berries	
1½ teaspoons Dijon mustard	1 medium red bell pepper, deseeded and diced
1 teaspoon granulated sugar	4 green onions, diced
1 teaspoon sea salt	1⅓ cups frozen corn, thawed
½ teaspoon freshly ground black pepper	
¼ cup white wine vinegar	¼ cup diced sun-dried tomatoes
½ cup extra-virgin olive oil	¼ cup chopped fresh Italian flat-leaf parsley
½ small red onion, peeled and diced	

1. Add the vegetable oil, water, and wheat berries to the Instant Pot.
2. Set the lid in place. Select the Multigrain mode and set the cooking time for 40 minutes on High Pressure. When the timer goes off, do a quick pressure release. Carefully open the lid.
3. Fluff the wheat berries with a fork. Drain and transfer to a large bowl.
4. Make the dressing by processing the mustard, sugar, salt, pepper, vinegar, olive oil, and red onion in a food processor until smooth.
5. Stir ½ cup of the dressing into the cooled wheat berries. Toss the seasoned wheat berries with the remaining ingredients.
6. Serve immediately. Cover and refrigerate any leftover dressing up to 3 days.

Saucy Mushroom Lettuce Cups

Prep time: 5 minutes | Cook time: 9 minutes | Serves 4

1 tablespoon vegetable oil
¼ cup minced shallots
2 tablespoons cooking sherry
4 cups cremini mushrooms, quartered
½ cup chopped water chestnuts
¼ cup low-sodium soy sauce
¼ cup vegetable broth
¼ cup fresh basil
8 butter lettuce leaves

1. Press the Sauté button on the Instant Pot and heat the oil. Add the scallions to the pot and sauté for 3 minutes, or until tender. Add the cooking sherry and continue to cook for 2 minutes. Stir in the remaining ingredients, except for the lettuce leaves.
2. Set the lid in place. Select the Manual mode and set the cooking time for 4 minutes on High Pressure. When the timer goes off, do a quick pressure release. Carefully open the lid.
3. Select the Sauté mode and cook the mushroom mixture, stirring frequently, until the sauce thickens. Let cool for 5 minutes.
4. Spoon equal amounts of the mushroom mixture into lettuce leaves and serve.

Egg and Veggie Mix

Prep time: 5 minutes | Cook time: 8 minutes | Serves 8

16 eggs, beaten
2 sweet potatoes, peeled and shredded
2 red bell peppers, deseeded and chopped
2 onions, chopped
2 garlic cloves, minced
4 teaspoons chopped fresh basil
Salt and black pepper, to taste
2 tablespoons oil

1. Add all the ingredients to the Instant Pot and stir to combine.
2. Set the lid in place. Select the Manual mode and set the cooking time for 8 minutes on High Pressure. When the timer goes off, do a quick pressure release. Carefully open the lid.
3. Serve immediately.

Energy Cookies

Prep time: 5 minutes | Cook time: 10 minutes | Serves 8

2 large eggs
1¼ cups almond butter
⅔ cup cocoa
powder
⅓ cup sugar
Salt, to taste
1 cup water

1. Place all the ingredients, except for the water, in a food processor and pulse until smooth. Form the mixture into 12 equal small balls and press them. Place a single layer of balls onto a cookie sheet.
2. Pour the water and insert the trivet in the Instant Pot. Put the sheet on the trivet.
3. Lock the lid. Select the Manual mode and set the cooking time for 10 minutes on High Pressure. Once the timer goes off, perform a natural pressure release for 10 minutes, then release any remaining pressure. Carefully open the lid.
4. Dish out the cookies and serve.

Stuffed Eggs

Prep time: 5 minutes | Cook time: 6 minutes | Serves 4

4 eggs
1½ tablespoons Greek yogurt
1½ tablespoons mayonnaise
½ teaspoon chopped jalapeño
¼ teaspoon onion
powder
¼ teaspoon paprika
¼ teaspoon lemon zests
Salt and black pepper, to taste
1 cup water, for the pot

1. Pour the water and insert the trivet in the Instant Pot. Place the eggs on the trivet.
2. Set the lid in place. Select the Manual mode and set the cooking time for 6 minutes on High Pressure. When the timer goes off, do a quick pressure release. Carefully open the lid.
3. Place the eggs into ice-cold water. Peel the eggs, and cut in half, lengthwise. Scoop out the egg yolks and mix them with the remaining ingredients. Fill the hollow eggs with the mixture and serve.

Red Wine Poached Pears

Prep time: 5 minutes | Cook time: 8 minutes | Serves 3

3 firm pears
½ teaspoon grated ginger
½ bottle red wine
½ grated cinnamon
1 cup granulated sugar
1 bay laurel leaf

1. Add all the ingredients to the Instant Pot and stir to combine.
2. Lock the lid. Select the Manual mode and set the cooking time for 8 minutes on High Pressure. Once the timer goes off, perform a natural pressure release for 10 minutes, then release any remaining pressure.
3. Carefully open the lid and transfer the pears to a bowl.
4. Select the Sauté mode and let the mixture simmer for 10 more minutes to reduce its consistency and drizzle the red wine sauce on pears.
5. Serve immediately.

Ginger-Garlic Egg Potatoes

Prep time: 5 minutes | Cook time: 10 minutes | Serves 3

2 eggs, whisked
1 teaspoon ground turmeric
1 teaspoon cumin seeds
2 tablespoons olive oil
2 potatoes, peeled and diced
1 onion, finely chopped
2 teaspoons ginger-garlic paste
½ teaspoon red chili powder
Salt and black pepper, to taste

1. Press the Sauté button on the Instant Pot and heat the oil. Add the cumin seed, ginger-garlic paste, and onions to the pot and sauté for 4 minutes. Stir in the remaining ingredients.
2. Set the lid in place. Select the Manual mode and set the cooking time for 6 minutes on High Pressure. When the timer goes off, do a quick pressure release. Carefully open the lid.
3. Serve immediately.

Rhubarb Strawberry Tarts

Prep time: 5 minutes | Cook time: 5 minutes | Serves 12

1 pound (454 g) rhubarb, cut into small pieces
½ pound (227 g) strawberries
¼ cup minced crystallized ginger
½ cup honey
1 cup water
12 tart shells, short crust
½ cup whipped cream

1. Add all the ingredients, except for the tart shells and whipped cream, to the Instant Pot and stir to combine.
2. Lock the lid. Select the Manual mode and set the cooking time for 5 minutes on High Pressure. Once the timer goes off, perform a natural pressure release for 10 minutes, then release any remaining pressure. Carefully open the lid.
3. Place the mixture in the tart shells. Top with whipped cream and serve.

Honey Carrots with Soy Sauce

Prep time: 5 minutes | Cook time: 6 minutes | Serves 4

8 medium carrots
1 cup water
1 clove garlic, finely chopped
1 tablespoon honey
2 tablespoons soy
sauce
½ tablespoon sesame seeds
Salt, to taste
Chopped green onions, for garnish

1. Add the carrots and water to the Instant Pot.
2. Set the lid in place. Select the Manual mode and set the cooking time for 3 minutes on High Pressure. When the timer goes off, do a quick pressure release. Carefully open the lid.
3. Remove the carrots. Drain the water.
4. Select the Sauté mode and add the remaining ingredients, except for the green onions and sesame seeds. Cook for 3 minutes, or until sticky.
5. Put the carrots back into the pot and coat well. Sprinkle with the green onions and seeds and serve.

Sweet Roasted Cashews

Prep time: 5 minutes | Cook time: 20 minutes | Serves 2

¾ cup cashews
¼ teaspoon salt
¼ teaspoon ginger powder
1 teaspoon minced

orange zest
4 tablespoons honey
1 cup water, for the pot

1. Stir together the honey, orange zest, ginger powder, and salt in a bowl. Add the cashews to the mixture and place it in a ramekin.
2. Pour the water and insert the trivet in the Instant Pot. Place the ramekin on the trivet.
3. Set the lid in place. Select the Manual mode and set the cooking time for 20 minutes on High Pressure. When the timer goes off, do a quick pressure release. Carefully open the lid.
4. Serve immediately.

White Beans with Fresh Tomato and Garlic

Prep time: 5 minutes | Cook time: 30 minutes | Serves 4

1 cup dried cannellini beans
4 cups vegetable broth
1 tablespoon vegetable oil
1 teaspoon salt

2 cloves garlic, minced
½ cup diced tomato
½ teaspoon dried sage
½ teaspoon freshly ground black pepper

1. Add the beans, broth, oil and salt to the Instant Pot and stir all ingredients until thoroughly combined.
2. Lock the lid. Select the Bean/Chili mode and set the cooking time for 30 minutes on High Pressure. Once the timer goes off, perform a natural pressure release for 10 minutes, then release any remaining pressure. Carefully open the lid.
3. Press the Sauté button and add the remaining ingredients and simmer uncovered for 10 minutes until thickened.
4. Serve warm.

Pepper and Olive Couscous Salad

Prep time: 5 minutes | Cook time: 7 minutes | Serves 4

1 cup couscous
2 cups water
1 medium red bell pepper, deseeded and diced
1 clove garlic, minced

½ cup mixed olives, pitted and chopped
1 teaspoon red wine vinegar
1 teaspoon salt
1 teaspoon olive oil

1. Stir together the couscous and water in the Instant Pot.
2. Lock the lid. Select the Manual mode and set the cooking time for 7 minutes on High Pressure. Once the timer goes off, perform a natural pressure release for 10 minutes, then release any remaining pressure. Carefully open the lid.
3. Fluff the couscous with a fork. Add all the remaining ingredients and stir until combined.
4. Refrigerate for 2 hours before serving.

Spinach Mushroom Treat

Prep time: 5 minutes | Cook time: 11 minutes | Serves 3

½ cup spinach
½ pound (227 g) fresh mushrooms, sliced
2 garlic cloves, minced
2 tablespoons chopped fresh thyme

1 onion, chopped
1 tablespoon olive oil
1 tablespoon chopped fresh cilantro, for garnish
Salt and black pepper, to taste

1. Press the Sauté button on the Instant Pot and heat the oil. Add the garlic and onions to the pot and sauté for 4 minutes. Stir in the remaining ingredients.
2. Set the lid in place. Select the Manual mode and set the cooking time for 7 minutes on High Pressure. When the timer goes off, do a quick pressure release. Carefully open the lid.
3. Serve garnished with the cilantro.

Egg-Crusted Zucchini

Prep time: 5 minutes | Cook time: 5 minutes | Serves 2

1 zucchini, cut into ½-inch round slices
½ teaspoon dried dill
½ teaspoon paprika
1 egg
1½ tablespoons

coconut flour
1 tablespoon milk
Salt and black pepper, to taste
1 tablespoon coconut oil

1. Whisk egg and milk in a bowl. Mix the salt, black pepper, paprika, dried dill, and flour in another bowl. Dip the zucchini slices in the egg mixture, then in the dry mixture.
2. Press the Sauté button on the Instant Pot and heat the oil. Add the zucchini slices to the pot and sauté for 5 minutes.
3. Serve immediately.

Tomato and Parsley Quinoa Salad

Prep time: 5 minutes | Cook time: 21 minutes | Serves 4

2 tablespoons olive oil
2 cloves garlic, minced
1 cup diced tomatoes
¼ cup chopped

fresh Italian flat-leaf parsley
1 tablespoon fresh lemon juice
1 cup quinoa
2 cups water
1 teaspoon salt

1. Press the Sauté button on the Instant Pot and heat the olive oil. Add the garlic and sauté for 30 seconds. Add the tomatoes, parsley and lemon juice. Sauté for an additional minute. Transfer the tomato mixture to a small bowl.
2. Add the quinoa and water to the Instant Pot.
3. Lock the lid. Select the Manual mode and set the cooking time for 20 minutes on High Pressure. Once the timer goes off, perform a natural pressure release for 10 minutes, then release any remaining pressure. Carefully open the lid.
4. Fluff the cooked quinoa with a fork. Stir in the tomato mixture and salt.
5. Serve immediately.

Mustard Flavored Artichokes

Prep time: 5 minutes | Cook time: 12 minutes | Serves 3

3 artichokes
3 tablespoons mayonnaise
1 cup water, for the pot

2 pinches paprika
2 lemons, sliced in half
2 teaspoons Dijon mustard

1. Mix mayonnaise, paprika, and mustard.
2. Pour the water and insert the trivet in the Instant Pot. Place the artichokes upwards and arrange the lemon slices on it.
3. Set the lid in place. Select the Manual mode and set the cooking time for 12 minutes on High Pressure. When the timer goes off, do a quick pressure release. Carefully open the lid.
4. Put the artichokes in the mayonnaise mixture. Serve.

Salty Edamame

Prep time: 5 minutes | Cook time: 25 minutes | Serves 4

1 cup shelled edamame
4 cups water
1 tablespoon vegetable oil

1 teaspoon coarse sea salt
1 tablespoon soy sauce

1. Add the edamame, water and oil to the Instant Pot and stir to combine thoroughly.
2. Lock the lid. Select the Bean/Chili mode and set the cooking time for 25 minutes on High Pressure. Once the timer goes off, perform a natural pressure release for 10 minutes, then release any remaining pressure. Carefully open the lid.
3. Drain the edamame and transfer to a serving bowl. Sprinkle with salt and serve with soy sauce on the side for dipping.

Leek and White Bean Purée

Prep time: 10 minutes | Cook time: 40 minutes | Serves 4

1 cup dried cannellini beans
5 cups vegetable broth, divided
1 tablespoon vegetable oil
½ teaspoon salt
1 cup thinly sliced leeks
1 teaspoon fresh lemon juice
2 cloves garlic, minced
¼ teaspoon dried tarragon

1. Add the beans, 4 cups of the broth, oil and salt to the Instant Pot, and stir until thoroughly combined.
2. Lock the lid. Select the Bean/Chili mode and set the cooking time for 30 minutes on High Pressure. Once the timer goes off, perform a natural pressure release for 10 minutes, then release any remaining pressure. Carefully open the lid.
3. Press the Sauté button and add the leeks, lemon juice, garlic and tarragon and simmer uncovered for 10 minutes to thicken.
4. Pour the bean mixture and the remaining 1 cup of the broth into a large food processor and blend until creamy.
5. Serve immediately.

Classic Baba Ghanoush

Prep time: 10 minutes | Cook time: 11 minutes | Serves 4 to 6

1 tablespoon sesame oil
1 large eggplant, peeled and diced
4 cloves garlic, peeled and minced
½ cup water
3 tablespoons fresh Italian flat-leaf parsley
½ teaspoon salt
2 tablespoons fresh lemon juice
2 tablespoons tahini
1 tablespoon extra-virgin olive oil

1. Press the Sauté button on the Instant Pot and heat the sesame oil. Add the eggplant and sauté for about 5 minutes, or until it begins to soften. Add the garlic and sauté for 30 seconds. Pour in the water

2. Set the lid in place. Select the Manual mode and set the cooking time for 6 minutes on High Pressure. When the timer goes off, do a quick pressure release. Carefully open the lid.
3. Strain the cooked eggplant and garlic and add to a food processor along with the parsley, salt, lemon juice and tahini. Pulse to process. Scrape down the sides of the food processor if necessary.
4. Add the olive oil and process until smooth.
5. Serve immediately.

Chickpea Mash

Prep time: 5 minutes | Cook time: 30 minutes | Makes 2 cups

1 cup dried chickpeas
4 cups water
¼ cup plus 1 tablespoon extra-virgin olive oil, divided
$1/_3$ cup fresh lemon juice
$1/_3$ cup tahini
2 teaspoons ground cumin
1 teaspoon minced garlic
¾ teaspoon salt
¾ teaspoon freshly ground black pepper

1. Add the chickpeas, water and 1 tablespoon of the oil to the Instant Pot.
2. Set the lid in place. Select the Bean/Chili mode and set the cooking time for 30 minutes on High Pressure. When the timer goes off, do a quick pressure release. Carefully open the lid.
3. Drain the chickpeas, carefully reserving the cooking liquid.
4. Place all the remaining ingredients along with the cooked chickpeas in a food processor and blend until creamy. If the consistency is too thick, add some of the reserved cooking liquid a little at a time until the hummus reaches a desired consistency.
5. Serve chilled or at room temperature alongside chips or prepared vegetables for dipping. The mixture can be stored in an airtight container in the fridge 1 to 2 days.

Cooked Guacamole

Prep time: 5 minutes | Cook time: 9 minutes | Serves 4

1 large onion, finely diced
4 tablespoons lemon juice
¼ cup cilantro, chopped
4 avocados, peeled
and diced
3 tablespoons olive oil
3 jalapeños, finely diced
Salt and black pepper, to taste

1. Press the Sauté button on the Instant Pot and heat the oil. Add the onions to the pot and sauté for 3 minutes, or until tender. Stir in the remaining ingredients.
2. Set the lid in place. Select the Manual mode and set the cooking time for 6 minutes on High Pressure. When the timer goes off, do a quick pressure release. Carefully open the lid.
3. Serve immediately.

Garlicky Green Lentil Mash

Prep time: 5 minutes | Cook time: 35 minutes | Serves 8

2 tablespoons olive oil, divided
1 cup diced yellow onion
3 cloves garlic, minced
1 teaspoon red wine
vinegar
2 cups dried green lentils
4 cups water
1 teaspoon salt
Pinch of freshly ground black pepper

1. Press the Sauté button on the Instant Pot and heat 1 tablespoon of the oil. Add the onions to the pot and sauté for 2 to 3 minutes, or until translucent. Add the garlic and vinegar, and sauté for 30 more seconds.
2. Add the remaining 1 tablespoon of the oil, lentils, water, and salt to the pot and stir to combine thoroughly.
3. Lock the lid. Select the Bean/Chili mode and set the cooking time for 30 minutes on High Pressure. Once the timer goes off, perform a natural pressure release for 10 minutes, then release any remaining pressure. Carefully open the lid.

4. Transfer the lentil mixture to a food processor and blend until smooth. Season with pepper and serve warm.

Cauliflower and Tomato Queso

Prep time: 10 minutes | Cook time: 5 minutes | Makes 4 cups

2 cups cauliflower florets
1 cup water
¾ cup thick-cut carrot coins
¼ cup raw cashews
¼ cup nutritional yeast
1 (10-ounce / 284-g) can diced tomatoes with green chiles
½ teaspoon smoked paprika
½ teaspoon salt
¼ teaspoon chili powder
¼ teaspoon jalapeño powder
⅛ teaspoon mustard powder
½ cup chopped bell pepper
2 tablespoons minced red onion
¼ cup minced cilantro

1. Drain the canned tomatoes and reserve the liquid. Set aside.
2. Add the cauliflower, water, carrots and cashews to the Instant Pot.
3. Set the lid in place. Select the Manual mode and set the cooking time for 5 minutes on High Pressure. When the timer goes off, do a quick pressure release. Carefully open the lid.
4. Pour the cooked mixture into a strainer over the sink and drain the extra water.
5. In a blender, put the drained mixture along with the nutritional yeast, liquid drained from the canned tomatoes, smoked paprika, salt, chili powder, jalapeño powder and mustard powder. Blend until smooth.
6. Transfer the blender contents into a mixing bowl and stir in the tomatoes and green chiles, bell pepper, minced onion and cilantro.
7. Serve at room temperature or warm.

Pecan and Cranberry Pilaf

Prep time: 5 minutes | Cook time: 30 minutes | Serves 4

1 cup long-grain white rice
2 cups vegetable broth
⅔ cup dried cranberries
1 teaspoon dried thyme
1 bay leaf
1 cup pecan pieces
2 tablespoons butter
Pinch of salt
Pinch of freshly ground black pepper

1. Add the rice, broth, cranberries, thyme, and bay leaf to the Instant Pot.
2. Lock the lid. Select the Rice mode and set the cooking time for 30 minutes on Low Pressure. Once the timer goes off, perform a natural pressure release for 10 minutes, then release any remaining pressure. Carefully open the lid.
3. Discard the bay leaf and stir in the remaining ingredients. Serve warm.

Thai Red Curry Mashed Chickpea

Prep time: 5 minutes | Cook time: 45 minutes | Serves 16

1 cup unsoaked chickpeas
2½ cups water
1 (13.6-ounce / 386-g) can full-fat coconut milk
1 to 2 tablespoon Thai red curry paste
2 tablespoons lime juice
Salt, to taste

1. Add the chickpeas and water to the Instant Pot.
2. Lock the lid. Select the Manual mode and set the cooking time for 45 minutes on High Pressure. Once the timer goes off, perform a natural pressure release for 20 minutes, then release any remaining pressure. Carefully open the lid.
3. Strain the chickpeas and add to a blender along with the coconut milk, curry paste and lime juice. Blend until smooth and season with salt.
4. Serve immediately.

Three Bean Salad with Parsley

Prep time: 10 minutes | Cook time: 30 minutes | Serves 8

⅓ cup apple cider vinegar
¼ cup granulated sugar
2½ teaspoons salt, divided
½ teaspoon freshly ground black pepper
¼ cup olive oil
½ cup dried chickpeas
½ cup dried kidney beans
1 cup frozen green beans pieces
4 cups water
1 tablespoon vegetable oil
1 cup chopped fresh Italian flat-leaf parsley
½ cup peeled and diced cucumber
½ cup diced red onion

1. For the dressing: In a small bowl, whisk together the vinegar, sugar, 1½ teaspoons of the salt and pepper. While whisking continuously, slowly add the olive oil. Once well combined, cover in plastic and refrigerate.
2. Add the chickpeas, kidney beans, green beans, water, vegetable oil, and the remaining 1 teaspoon of the salt to the Instant Pot. Stir to combine.
3. Lock the lid. Select the Manual mode and set the cooking time for 30 minutes on High Pressure. Once the timer goes off, perform a natural pressure release for 10 minutes, then release any remaining pressure. Carefully open the lid.
4. Transfer the cooked beans to a large mixing bowl. Stir in all the remaining ingredients along with the dressing. Toss to combine thoroughly. Cover and refrigerate for 2 hours before serving.

Red Peppers Stuffed with Couscous

Prep time: 5 minutes | Cook time: 21 minutes | Serves 4

1 cup couscous	1 teaspoon dried
2 cups water	oregano
2 tablespoons	1 teaspoon salt
toasted pine nuts	4 large red bell
4 ounces (113 g)	peppers, stemmed
crumbled cashew	and cored
cheese	

1. Preheat the oven to 350ºF (180ºC).
2. Add the couscous and water to the Instant Pot.
3. Lock the lid. Select the Manual mode and set the cooking time for 6 minutes on High Pressure. Once the timer goes off, perform a natural pressure release for 10 minutes, then release any remaining pressure. Carefully open the lid.
4. Fluff the couscous and add the remaining ingredients, except for the bell peppers. Stir well to combine.
5. Stuff ¼ of the couscous mixture into each bell pepper and place in a baking pan. Bake in the preheated oven for 15 minutes, or until the peppers begin to soften.
6. Let cool for 5 minutes before serving.

Creamy Corn Polenta

Prep time: 5 minutes | Cook time: 10 minutes | Serves 4

3½ cups water	1 cup corn kernels
½ cup coarse	1 teaspoon dried
polenta	thyme
½ cup fine yellow	1 teaspoon salt
cornmeal	

1. Add all the ingredients to the Instant Pot and stir to combine.
2. Set the lid in place. Select the Manual mode and set the cooking time for 10 minutes on High Pressure. When the timer goes off, do a quick pressure release. Carefully open the lid.
3. Serve warm.

Rice-Stuffed Grape Leaves

Prep time: 15 minutes | Cook time: 21 minutes | Serves 16

⅓ cup olive oil	2 cups vegetable
4 green onions,	broth
chopped	1 teaspoon salt
⅓ cup minced fresh	¼ teaspoon freshly
mint	ground black pepper
⅓ cup minced fresh	½ teaspoon lemon
Italian flat-leaf	zest
parsley	1 (16-ounce / 454-
3 cloves garlic,	g) jar grape leaves
minced	2 cups water
1 cup long-grain	½ cup fresh lemon
white rice	juice

1. Press the Sauté button on the Instant Pot and heat the oil. Add the green onions, mint and parsley to the pot and sauté for 2 minutes, or until the scallions are soft. Add the garlic and sauté for an additional 30 seconds. Add the rice and stir-fry for 1 minute. Stir in the broth, salt, pepper, and lemon zest.
2. Set the lid in place. Select the Manual mode and set the cooking time for 8 minutes on High Pressure. When the timer goes off, do a quick pressure release. Carefully open the lid. Transfer the rice mixture to a medium bowl.
3. Drain the grape leaves. Rinse them thoroughly in warm water and then arrange them rib side up on a clean work surface. Trim away any thick ribs.
4. Spoon about 2 teaspoons of the rice mixture on each grape leaf. Fold the sides of each leaf over the filling and then roll it from the bottom to the top. Repeat with the remaining leaves. Arrange the stuffed leaves, seam-side down, in a single layer in the steamer basket insert.
5. Pour the water into the Instant Pot. Set the steam basket insert into the pot and pour the lemon juice over the stuffed grape leaves.
6. Set the lid in place. Select the Steam mode and set the cooking time for 10 minutes on High Pressure. When the timer goes off, do a quick pressure release. Carefully open the lid.
7. Remove the steamer basket from the pot and let the stuffed leaves rest for 5 minutes. Serve hot or cold.

Fast Single-Serve Paella

Prep time: 10 minutes | Cook time: 14 minutes | Serves 4

3 tablespoons olive oil
1 medium sweet onion, peeled and chopped
1 cup peeled and grated carrot
1 medium red bell pepper, deseeded and chopped
1 cup fresh green peas
1 clove garlic, minced
1 cup basmati rice
1½ teaspoons turmeric powder
2 cups vegetable broth
¼ cup chopped fresh Italian flat-leaf parsley
Pinch of salt
Pinch of freshly ground black pepper

1. Press the Sauté button on the Instant Pot and heat the oil. Add the onion, carrot, bell pepper and peas and sauté for 5 minutes, or until they begin to soften.
2. Add the garlic, rice and turmeric to the pot and stir until well coated. Add the broth and parsley.
3. Lock the lid. Select the Manual mode and set the cooking time for 9 minutes on High Pressure. Once the timer goes off, perform a natural pressure release for 10 minutes, then release any remaining pressure. Carefully open the lid.
4. Season with salt and pepper before serving.

Tomato Black Bean Dip

Prep time: 5 minutes | Cook time: 35 minutes | Serves 12

1 tablespoon olive oil
1 small yellow onion, peeled and diced
3 cloves garlic, minced
1 cup dried black beans
2 cups water
1 (14.5-ounce / 411-g) can diced tomatoes
2 (4-ounce / 113-g) cans mild green chilies, finely chopped
1 teaspoon chili powder
½ teaspoon dried oregano
¼ cup finely chopped fresh cilantro
1 cup shredded cashew cheese
Pinch of salt

1. Press the Sauté button on the Instant Pot and heat the oil. Add the onions and sauté for 3 minutes, or until soft. Add the garlic and sauté for 30 seconds. Transfer the onions and garlic to a small bowl and set aside.
2. Stir in the beans, water, tomatoes, chilies, chili powder and oregano.
3. Set the lid in place. Select the Bean/Chili mode and set the cooking time for 30 minutes on High Pressure. When the timer goes off, do a quick pressure release. Carefully open the lid.
4. Transfer the mixture to a food processor. Add the onion and garlic mixture along with the cilantro and cheese and process until smooth. Taste for seasoning and add salt if desired.
5. Transfer the dip to a serving bowl. Serve warm.

Barbecue Wasabi Chickpeas

Prep time: 5 minutes | Cook time: 34 to 35 minutes | Serves 4

2 tablespoons vegetable oil, divided
½ cup diced yellow onion
1 tablespoon wasabi powder
4 cups plus 1 tablespoon water, divided
1 cup dried chickpeas
1 cup barbecue sauce

1. Press the Sauté button on the Instant Pot and heat 1 tablespoon of the oil. Add the onions and sauté for 4 to 5 minutes, or until translucent.
2. Reconstitute the wasabi powder by combining it with 1 tablespoon of the water, then add to the sautéed onions. Remove from the pot and set aside.
3. Add the remaining 4 cups of the water, chickpeas, and 1 tablespoon of the oil to the pot and stir to combine thoroughly.
4. Lock the lid. Select the Bean/Chili mode and set the cooking time for 30 minutes on High Pressure. Once the timer goes off, perform a natural pressure release for 10 minutes, then release any remaining pressure. Carefully open the lid.
5. Add the onion mixture and barbecue sauce and stir to combine thoroughly.
6. Serve immediately.

Chinese Sesame Baby Carrots

Prep time: 10 minutes | Cook time: 2 minutes | Serves 2

½ pound (227 g) baby carrots, trimmed and scrubbed
¼ cup orange juice
½ cup water
1 tablespoon raisins
½ tablespoon soy sauce
1 tablespoon Shaoxing wine
½ teaspoon garlic powder
½ teaspoon shallot powder
½ teaspoon mustard powder
¼ teaspoon cumin seeds
1 teaspoon butter, at room temperature
1 tablespoon toasted sesame seeds

1. Place all the ingredients, except for the sesame seeds, in the Instant Pot.
2. Set the lid in place. Select the Manual mode and set the cooking time for 2 minutes on High Pressure. When the timer goes off, do a quick pressure release. Carefully open the lid.
3. Serve topped with the sesame seeds.

Traditional Steamed Spring Rolls

Prep time: 10 minutes | Cook time: 5 minutes | Serves 12

1 cup shredded napa cabbage
1 cup sliced bamboo shoots
¼ cup chopped fresh cilantro
2 cloves garlic, minced
5 shiitake mushrooms, sliced
2 medium carrots, peeled and grated
1 teaspoon soy sauce
1 teaspoon rice wine vinegar
12 spring roll wrappers
2 cups water

1. In a bowl, stir together all the ingredients, except for the roll wrappers and water.
2. Place the spring roll wrappers on a clean work surface. Divided the cabbage mixture equally among the wrappers, making a row down the center. Roll up the wrappers, tuck in the ends, and place side by side in the steamer basket.

3. Add the water to the Instant Pot and insert the steamer basket.
4. Lock the lid. Select the Steam mode and set the cooking time for 3 minutes on High Pressure. Once the timer goes off, perform a natural pressure release for 10 minutes, then release any remaining pressure. Carefully open the lid.
5. Remove the rolls from the pot and serve warm.

Black-Eyed Pea Salad

Prep time: 10 minutes | Cook time: 30 minutes | Makes 5 cups

1 cup dried black-eyed peas
4 cups water
1 pound (454 g) cooked corn kernels
½ medium red onion, peeled and diced
½ medium green bell pepper, deseeded and diced
1 pickled jalapeño, finely chopped
1 medium tomato, diced
2 tablespoons chopped fresh cilantro
¼ cup red wine vinegar
2 tablespoons extra-virgin olive oil
1 teaspoon salt
½ teaspoon freshly ground black pepper
½ teaspoon ground cumin

1. Add the black-eyed peas and water to the Instant Pot.
2. Lock the lid. Select the Bean/Chili mode and set the cooking time for 30 minutes on High Pressure. Once the timer goes off, perform a natural pressure release for 20 minutes, then release any remaining pressure. Carefully open the lid.
3. Drain the peas and transfer to a large mixing bowl. Add all the remaining ingredients to the beans and stir until thoroughly combined.
4. Refrigerate for 1 to 2 hours before serving.

Chapter 9 Vegetable Mains

Mushroom and Cabbage Dumplings

Prep time: 20 minutes | Cook time: 15 to 16 minutes | Makes 12 dumplings

1 tablespoon olive oil
1 cup minced shiitake mushrooms
1½ cups minced cabbage
½ cup shredded carrot
2 tablespoons soy sauce
1 tablespoon rice wine vinegar
1 teaspoon grated fresh ginger
12 round dumpling wrappers
1½ cups water

1. Select the Sauté setting of the Instant Pot. Heat the oil until shimmering.
2. Add the mushrooms and sauté for 3 or 4 minutes until the mushrooms release the juices.
3. Add the cabbage, carrot, soy sauce and rice wine vinegar and sauté for 5 minutes or until the mixture is dry. Mix in the ginger.
4. Line a steamer with parchment paper. Prepare a small bowl of water.
5. Put a wrapper on the clean work surface and rub the water around the edge of the wrapper. Add 1 tablespoon of the vegetable filling to the middle of the wrapper and fold in half. Press to make a dumpling. Then put the dumpling in the steamer. Repeat with remaining wrappers and fillings.
6. Arrange the trivet in the pot. Put the steamer on the trivet and pour the water in the pot.
7. Put the lid on. Select the Steam setting and set the timer for 7 minutes on High Pressure.
8. When timer beeps, use a natural pressure release for 5 minutes, then release any remaining pressure. Open the lid.
9. Serve hot.

Mini Tofu and Vegetable Frittatas

Prep time: 15 minutes | Cook time: 25 to 26 minutes | Serves 4

1 tablespoon olive oil
½ cup minced onion
½ cup minced mushrooms
⅓ cup minced bell pepper
⅓ cup grated carrot
⅓ cup minced kale, collards or spinach
1 (14-ounce / 397-g) package firm tofu, quickly pressed to remove most of the liquid
2 tablespoons nutritional yeast
2 teaspoons Italian herb seasoning
1½ teaspoons salt
½ teaspoon ground turmeric
Salt and ground black pepper, to taste
1½ cups water

1. Select the Sauté setting of the Instant Pot. Heat the oil until shimmering, add the onion and sauté until translucent, 5 minutes.
2. Add the mushrooms and cook for 3 minutes or until they release juices, then add the bell pepper and carrot, and sauté for 2 or 3 minutes or until the mixture is dry. Stir in the kale and set aside to cool.
3. Add the tofu, nutritional yeast, Italian herb seasoning, salt, and turmeric to the blender. Blend until smooth.
4. Combine the cooled vegetables and tofu mixture in a bowl. Sprinkle with salt and pepper.
5. Grease 4 ramekins and divide the mixture among them. Cover with foil. Put the trivet in the Instant Pot and pour in the water. Arrange the ramekins on the trivet.
6. Put the lid on. Set to Manual mode and set cooking time for 15 minutes at High Pressure.
7. When timer beeps, allow a natural pressure release for 5 minutes, then release any remaining pressure. Open the lid.
8. Serve hot.

Kashmiri Tofu

Prep time: 20 minutes | Cook time: 20 minutes | Serves 4

8 small dried red chilies
5 cloves
3 tablespoons coriander seeds
5 green cardamoms
2 tablespoons unsalted butter
½ tablespoon olive oil
½ tablespoon grated garlic
½ tablespoon grated ginger
2 small red onions, cubed
4 large tomatoes
½ teaspoon kashmiri red chili powder
¾ cup water, divided
1 small green bell pepper, diced, divided
1 small red bell pepper, diced, divided
1 pound (454 g) extra-firm tofu, cubed
1½ teaspoons fenugreek leaves, crushed
3 tablespoons heavy cream
1 teaspoon sugar
2 tablespoons cilantro, chopped

1. In a pan over medium heat, roast the red chilies, cloves, coriander seeds, and green cardamoms for 6 minutes or until fragrant.
2. Turn off the heat. Transfer them to a spice grinder and grind to a fine powder. Set aside.
3. Press the Sauté button on the Instant Pot. Add the butter and oil to the pot and then add the garlic and ginger and sauté for a few seconds.
4. Add the onion and sauté for 2 minutes until softened. Add the tomatoes and sauté for 3 minutes.
5. Add the kashmiri red chili powder, salt, and the prepared spice mix. Mix until well combined and then add ½ cup of water and half of the bell peppers.
6. Close the pot, and then press the Manual button. Set cooking time for 4 minutes on High Pressure.
7. When timer beeps, do a quick pressure release.
8. Open the pot and press the Sauté button. Add the remaining water and then stir in the cubed tofu and the remaining half of the bell peppers.
9. Fold in the fenugreek leaves, heavy cream, sugar, and cilantro and simmer for 4 minutes.
10. Serve hot.

Soya Granules and Green Pea Tacos

Prep time: 20 minutes | Cook time: 8 minutes | Serves 8

2 cups soya granules, soaked in water for at least 20 minutes, drained
½ cup frozen green peas, soaked in water for at least 5 minutes, drained
1 tablespoon olive oil
1 medium red onion, chopped
2 teaspoons ginger garlic paste
3 jalapeños, deseeded, sliced, plus more for garnish
1 tablespoon tomato paste
¾ teaspoon taco seasoning
½ teaspoon garam masala
½ teaspoon coriander powder
1 teaspoon salt
1 cup plus 2 tablespoons water
2 tablespoons cilantro, chopped, plus more for garnish
2 teaspoons lime juice
8 small corn tortillas
Sliced onions, for garnish
Salsa, for garnish
Diced avocados, for garnish

1. Press the Sauté button on the Instant Pot. Add the oil and then add the chopped onion. Cook the onion for 2 minutes until softened.
2. Add the ginger garlic paste and cook for another minute
3. Add the sliced jalapeños and cook for 30 seconds. Add the soya granules to the pot along with the green peas.
4. In a small bowl, mix the tomato paste with 2 tablespoons of water, then add it to the pot, along with the taco seasoning, garam masala, coriander powder and salt, and mix until well combined. Add the remaining water and close the lid.
5. Press the Manual button and set the timer for 4 minutes at High Pressure.
6. When timer beeps, let the pressure release naturally for 5 minutes, then release any remaining pressure.
7. Remove the lid, add the cilantro and lime juice and mix.
8. Warm the tortillas and fill with the prepared keema filling. Top with sliced onions, jalapeños, cilantro, salsa and diced avocados and serve.

Ritzy Green Pea and Cauliflower Curry

Prep time: 20 minutes | Cook time: 8 minutes | Serves 4

3 large tomatoes
4 large cloves garlic
1-inch piece ginger
1 green chili
12 raw cashews
1½ tablespoons olive oil
1 bay leaf
3 green cardamoms
6 peppercorns
3 cloves
1 large red onion, chopped
1½ teaspoons coriander powder
1 teaspoon garam masala
½ teaspoon red chili powder
½ teaspoon turmeric powder
1 teaspoon salt
¼ cup plain yogurt, at room temperature
½ cup plus 2 tablespoons coconut milk
¼ cup water
1 large head cauliflower, cut into florets
½ cup frozen green peas Cilantro, for garnish

1. Using a blender, purée the tomatoes, garlic, ginger, green chili and cashews to a smooth paste. Set aside.
2. Press the Sauté button on the Instant Pot. Add the oil and then add the bay leaf, green cardamoms, peppercorns and cloves. Sauté for a few seconds until the spices are fragrant and then add the onion. Cook the onion until soft, around 2 minutes.
3. Add the puréed tomato mixture. Cook for 2 minutes and then add the coriander powder, garam masala, red chili powder, turmeric powder and salt. Stir to combine the spices and cook them for 30 seconds.
4. Add the yogurt, whisking continuously until well combined.
5. Add the coconut milk and the water and mix to combine.
6. Add the cauliflower florets and peas and toss to combine them with the masala.
7. Close the lid and press the Manual button. Set the timer for 3 minutes on Low Pressure.
8. When timer beeps, do a quick pressure release.
9. Open the pot, give them a stir. Garnish with cilantro and serve.

Baby Eggplants with Coconut

Prep time: 20 minutes | Cook time: 10 minutes | Serves 4

¼ cup dried coconut powder
1 tablespoon coriander powder
1 teaspoon cumin powder
½ teaspoon red chili powder
½ teaspoon garam masala
¼ teaspoon turmeric powder
1 teaspoon salt, divided
12 baby eggplants (1 pound / 454 g in total), each eggplant is 2 inches, rinsed and patted dry
1 tablespoon olive oil
½ teaspoon mustard seeds
1 medium red onion, chopped
1 teaspoon ginger garlic paste
2 medium tomatoes, chopped
¾ cup water, divided
Cilantro, for garnish

1. In a bowl, mix the coconut powder, coriander powder, cumin powder, red chili powder, garam masala, turmeric powder and ½ teaspoon salt.
2. Make crosswise and lengthwise slits through the flesh of each eggplant, but without cutting all the way through. Carefully open the eggplants up and divide half of the coconut mixture in each baby eggplant. Reserve remaining half of the coconut stuffing for the curry. Set the stuffed eggplants and reserved stuffing mixture aside.
3. Press the Sauté button on the Instant Pot. Add the oil and the mustard seeds and let them heat until they pop.
4. Add the onion and cook for 2 minutes until soft and translucent.
5. Add the ginger garlic paste and cook for 1 minute, then add the tomatoes and ¼ cup of water. Cook the tomatoes for 2 minutes until they turn soft, and then add the reserved coconut stuffing. Cook for 1 minute and then add ½ cup of water and ½ teaspoon of salt and mix well.
6. Put the stuffed eggplants on top of the masala and close the lid.
7. Press the Manual button. Set cooking time for 4 minutes on High Pressure.
8. When timer beeps, do a quick pressure release.
9. Open the pot, garnish with cilantro and serve.

Tofu and Greens with Fenugreek Sauce

Prep time: 25 minutes | Cook time: 15 to 18 minutes | Serves 3

1 yellow onion, quartered
15 cashews
3 cloves garlic
1-inch piece ginger
1 green chili
4 green cardamoms
1½ cups water, divided
1½ tablespoons olive oil
1 bay leaf
1 teaspoon coriander powder
¼ teaspoon garam masala
¼ teaspoon turmeric powder
¼ teaspoon red chili powder
1 teaspoon salt
1½ cups fenugreek leaves, stems removed, chopped
6 ounces (170 g) extra-firm tofu, cubed
1 teaspoon fenugreek leaves, crushed
¼ cup heavy cream
½ teaspoon sugar
1 cup broccoli florets
10 thin asparagus stalks, hard end removed and then cut into 1-inch pieces

1. Put the onion and cashews into the steamer basket. Pour 1 cup of water in the Instant Pot and then put the steamer basket inside it.
2. Close the lid and then press the Steam button. Set cooking time for 2 minutes on High Pressure.
3. When timer beeps, do a quick pressure release. Open the lid.
4. Transfer the steamed onion and cashews to a blender and add the garlic, ginger, green chili, green cardamoms and ½ cup of water and purée to a smooth paste.
5. Press the Sauté button on the Instant Pot. Add the oil and then add the bay leaf along with the prepared onion paste. Cook the onion paste for 4 to 5 minutes, until there's no smell of raw onion, and then stir in the coriander powder, garam masala, turmeric powder, red chili powder and salt. Cook for 1 minute, then add the chopped fenugreek leaves and cook for another 1 to 2 minutes.
6. Add 1 cup of water and the tofu, mix well and then close the lid. Press the Manual button and set the timer for 3 minutes on High Pressure.
7. When timer beeps, do a quick pressure release.
8. Open the lid and press the Sauté button. Add the fenugreek leaves, heavy cream, sugar, broccoli florets and asparagus.
9. Cover the pot and let it simmer for 4 to 5 minutes. Serve warm.

Jamaican Pumpkin and Potato Curry

Prep time: 15 minutes | Cook time: 6 minutes | Serves 6

2 tablespoons vegetable oil
3 cloves garlic, minced
1 tablespoon minced fresh ginger
1 cup chopped onion
1 tablespoon plus 1½ teaspoons Jamaican curry powder
1 stemmed, deseeded, and sliced Scotch bonnet pepper
3 sprigs fresh thyme
1 teaspoon kosher salt
½ teaspoon ground allspice
4 cups (1-inch cubes) peeled pumpkin
1½ cups (1-inch cubes) peeled potatoes
2 cups stemmed, deseeded, and diced red, yellow bell peppers
1 cup water

1. Select Sauté on the Instant Pot. Heat the vegetable oil.
2. Add the garlic and ginger. Sauté for a minute or until fragrant.
3. Add the onion and sauté for 2 minutes or until translucent.
4. Fold in the curry powder, Scotch bonnet pepper, thyme, salt, and allspice. Stir to coat well. Add the pumpkin, potatoes, bell peppers, and water.
5. Lock the lid. Select Manual mode and set the timer for 3 minutes at High Pressure.
6. When timer beeps, perform a natural pressure release for 10 minutes, then release any remaining pressure. Open the lid.
7. Serve immediately.

Minty Paneer Cubes with Cashews

Prep time: 20 minutes | Cook time: 10 to 11 minutes | Serves 4

1½ cups cilantro, roughly chopped
¾ cup mint leaves
1 small red onion
2 green chilies
15 cashews
1-inch piece ginger
2 cloves garlic
¼ teaspoon ground black pepper
1¼ cups water, divided
1 tablespoon olive oil or unsalted butter
1 bay leaf
¾ teaspoon cumin seeds
½ cup yogurt,
whisked with ¼ teaspoon cornstarch
½ teaspoon cumin powder
½ teaspoon coriander powder
¼ teaspoon crushed red pepper, optional
½ teaspoon salt
2 teaspoons heavy cream
Garam masala, to sprinkle
½ teaspoon sugar
1 cup paneer, cut into cubes
Sliced onions, for serving

1. In a blender, grind together the cilantro, mint leaves, onion, green chilies, cashews, ginger, garlic, black pepper and ¼ cup of water to form a smooth paste. Set it aside.
2. Press the Sauté button on the Instant Pot. Add the oil, bay leaf and cumin seeds and let the cumin seeds sizzle for a few seconds.
3. Then add the prepared cilantro mint paste to the pot and cook for 2 to 3 minutes, or until the raw smell of the onion in the paste goes away.
4. Whisk the yogurt with the cornstarch and then fold into the pot. Cook for 2 minutes.
5. Add cumin powder, coriander powder, crushed red pepper and ¾ cup of water and cook for a few seconds.
6. Close the lid, and then press the Soup button and set the cooking time for 3 minutes on High Pressure.
7. When timer beeps, do a quick pressure release.
8. Open the pot, stir the curry and press the Sauté button. Add ¼ cup of water along with the salt, heavy cream, garam masala and sugar. Mix well and then add the paneer cubes.
9. Let the curry simmer for 2 minutes. Serve with sliced onions on the side.

Potatoes and Cauliflower Masala

Prep time: 15 minutes | Cook time: 13 to 14 minutes | Serves 4

1 tablespoon vegetable oil
½ teaspoon cumin seeds
1 large red onion, finely chopped
1½ teaspoons ginger garlic paste
2 medium tomatoes, chopped
½ teaspoon dried mango powder
¼ teaspoon garam masala
¼ teaspoon red chili powder
1 teaspoon coriander powder
½ teaspoon turmeric powder
¾ teaspoon salt
6 tablespoons water, divided
2 medium potatoes, diced into 1-inch pieces
1 (1-pound / 454-g) medium head cauliflower, cut into medium to large florets
2 tablespoons cilantro, chopped, plus more for garnish

1. Press the Sauté button on the Instant Pot. Add the oil and the cumin seeds and let them sizzle for a few seconds.
2. Add the chopped onion and cook for 3 minutes until soft and translucent.
3. Add the ginger garlic paste and cook for another minute or until fragrant.
4. Add the tomatoes and cook for 2 minutes or until the tomatoes are soft.
5. Add the dried mango powder, garam masala, red chili powder, coriander powder, turmeric powder, and salt and mix to combine.
6. Cook the spices for 30 seconds, and then add 2 tablespoons of water and diced potatoes.
7. Toss to coat well. Cover the pot and let the potatoes cook for 3 to 4 minutes, stirring once halfway through.
8. Remove the lid, add 4 tablespoons of water and mix well to deglaze the pot.
9. Put the cauliflower florets on top. Sprinkle 2 tablespoons of cilantro on top of the cauliflower.
10. Close the pot. Press the Manual button and set the timer for 3 minutes on Low Pressure. When timer beeps, do a quick pressure release.
11. Open the pot and gently mix the cauliflower with the potatoes and the masala. Transfer them to a serving bowl, garnish with more cilantro and serve.

Simple Spiced Russet Potatoes

Prep time: 15 minutes | Cook time: 12 minutes | Serves 3 to 4

2 large russet potatoes, cut in half and skin left on
1 tablespoon olive oil
1¼ teaspoon cumin seeds
2 teaspoons coriander seeds, roughly crushed
2 green chilies, sliced
1-inch piece ginger, chopped
½ teaspoon turmeric powder
⅛ teaspoon red chili powder
½ teaspoon salt
2 teaspoons lemon juice
Cilantro, to garnish

1. Add 1 cup of water to the Instant Pot. Put the trivet inside the pot, then put the potatoes, cut side up, on top of the trivet.
2. Secure the lid. Press the Manual button and set the timer for 10 minutes on High Pressure.
3. When timer beeps, let the pressure release naturally for 5 minutes, then release any remaining pressure. Open the lid.
4. Carefully remove the potatoes from the trivet. When they have cooled down a bit, peel the potatoes and dice them into small pieces.
5. Drain the water from the pot, wipe it dry and then put it back into the Instant Pot.
6. Press the Sauté button, add the oil and then the cumin seeds. Let the seeds sizzle for a few seconds, then add the coriander seeds and green chilies. Sauté for a few seconds and then add the ginger. Sauté for a minute until the ginger is golden.
7. Add the potatoes, turmeric powder, red chili powder and salt and mix, until all the potato pieces are well coated with the spices. Mix gently.
8. Add the lemon juice and toss to combine. Garnish with cilantro and serve.

Tofu and Mango Curry

Prep time: 15 minutes | Cook time: 9 minutes | Serves 2

8 ounces (227 g) extra-firm tofu, pressed to remove the moisture, cubed
¼ teaspoon smoked paprika
¼ teaspoon crushed red pepper
1¼ teaspoon salt, divided
⅛ teaspoon ground black pepper
2 tablespoons olive oil, divided
½ teaspoon mustard seeds
2 dried red chilies
½ medium white onion, diced
1½-inch piece ginger, grated
¾ cup gresh mango purée
½ cup coconut milk
1 teaspoon curry powder
½ cup water
Juice of ½ lemon
Cilantro, to garnish

1. Toss the tofu cubes with smoked paprika, crushed red pepper, ¼ teaspoon salt and ground black pepper.
2. Press the Sauté button on the Instant Pot. Add 1 tablespoon of oil to the pot, then add the spiced tofu cubes and cook for 4 minutes, or until lightly browned on all sides. Remove the tofu cubes to a bowl and set aside.
3. Add another tablespoon of oil to the pot, then add the mustard seeds. Let the mustard seeds pop and then add the dried red chilies. Sauté for a few seconds, then add the onion and ginger. Cook the onion and ginger for a minute until the onion turns a little soft.
4. Add the mango purée, coconut milk, and curry powder, then add 1 teaspoon of salt and let it all cook for a minute.
5. Add the water along with the sautéed tofu cubes and close the lid. Press the Manual button and set the timer for 3 minutes on High Pressure.
6. When timer beeps, do a quick pressure release. Open the lid.
7. Stir in the lemon juice, then transfer the curry to a serving bowl. Garnish with cilantro and serve.

Creamy Mushrooms and Green Beans

Prep time: 15 minutes | Cook time: 5 minutes | Serves 8

2 cups finely chopped mushrooms
1 cup chopped onion
3 cloves garlic, minced
1 teaspoon kosher salt
½ teaspoon black pepper
¼ cup water
1 pound (454 g)

trimmed fresh green beans
2 tablespoons diced cream cheese, at room temperature
¼ cup half-and-half
Sliced toasted almonds (optional)
Fried onions (optional)

1. In the Instant Pot, combine the mushrooms, onion, garlic, salt, pepper, and water. Put the green beans on top. Set the cream cheese on top of the beans.
2. Lock the lid. Select Manual mode and set the timer for 3 minutes on High Pressure.
3. When timer beeps, use a quick pressure release. Open the lid.
4. Select Sauté mode. Stir in the half-and-half. Cook, stirring frequently, until the sauce has thickened, about 2 minutes.
5. Transfer them to a serving bowl. Top with almonds and fried onions, and serve.

Cheesy Spaghetti Squash and Spinach

Prep time: 10 minutes | Cook time: 8 minutes | Serves 4

1 large spaghetti squash, cut into 8 pieces
1½ cups water
3 tablespoons olive oil
8 cloves garlic, thinly sliced
½ cup slivered

almonds
1 teaspoon red pepper flakes
4 cups chopped fresh spinach
1 teaspoon kosher salt
1 cup shredded Parmesan cheese

1. Pour the water into the Instant Pot. Put a trivet in the pot. Set the squash on the trivet.

2. Lock the lid. Select Manual mode and set the timer for 7 minutes on High Pressure.
3. When timer beeps, perform a natural pressure release for 10 minutes, then release any remaining pressure.
4. Remove the squash, and cut it in half lengthwise. Use a fork to scrape the strands of one half into a large bowl. Measure out 4 cups. Reserve the other half for other use.
5. Set the squash shell aside to use as a serving vessel. Clean the pot.
6. Select Sauté mode. When the pot is hot, add the olive oil. Once the oil is hot, add the garlic, almonds, and pepper flakes. Cook, stirring constantly and being careful not to burn the garlic for 1 minute.
7. Add the spinach, salt, and spaghetti squash. Stir well to thoroughly combine ingredients until the spinach wilts.
8. Transfer the mixture to the reserved squash shell. Sprinkle with the Parmesan cheese before serving.

Lemony Peas with Bell Pepper

Prep time: 5 minutes | Cook time: 1 minutes | Serves 4

2 cups frozen peas
1 cup stemmed, deseeded, and diced red bell pepper
1 cup thinly sliced onion
1 tablespoon butter, melted
2 tablespoons water

1 teaspoon kosher salt
½ teaspoon black pepper
2 tablespoons chopped fresh mint
Zest of 1 lemon
1 tablespoon fresh lemon juice

1. In the Instant Pot, combine the peas, bell pepper, onion, butter, water, salt, and pepper. Stir to mix well.
2. Lock the lid. Select Manual mode and set the timer for 1 minute on High Pressure.
3. When timer beeps, use a quick pressure release. Open the lid.
4. Stir in the mint along with the lemon zest and juice and serve.

Traditional Indian Dal

Prep time: 20 minutes | Cook time: 16 to 20 minutes | Serves 4 to 6

1½ cups yellow lentils
3 tablespoons unrefined virgin coconut oil, divided
1 large yellow onion, chopped
5 garlic cloves, minced
1½-inch piece fresh ginger, grated
2 serrano peppers, deseeded and diced
1 teaspoon ground cumin
1 teaspoon ground coriander
1 teaspoon ground turmeric
1 teaspoon garam masala
½ teaspoon Indian red chile powder
2 bay leaves
4 cups water
1 teaspoon kosher salt
3 small tomatoes, chopped
2 shallots, thinly sliced
½ teaspoon black mustard seeds
1 teaspoon cumin seeds
3 dried red chile peppers
Juice of ½ lime, plus more to taste
½ cup roughly chopped fresh cilantro

1. Soak the lentils in cold water for 15 minutes and then drain them.
2. Select the Sauté setting on the Instant Pot and let the pot heat up for a few minutes before adding 1 tablespoon of the coconut oil, followed by the onion. Cook until the onion is translucent, 3 to 4 minutes.
3. Add the garlic, ginger, and serranos, and cook for 1 to 2 minutes, stirring frequently to prevent sticking.
4. Add the ground cumin, coriander, turmeric, garam masala, chile powder, and bay leaves and stir vigorously for 30 seconds until very aromatic.
5. Pour in the water, using a wooden spoon to scrape up any browned bits on the bottom of the pot. Add the soaked and drained lentils, salt, and tomatoes. Stir to combine.
6. Lock the lid. Select the Manual mode and set the cooking time for 10 minutes on High Pressure. Once the timer goes off, perform a natural pressure release for 10 minutes, then release any remaining pressure.
7. While the pot is depressurizing, make the tadka. Heat a medium skillet on the stove over medium-high heat. Add the remaining 2 tablespoons of the coconut oil and, once shimmering, add the shallots. Stir and cook until the shallots turn golden and are beginning to crisp, 2 to 3 minutes. Add the mustard seeds, cumin seeds, and dried red chiles. Cook, stirring frequently, until the seeds are beginning to pop, 30 to 60 seconds. Remove from the heat.
8. Open the pot and discard the bay leaves. Carefully pour the tadka over the dal. Stir to combine well. Add the lime juice and cilantro and taste for seasonings, adding more lime juice as needed.
9. Serve immediately.

Jackfruit and Tomatillos Tinga

Prep time: 15 minutes | Cook time: 21 minutes | Serves 4

1 tablespoon olive oil
1½ cups minced onion
6 cloves garlic, minced
2 tablespoons minced jalapeño
1 (20-ounce / 565-g) can jackfruit in brine, rinsed, shredded
1 (14.5-ounce /
411-g) can diced tomatoes
1 cup diced tomatillos
1½ teaspoons dried thyme
1 teaspoon dried oregano
¼ cup water
½ teaspoon ground cumin
Salt, to taste

1. Select the Sauté setting of the Instant Pot and heat the oil until shimmering.
2. Add the onion and sauté for 5 minutes or until transparent. Then add the garlic and jalapeño and sauté for 1 minute more.
3. Add the jackfruit, tomatoes, tomatillos, thyme, oregano, water, and cumin to the pot and stir to combine.
4. Put the lid on. Select the Manual setting and set the timer for 15 minutes on High Pressure.
5. When timer beeps, allow the pressure to release naturally for 5 minutes, then release any remaining pressure. Open the lid.
6. Sprinkle with salt and serve.

Grape Leaves with Rice and Nuts

Prep time: 15 minutes | Cook time: 4 minutes | Serves 4

1 cup chopped onion
1 cup chopped tomato
1 cup basmati rice, rinsed and drained
1 cup pine nuts
8 ounces (227 g) brined grape leaves, drained and chopped
2 tablespoons olive oil
3 cloves garlic, minced
1 tablespoon dried parsley
1½ teaspoons ground allspice
1 teaspoon kosher salt
1 teaspoon black pepper
1 cup water
⅓ cup fresh lemon juice
¼ cup chopped fresh mint

1. In the Instant Pot, combine the onion, tomato, rice, pine nuts, grape leaves, olive oil, garlic, parsley, allspice, salt, pepper, and water. Stir to combine.
2. Lock the lid. Select Manual mode and set the timer for 4 minutes on High Pressure.
3. When timer beeps, perform a natural pressure release for 10 minutes, then release any remaining pressure. Open the lid.
4. Stir in the lemon juice and mint and serve.

Vegetarian Caponata

Prep time: 15 minutes | Cook time: 6 minutes | Serves 6

4 cups (1-inch cubes) peeled eggplant
1 cup chopped tomato
1 cup chopped onion
3 cloves garlic, minced
2 tablespoons tomato paste
2 tablespoons balsamic vinegar
2 tablespoons granulated sugar
2 tablespoons olive oil
¼ cup water
1 teaspoon kosher salt
½ teaspoon coarsely ground black pepper
¼ cup capers
¼ cup sliced green olives
¼ cup chopped fresh parsley

1. In the Instant Pot, combine the eggplant, tomato, onion, garlic, tomato paste,

vinegar, sugar, olive oil, water, salt, and pepper. Stir to mix well.
2. Secure the lid. Select Manual mode and set cooking time for 2 minutes at High Pressure.
3. When timer beeps, perform a natural pressure release for 5 minutes, then release any remaining pressure. Open the lid.
4. Select Sauté mode of the Instant Pot. Sauté for 4 minutes or until thick and caramelized. Stir in the capers and olives.
5. Transfer to a serving platter. Top with the parsley and serve.

Green Beans with Coconut

Prep time: 10 minutes | Cook time: 3 minutes | Serves 4

2 tablespoons vegetable oil
1 teaspoon mustard seeds
1 teaspoon cumin seeds
1 cup diced onion
1 teaspoon ground turmeric
1 teaspoon kosher salt
½ teaspoon cayenne pepper
1 (12-ounce / 340-g) package frozen green beans
¼ cup unsweetened shredded coconut
½ cup water
¼ cup chopped fresh cilantro

1. Select Sauté mode on the Instant Pot. When the pot is hot, add the oil. Once the oil is hot, add the mustard seeds and cumin seeds, and allow to sizzle for 15 to 20 seconds.
2. Stir in the onion. Add the turmeric, salt, and cayenne and stir to coat. Add the green beans, coconut, and water; stir to combine.
3. Lock the lid. Select Manual mode and set the timer for 2 minutes at High Pressure.
4. When timer beeps, use a quick pressure release. Open the lid.
5. Transfer to a serving dish and garnish with the cilantro. Serve warm.

Easy Braised Kale with Tomatoes

Prep time: 5 minutes | Cook time: 5 minutes | Serves 4

2 cups diced tomatoes
1 teaspoon ground turmeric
½ teaspoon ground coriander
1 cup chopped onion

3 cloves garlic, minced
2 teaspoons smoked paprika
½ cup water
6 cups chopped kale
Juice of 1 lemon

1. In the Instant Pot, combine the tomatoes, turmeric, coriander, onion, garlic, paprika, and water. Stir to combine. Stir in the kale.
2. Lock the lid. Select Manual mode and set the timer for 5 minutes on High Pressure.
3. When timer beeps, perform a natural pressure release for 10 minutes, then release any remaining pressure. Open the lid.
4. Stir in the lemon juice and serve.

Sumptuous Vegetable and Tofu Curry

Prep time: 5 minutes | Cook time: 6 minutes | Serves 4

2 cups diced peeled butternut squash
2 cups chopped bok choy
1 cup button or cremini mushrooms, trimmed and quartered
1 cup stemmed,

deseeded, and roughly chopped yellow bell pepper
1 block Japanese curry paste, diced
2 cups water
1 (14-ounce / 397-g) package firm tofu, diced

1. In the Instant Pot, combine the butternut squash, bok choy, mushrooms, bell pepper, curry paste, and water. Stir to mix well.
2. Lock the lid. Select Manual mode and set the timer for 4 minutes at High Pressure.
3. When timer beeps, perform a natural pressure release for 10 minutes, then release any remaining pressure.
4. Open the lid. Stir in the tofu. Set the pot to Sauté mode and sauté for 2 minutes or until the tofu is lightly browned.
5. Serve immediately.

Potatoes and Carrots with Cabbage

Prep time: 10 minutes | Cook time: 2 minutes | Serves 6

1 teaspoon ground turmeric
1 teaspoon ground cumin
1 teaspoon smoked paprika
2 tablespoons vegetable oil
1 teaspoon kosher salt
¼ cup water

2 cups peeled and chopped (1-inch pieces) russet potatoes
3 medium carrots, peeled and cut into 2-inch pieces
1 cup chopped onion
3 cups coarsely chopped cabbage

1. In the Instant Pot, combine the turmeric, cumin, paprika, oil, salt, and water. Stir to mix well.
2. Add the potatoes, carrots, and onion. Stir to combine well. Arrange the cabbage on top.
3. Lock the lid. Select Manual mode and set the timer for 2 minutes on High Pressure.
4. When timer beeps, use a quick pressure release. Open the lid.
5. Serve immediately.

Sweet and Sour Cabbage

Prep time: 5 minutes | Cook time: 3 minutes | Serves 4

6 cups chopped red cabbage
3 small apples, unpeeled, cored, and cut into 1-inch wedges
$1/_3$ cup apple cider vinegar
¼ teaspoon ground cloves

2 bay leaves
2 tablespoons butter, melted
2 tablespoons granulated sugar
1 teaspoon kosher salt
½ teaspoon black pepper

1. In the Instant Pot, combine all the ingredients. Stir to mix well.
2. Lock the lid. Select Manual mode and set the timer for 3 minutes at High Pressure.
3. When timer beeps, use a quick pressure release. Open the lid.
4. Remove the bay leaves before serving.

Glazed Brussels Sprouts and Cranberries

Prep time: 10 minutes | Cook time: 3 minutes | Serves 6

1½ cups marmalade
2 pounds (907 g) small Brussels sprouts, rinsed and trimmed
1 cup dried cranberries
½ cup orange
2 tablespoons butter, melted
1 teaspoon kosher salt
½ teaspoon cayenne pepper

1. Pour the water into the Instant Pot. Put a steamer basket in the pot. Put the Brussels sprouts and cranberries in the steamer basket.
2. Lock the lid. Select Manual mode and set the timer for 3 minutes on High Pressure.
3. When timer beeps, use a quick pressure release. Open the lid.
4. Transfer the Brussels sprouts and cranberries to a serving bowl. Add the orange marmalade, butter, salt, and cayenne. Toss to combine well. Serve hot.

Potato Cubes with Avocado Sauce

Prep time: 15 minutes | Cook time: 8 minutes | Serves 4

1 cup water
4 to 6 medium russet potatoes, scrubbed and cut in large cubes (4 to 5 cups)
1 avocado, peeled and pitted
2 tablespoons freshly squeezed lime juice
2 teaspoons onion powder, divided
1 teaspoon garlic powder, divided
Pinch salt
1 tablespoon olive oil
½ teaspoon smoked paprika
¼ teaspoon ground chipotle pepper

1. Put the potatoes in a steamer basket.
2. Put a trivet in the Instant Pot, pour in the water, and set the basket on top.
3. Lock the lid. Select Manual mode and set the timer for 6 minutes at High Pressure.

4. Once the cook time is complete, let the pressure release naturally for 10 minutes, then release any remaining pressure. Open the lid and let sit.
5. Meanwhile, in a blender, combine the avocado, lime juice, 1 teaspoon of onion powder, ½ teaspoon of garlic powder, and the salt. Pulse to purée. Transfer to a serving bowl.
6. Unlock the lid. Remove the basket from the pot.
7. Select Sauté mode of the Instant Pot. Return the potatoes to the pot and add the olive oil, remaining 1 teaspoon of onion powder, remaining ½ teaspoon of garlic powder, paprika, and chipotle pepper.
8. Sauté for 2 minutes, or until any liquid has evaporated. Serve the potatoes with the puréed avocado sauce.

Okra with Tomatoes

Prep time: 10 minutes | Cook time: 2 minutes | Serves 4

1 (14.5-ounce / 411-g) can diced tomatoes
2 tablespoons apple cider vinegar
1 cup diced onion
3 cloves garlic, minced
2 vegetable bouillon cubes, crushed
¼ teaspoon ground allspice
1 teaspoon smoked paprika
1 teaspoon kosher salt
½ cup water, divided
1½ pounds (680 g) fresh okra
2 tablespoons tomato paste
1 tablespoon fresh lemon juice

1. In the Instant Pot, combine the tomatoes, vinegar, onion, garlic, bouillon cubes, allspice, paprika, salt, and ¼ cup of the water. Put the okra on top.
2. Secure the lid. Select Manual mode and set the cooking time for 2 minutes at High Pressure.
3. When timer beeps, perform a natural pressure release for 5 minutes, then release any remaining pressure.
4. In a small bowl, Dissolve the tomato paste into the remaining water.
5. Mix the tomato paste mixture and lemon juice into the pot and serve.

Simple Ratatouille

Prep time: 15 minutes | Cook time: 10 minutes | Serves 4 to 6

2 teaspoons olive oil
1 onion, diced
4 garlic cloves, minced
1 eggplant, cubed
4 tomatoes, diced
2 bell peppers, any color, deseeded and

chopped
1 cup water
1½ tablespoons dried basil
½ teaspoon salt
Freshly ground black pepper, to taste

1. Select Sauté mode on the Instant Pot. Heat the oil until shimmering. Add the onion and garlic, and sauté for 4 minutes or until the onion is softened.
2. Add the eggplant, tomatoes, bell peppers, water, and basil.
3. Close and lock the lid, then set the time for 6 minutes on High Pressure.
4. Once the cook time is complete, let the pressure release naturally for 20 minutes, then release any remaining pressure.
5. Carefully unlock the lid. Let cool for a few minutes, then season with salt and pepper. Serve warm.

Lemony Asparagus and English Peas

Prep time: 5 minutes | Cook time: 2 minutes | Serves 4

1 to 2 cloves garlic, minced
2 cups fresh English peas
2 cups asparagus, cut into pieces

¼ cup vegetable broth
Zest and juice of 1 lemon
2 to 3 tablespoons toasted pine nuts

1. Add the garlic, peas, asparagus and broth to the Instant Pot.
2. Set the lid in place. Select the Manual mode and set the cooking time for 2 minutes on Low Pressure. When the timer goes off, do a quick pressure release. Carefully open the lid.
3. Add the lemon zest and juice and stir. Transfer to a bowl or plate. Garnish with the nuts.
4. Serve immediately.

Sumptuous Vegetable Mix

Prep time: 15 minutes | Cook time: 23 to 24 minutes | Serves 3

1 tablespoon olive oil
½ carrot, peeled and minced
½ celery stalk, minced
½ small onion, minced
1 garlic clove, minced
½ teaspoon crushed dried sage
½ teaspoon crushed dried rosemary
4 ounces (113 g) fresh Portabella mushrooms, sliced
4 ounces (113 g) fresh white mushrooms, sliced
¼ cup red wine

1 Yukon Gold potato, peeled and diced
¾ cup fresh green beans, trimmed and chopped
1 cup chopped tomatoes
½ cup tomato paste
½ tablespoon balsamic vinegar
3 cups water
Salt and freshly ground black pepper, to taste
2 ounces (57 g) frozen peas
½ lemon juice
2 tablespoons chopped fresh cilantro for garnishing

1. Press the Sauté button on the Instant Pot and heat the oil. Add the onion, tomatoes and celery into the Instant Pot and sauté for 5 minutes.
2. Stir in the herbs and garlic and cook for 1 minute.
3. Add the mushrooms and sauté for 5 minutes. Stir in the wine and cook for a further 2 minutes
4. Add the diced potatoes and mix. Cover the pot with a lid and let the potatoes cook for 2 to 3 minutes.
5. Add the green beans, carrots, tomato paste, peas, salt, pepper, water and vinegar.
6. Set the lid in place. Select the Manual mode and set the cooking time for 8 minutes on High Pressure. When the timer goes off, do a quick pressure release. Carefully open the lid.
7. Stir the veggies and then add the lemon juice and cilantro.
8. Serve immediately.

Carrots with Ginger-Almond Cream

Prep time: 15 minutes | Cook time: 6 to 7 minutes | Serves 3 to 4

1½ pounds (680 g) carrots, scrubbed and peeled
2 tablespoons butter
1 tablespoon pure maple syrup
½ teaspoon garlic powder
½ teaspoon kosher salt
Freshly cracked black pepper, to taste
Ginger-Almond Cream:
2 tablespoons no-added-sugar creamy
almond butter
2 teaspoons rice vinegar
1 teaspoon pure maple syrup
1 teaspoon reduced-sodium tamari
1-inch piece fresh ginger, grated
¼ cup water
For Serving:
¼ cup finely chopped fresh cilantro
2 teaspoons toasted white sesame seeds

1. For carrots that are relatively uniform in width and not too fat, simply trim the ends and tops so that they fit lying flat in the Instant Pot.
2. For carrots that are much fatter on the top and much skinnier at the bottom, halve the carrots crosswise, then slice the fat tops lengthwise and keep the skinnier bottoms whole.
3. Select the Sauté setting on the Instant Pot and melt the butter. Add the carrots, toss around in the butter, and cook for 2 minutes.
4. Add the maple syrup, garlic powder, salt, and pepper and toss to coat the carrots evenly.
5. Set the lid in place. Select the Manual mode and set the cooking time for 3 minutes on High Pressure.
6. Meanwhile, make the ginger-almond cream: In a bowl, whisk together the almond butter, vinegar, maple syrup, tamari, ginger, and water until smooth.
7. When the timer goes off, do a quick pressure release. Carefully open the lid.
8. Using a slotted spoon, transfer the carrots to a serving dish. Keep the liquid remaining in the pot and add all the ingredients for the ginger-almond cream to the pot.
9. Select the Sauté setting. Whisk the ingredients together and cook until the sauce is thick but pourable, 1 to 2 minutes. Using oven mitts, remove the inner pot and pour the cream on top of the carrots. Garnish with the cilantro and sesame seeds.
10. Serve immediately.

Swiss Chard and White Beans

Prep time: 10 minutes | Cook time: 4 to 5 minutes | Serves 4 to 6

2 bunches Swiss chard, thick bottom stems discarded, leaves sliced into 1-inch-wide ribbons
2 tablespoons olive oil
4 garlic cloves, thinly sliced
1 large red onion, cut into ⅜-inch-thick slices
½ teaspoon kosher salt
½ teaspoon crushed
red pepper flakes
⅓ cup low-sodium vegetable broth
½ cup golden raisins
1½ cups cooked cannellini beans
⅓ cup toasted pine nuts
10 pitted green olives, sliced
2 tablespoons capers, drained
Grated zest of 1 large lemon

1. Thoroughly wash and dry the chard leaves.
2. Select the Sauté setting on the Instant Pot and heat the oil. Add the garlic. Cook, tossing frequently to prevent burning, until the garlic is lightly golden, 1 to 2 minutes.
3. Add the onion and season with the salt and pepper flakes. Cook for 2 minutes, tossing occasionally, then select the Cancel setting.
4. Add the chard leaves, vegetable broth, and raisins. Using a large spoon, mix together the ingredients. Press down the pile of chard with the spoon to ensure the mixture is below the Instant Pot's maximum capacity line.
5. Set the lid in place. Select the Manual mode and set the cooking time for 1 minute on High Pressure. When the timer goes off, do a quick pressure release. Carefully open the lid.
6. Transfer the cooked vegetables to a large bowl. Add the cannellini beans, toasted nuts, olives, capers, and lemon zest. Toss to combine and serve.

Citrus Carrots and Kale

Prep time: 15 minutes | Cook time: 10 to 11 minutes | Serves 4

Kale and Carrots:

2 tablespoons olive oil
2 medium yellow onions, diced
8 garlic cloves, chopped
6 medium carrots, sliced into ½-inch-thick half-moons
1 teaspoon kosher salt

Freshly cracked black pepper, to taste
1 large bunch Tuscan kale, thick stems removed, leaves sliced into 1-inch pieces
1/3 cup low-sodium vegetable broth
6 sprigs fresh thyme

Citrus Dressing:

Grated zest and juice of 1 small orange
1 tablespoon balsamic vinegar
½ teaspoon Dijon mustard
¼ teaspoon kosher

salt
Freshly cracked black pepper, to taste
For Serving:
2 tablespoons hemp seeds

1. Prepare the kale and carrots: Select the Sauté setting on the Instant Pot and let the pot heat up for a few minutes before adding the olive oil. Once the oil is hot, add the onions. Cook until the onions are just beginning to soften, about 3 minutes. Add the garlic and carrots with a pinch each of salt and pepper and cook until the carrots are slightly softened, 4 to 5 minutes.
2. Add the sliced kale, packing it down, followed by the vegetable broth, thyme sprigs, salt and pepper. Use a long-handled spoon to toss the mixture together and to push down the kale to ensure it is below the Instant Pot's maximum capacity line.
3. Set the lid in place. Select the Manual mode and set the cooking time for 3 minutes on High Pressure.
4. Meanwhile, make the citrus dressing: In a small bowl, combine the orange zest, orange juice, vinegar, mustard, salt, and pepper and whisk until smooth.
5. When the timer goes off, do a quick pressure release. Carefully open the lid.

6. Discard the thyme sprigs. Using a slotted spoon, transfer the kale and carrots to a serving dish, leaving behind any remaining liquid. Top with the citrus dressing and hemp seeds, stirring gently to coat.
7. Serve immediately.

Mashed Root Vegetables

Prep time: 15 minutes | Cook time: 9 to 10 minutes | Serves 8

1 head garlic, roasted
1 cup water
1 tablespoon olive oil
1 medium yellow onion, roughly chopped
1 pound (454 g) carrots, peeled and cut into large cubes
1 pound (454 g) sweet potatoes, peeled and cut into pieces slightly larger

than the carrots
1 small head cauliflower, roughly chopped into florets
1 large sprig fresh rosemary
6 sprigs fresh thyme
1¼ teaspoons kosher salt, divided
Freshly cracked black pepper, to taste
1/3 cup low-sodium vegetable broth
2 tablespoons butter

1. Select the Sauté setting and let the pot heat up for a few minutes before adding the olive oil. Once the oil is hot, add the onion. Cook until the onion is lightly browned, 4 to 5 minutes.
2. Add the carrots, sweet potatoes, cauliflower, rosemary, and thyme. Squeeze the roasted garlic cloves directly into the Instant Pot and season with ¾ teaspoon of the salt and pepper. Pour the vegetable broth on top and stir all the ingredients to combine.
3. Set the lid in place. Select the Manual mode and set the cooking time for 5 minutes on High Pressure. When the timer goes off, do a quick pressure release. Carefully open the lid.
4. Add the butter and the remaining ½ teaspoon of the salt. Using an immersion blender, blend all the ingredients together until smooth.
5. Serve warm.

Sweet Potato Salad with Parsley

Prep time: 10 minutes | Cook time: 17 minutes | Serves 4

¼ cup olive oil
1 medium yellow onion, peeled and diced
2 cloves garlic, minced
1 teaspoon ground cumin
1 teaspoon paprika
¼ cup fresh lemon juice
1 cup water

3 cups peeled and cubed sweet potatoes
¼ cup chopped green olives
3 tablespoons chopped fresh Italian flat-leaf parsley
Pinch of salt
Pinch of freshly ground black pepper

1. Press the Sauté button on the Instant Pot and heat the oil. Add the onion and sauté for 5 minites, or until it begins to turn golden brown. Add the garlic, cumin, paprika, and lemon juice and cook for about 2 minutes. Transfer to a large bowl and set aside.
2. Add the water and the sweet potatoes to the pot.
3. Lock the lid. Select the Manual mode and set the cooking time for 10 minutes on High Pressure. Once the timer goes off, perform a natural pressure release for 10 minutes, then release any remaining pressure. Carefully open the lid.
4. Drain the sweet potatoes in a colander. Toss the potatoes with the onion mixture. Add the olives and parsley and season with salt and pepper, and serve warm.

Green Beans with Maple-Tahini Dressing

Prep time: 15 minutes | Cook time: 5 minutes | Serves 4

Green Beans:
1 pound (454 g) green beans, ends trimmed
½ cup water
¾ teaspoon kosher salt
Freshly cracked

black pepper, to taste
1 tablespoon olive oil
2 garlic cloves, minced
2 shallots, diced

Maple-Tahini Dressing:
2½ tablespoons tahini
2 tablespoons fresh lemon juice
1½ tablespoons extra-virgin olive oil
1 tablespoon pure maple syrup
1 garlic clove, finely

minced
¼ teaspoon kosher salt, plus more to taste
¼ teaspoon freshly cracked black pepper
2 tablespoons warm water

Salad Add-Ons:
½ cup cherry tomatoes, halved
⅓ cup toasted almonds, roughly

chopped
1 small bunch fresh mint leaves, torn into pieces

1. Cook the green beans: Place the green beans in the Instant Pot. Add the water, salt and pepper.
2. Set the lid in place. Select the Manual mode and set the cooking time for 1 minute on High Pressure.
3. Meanwhile, make the maple-tahini dressing: In a small bowl, combine the tahini, lemon juice, extra-virgin olive oil, maple syrup, garlic, salt, and pepper and whisk together until smooth and creamy. Then add the warm water and whisk until it has a pourable consistency. Taste for seasonings and adjust accordingly.
4. When the timer goes off, do a quick pressure release. Carefully open the lid.
5. Using oven mitts, carefully remove the inner pot and drain the green beans in a colander.
6. Return the inner pot to the Instant Pot. Select the Sauté setting and heat the olive oil until shimmering.
7. Add the garlic and shallots. Cook until browned, about 3 minutes. Return the green beans to the pot, stir to combine, and cook for 1 minute.
8. Transfer the green bean mixture to a serving dish and drizzle with the dressing, tossing to coat. Sprinkle on the cherry tomatoes, almonds, and torn mint leaves and serve.

Sesame-Garlic Green Beans

Prep time: 5 minutes | Cook time: 5 minutes | Serves 4

5 cups green beans, trimmed	1 tablespoon sesame oil
4 cloves garlic, sliced	1 tablespoon toasted sesame seeds
½ cup vegetable broth	¼ cup chopped red bell pepper

1. Combine the green beans, garlic and vegetable broth in the Instant Pot.
2. Set the lid in place. Select the Manual mode and set the cooking time for 5 minutes on High Pressure. When the timer goes off, do a quick pressure release. Carefully open the lid.
3. Remove the green beans and drain them thoroughly, reserving the sliced garlic.
4. Transfer the green beans to a bowl, along with the reserved garlic. Add the sesame oil and the toasted sesame seeds. Toss to coat.
5. Garnish the dish with chopped red bell pepper before serving.

Potato and Spinach Risotto

Prep time: 10 minutes | Cook time: 16 to 18 minutes | Serves 6

2 medium leeks, white part only	½ cup dry white wine
¼ cup plus 1 tablespoon olive oil, divided	2 cups mushroom broth
3 sprigs fresh thyme	4 cups fresh spinach leaves
3 pounds (1.4 kg) russet potatoes, peeled and diced into cubes	Pinch of salt
	Pinch of freshly ground black pepper

1. Thinly slice leeks crosswise into semicircles and rinse.
2. Press the Sauté button on the Instant Pot and add ¼ cup of the olive oil. Add the leeks and sauté until translucent. Add the thyme and continue to sauté for 4 minutes, then transfer to a medium bowl.
3. In the medium bowl, toss the potatoes with 1 tablespoon olive oil to thinly coat.

Add the potatoes to the pot and sauté for 5 minutes.

4. Add the wine and deglaze the pot, then cook until the wine has almost evaporated, about 2 to 4 minutes. Add the leek mixture and the broth to the potatoes in the pot.
5. Lock the lid. Select the Manual mode and set the cooking time for 5 minutes on High Pressure. Once the timer goes off, perform a natural pressure release for 10 minutes, then release any remaining pressure. Carefully open the lid.
6. Add the spinach to the pot and stir until it is wilted and all the ingredients have been combined.
7. Season with salt and pepper and serve.

Eggplant Curry with Spinach

Prep time: 15 minutes | Cook time: 22 minutes | Serves 4

¾ cup lentils, soaked and rinsed	cumin
1 teaspoon olive oil	2 tomatoes, chopped
½ onion, chopped	1 cup chopped eggplant
4 garlic cloves, chopped	1 cup cubed sweet potatoes
1 teaspoon chopped ginger	¾ teaspoon salt
1 hot green chili, chopped	2 cups water
¼ teaspoon turmeric	1 cup baby spinach leaves
½ teaspoon ground	

1. Press the Sauté button on the Instant Pot and heat the oil. Add the garlic, ginger, chili and salt into the Instant Pot and sauté for 3 minutes.
2. Stir in the tomatoes and all the spices. Cook for 5 minutes.
3. Add all the remaining ingredients, except for the spinach leaves.
4. Lock the lid. Select the Manual mode and set the cooking time for 12 minutes on High Pressure. Once the timer goes off, perform a natural pressure release for 15 minutes, then release any remaining pressure. Carefully open the lid.
5. Select the Sauté mode. Stir in the spinach leaves and let the pot simmer for 2 minutes.
6. Serve warm.

Cauliflower Butternut Squash

Prep time: 10 minutes | Cook time: 7 minutes | Serves 3

½ medium onion, diced
2 teaspoons oil
1 garlic clove, minced
½ cup tomato paste
½ pound (227 g) frozen cauliflower
½ pound (227 g) frozen, cubed
butternut squash
½ cup vegetable broth
½ teaspoon paprika
¼ teaspoon dried thyme
2 tablespoons chopped fresh cilantro
2 pinches sea salt

1. Press the Sauté button on the Instant Pot and heat the oil. Add the onion and garlic into the Instant Pot and sauté for 2 minutes.
2. Add the broth, tomato paste, cauliflower, butternut, and all the spices, to the pot.
3. Set the lid in place. Select the Manual mode and set the cooking time for 5 minutes on High Pressure. When the timer goes off, do a quick pressure release. Carefully open the lid.
4. Stir well, garnish with the fresh cilantro and serve hot.

Celery and Carrots Chickpea Rice

Prep time: 10 minutes | Cook time: 13 minutes | Serves 4

1 cup long-grain white rice
½ cup chickpeas, soaked
½ large onion, chopped
2 large carrots, diced
2 celery sticks, chopped
½ small leek, chopped
1 tablespoon olive oil
½ tablespoon ginger paste
½ teaspoon garlic paste
½ tablespoon Worcester sauce
½ teaspoon chopped coriander
½ teaspoon chopped parsley
2½ cups water
Salt and pepper, to taste

1. Press the Sauté button on the Instant Pot and heat the oil. Add the onion, ginger and garlic paste in the Instant Pot and sauté for 5 minutes.

2. Stir in the remaining vegetables and stir-fry for 3 minutes.
3. Add the remaining ingredients
4. Lock the lid. Select the Manual mode and set the cooking time for 5 minutes on High Pressure. Once the timer goes off, perform a natural pressure release for 10 minutes, then release any remaining pressure. Carefully open the lid.
5. Stir well and serve warm.

Spicy and Sweet Braised Red Cabbage

Prep time: 10 minutes | Cook time: minutes | Makes 7 cups

1 tablespoon olive oil
1 medium red cabbage, roughly chopped
1¼ teaspoons kosher salt, divided
2 large carrots, grated
1 apple, unpeeled and grated
1¼ cups low-sodium vegetable broth
¼ cup apple cider vinegar
1½ tablespoons reduced-sodium tamari
1 tablespoon organic brown sugar
½ cup dried sour cherries
1 teaspoon crushed red pepper flakes
2 teaspoons white sesame seeds

1. Select the Sauté setting on the Instant Pot and let the pot heat up for a few minutes before adding the olive oil. Once the oil is hot, add the cabbage. Add ½ teaspoon of the kosher salt and cook, stirring occasionally, until the cabbage begins to brown, about 4 minutes.
2. Top the cabbage with the carrots and apple, then pour in the vegetable broth, vinegar, and tamari and add the brown sugar, dried cherries, pepper flakes, and the remaining ¾ teaspoon of the salt. Stir well to combine.
3. Set the lid in place. Select the Manual mode and set the cooking time for 3 minutes on High Pressure. When the timer goes off, do a quick pressure release. Carefully open the lid.
4. Transfer the cabbage to a serving dish and serve garnished with the sesame seeds.

Smoky Brussels Sprouts with Pecans

Prep time: 5 minutes | Cook time: 2 minutes | Serves 4

2 cups small baby Brussels sprouts	¼ cup chopped pecans
¼ cup water	2 tablespoons maple syrup
½ teaspoon liquid smoke	Salt, to taste

1. Add the Brussels sprouts, water and liquid smoke to the Instant Pot and mix well.
2. Set the lid in place. Select the Manual mode and set the cooking time for 2 minutes on High Pressure. When the timer goes off, do a quick pressure release. Carefully open the lid.
3. Select the Sauté mode and add the pecans and maple syrup and reduce the liquid. Remove from the heat once tender and season with salt.
4. Serve immediately.

Summer Vegetable Plate

Prep time: 10 minutes | Cook time: 10 minutes | Serves 4

Bottom Layer:

4 large ears corn, shucked and cleaned	1 lime
1 cup water	Salt, to taste

Middle Layer:

4 cups (400 g) green beans, broken in half if large	smoke
½ teaspoon liquid	¼ to ½ teaspoon salt

Top Layer:

2 medium summer squash, sliced	chopped fresh thyme, basil and oregano
2 tablespoons	

1. For the bottom layer, arrange the corn in the Instant Pot liner and pour in the water.
2. For the middle layer, sprinkle the green beans with the liquid smoke and salt, then seal in a foil packet and set on top of the corn.

3. For the top layer, toss the squash and herbs together, then seal in a foil packet and place on top of the green bean layer.
4. Lock the lid. Select the Manual mode and set the cooking time for 10 minutes on High Pressure. Once the timer goes off, perform a natural pressure release for 15 minutes, then release any remaining pressure. Carefully open the lid. Lift out the packets.
5. Before serving, squeeze lime juice on the corn and sprinkle with salt.

Cauliflower and Mushroom Stroganoff

Prep time: 10 minutes | Cook time: 17 minutes | Serves 4

1 tablespoon olive oil	dill
1 cup minced onion	2 cups cauliflower florets, wrapped in foil
1½ teaspoons minced garlic	½ cup unsweetened almond milk
2 teaspoons paprika	1 tablespoon nutritional yeast
2 pounds (907 g) mushrooms, sliced	½ teaspoon dill
½ cup water	Salt and pepper, to taste
1 vegetable bouillon cube	
1½ teaspoons dried	

1. Press the Sauté button on the Instant Pot and heat the oil. Add the onion and sauté until transparent, 5 minutes. Then add the garlic and paprika and sauté for 2 more minutes.
2. Add the mushrooms, water, bouillon cube and dill to the onion mixture and stir to combine. Top with the cauliflower foil packet.
3. Set the lid in place. Select the Manual mode and set the cooking time for 10 minutes on High Pressure. When the timer goes off, do a quick pressure release. Carefully open the lid.
4. Transfer the cooked cauliflower to a blender along with the almond milk, nutritional yeast and dill. Blend until smooth and season with salt and pepper to taste. Pour the sauce into the Instant Pot and mix with the mushrooms.
5. Serve warm.

Sesame Teriyaki Vegetables

Prep time: 10 minutes | Cook time: 18 minutes | Serves 4

¾ large yellow onion, chopped
1½ medium carrots, diced
1½ ribs celery, chopped
1 medium portabella mushroom, diced
¾ tablespoon chopped garlic
2 cups water
1 pound (454 g) white potatoes, peeled and diced
¼ cup tomato paste
½ tablespoon sesame oil
2 teaspoons sesame seeds
½ tablespoon paprika
1 teaspoon fresh rosemary
¾ cup peas
¼ cup chopped fresh parsley

1. Press the Sauté button on the Instant Pot and heat the oil. Add the sesame seeds and all the vegetables in the Instant Pot and sauté for 5 minutes.
2. Stir in the remaining ingredients.
3. Lock the lid. Select the Manual mode and set the cooking time for 13 minutes on High Pressure. Once the timer goes off, perform a natural pressure release for 10 minutes, then release any remaining pressure. Carefully open the lid.
4. Garnish with the fresh parsley and serve hot.

Veggie Bolognese

Prep time: 15 minutes | Cook time: 7 minutes | Serves 8

½ head cauliflower, cut into rough florets
1 (10-ounce / 284-g) can mushrooms
2 cups shredded carrot
2 cups eggplant chunks
2 (28-ounce / 794-g) cans crushed tomatoes
1 cup water
6 cloves garlic, minced
2 tablespoons tomato paste
2 tablespoons agave nectar
2 tablespoons balsamic vinegar
1½ tablespoons dried oregano
1 tablespoon dried basil
1½ teaspoons dried rosemary
Salt and pepper, to taste

1. Add the cauliflower florets to a food processor and pulse until the pieces are tiny and look like couscous. Scrape out into the Instant Pot liner.
2. Add the mushrooms to the food processor and pulse until small, then add them to the Instant Pot liner. Repeat with the carrots and eggplant, until all the veggies are minced and in the Instant Pot liner.
3. Mix in the crushed tomatoes, water, garlic, tomato paste, agave nectar, balsamic vinegar, oregano, basil and rosemary.
4. Lock the lid. Select the Manual mode and set the cooking time for 7 minutes on High Pressure. Once the timer goes off, perform a natural pressure release for 10 minutes, then release any remaining pressure. Carefully open the lid.
5. Season with salt and pepper and serve.

Simple Veggie Lasagne

Prep time: 10 minutes | Cook time: 12 minutes | Serves 4

2 tablespoons olive oil
1 medium onion, chopped
½ green pepper, chopped
2 carrots, chopped
1 medium zucchini, chopped
1 cup sliced bell pepper
1 large can diced tomatoes
3 cups vegetable broth
½ box lasagne noodles
½ teaspoon onion powder
1 teaspoon black pepper
1 teaspoon oregano
Sea salt, to taste

1. Press the Sauté button on the Instant Pot and heat the oil. Add the green pepper, onion and carrots in the Instant Pot and sauté for 5 minutes.
2. Stir in the zucchini, bell pepper and all the spices to cook for 3 minutes
3. Add the broth, tomatoes, and lasagne noodles to the pot.
4. Set the lid in place. Select the Manual mode and set the cooking time for 4 minutes on High Pressure. When the timer goes off, do a quick pressure release. Carefully open the lid.
5. Serve hot.

Classic Brazilian Potato Curry

Prep time: 10 minutes | Cook time: 30 minutes | Serves 2

2 large potatoes, peeled and diced
1 small onion, peeled and diced
8 ounces (227 g) fresh tomatoes
1 tablespoon olive oil
1 cup water
2 tablespoons grated
garlic cloves, divided
½ tablespoon rosemary
½ tablespoon cayenne pepper
1½ tablespoons thyme
Salt and pepper, to taste

1. Pour the water into the Instant Pot and place the trivet inside.
2. Place the potatoes and 1 tablespoon of the garlic over the trivet and sprinkle some salt and pepper on top.
3. Lock the lid. Select the Steam mode and set the cooking time for 20 minutes on High Pressure. Once the timer goes off, perform a natural pressure release for 15 minutes, then release any remaining pressure. Carefully open the lid.
4. Put the potatoes to one side and empty the pot.
5. Select the Sauté mode. Add the remaining ingredients to the pot and cook for 10 minutes. Use an immerse blender to purée the cooked mixture.
6. Stir in the steamed potatoes and serve hot.

Spinach Potato Corn Mix

Prep time: 10 minutes | Cook time: 13 minutes | Serves 6

1 tablespoon olive oil
3 scallions, chopped
½ cup chopped onion
2 large white potatoes, peeled and diced
1 tablespoon grated ginger
3 cups frozen corn kernels
1 cup vegetable stock
2 tablespoons light soy sauce
2 large cloves garlic, diced
1/3 teaspoon white pepper
1 teaspoon salt
3 to 4 handfuls baby spinach leaves
Juice of ½ lemon

1. Press the Sauté button on the Instant Pot and heat the oil. Add the ginger, garlic and onions in the Instant Pot and sauté for 5 minutes.
2. Add all the remaining ingredients, except for the spinach leaves and lime juice.
3. Set the lid in place. Select the Manual mode and set the cooking time for 5 minutes on High Pressure. When the timer goes off, do a quick pressure release. Carefully open the lid.
4. Select the Sauté mode. Add the spinach and cook for 3 minutes.
5. Drizzle the lime juice over the dish and serve hot.

Vegetable Mix Chili

Prep time: 15 minutes | Cook time: 10 minutes | Serves 3

½ tablespoon olive oil
1 small yellow onion, chopped
4 garlic cloves, minced
¾ (15-ounce / 425-g) can diced tomatoes
1 ounce (28 g) sugar-free tomato paste
½ (4-ounces / 113-g) can green chilies with liquid
1 tablespoon Worcestershire
sauce
2 tablespoons red chili powder
½ cup diced carrots
½ cup chopped scallions
½ cup chopped green bell pepper
¼ cup peas
1 tablespoon ground cumin
½ tablespoon crushed dried oregano
Salt and freshly ground black pepper, to taste

1. Press the Sauté button on the Instant Pot and heat the oil. Add the onion, and garlic into the Instant Pot and sauté for 5 minutes.
2. Stir in the remaining vegetables and stir-fry for 3 minutes. Add the remaining ingredients.
3. Lock the lid. Select the Manual mode and set the cooking time for 2 minutes on High Pressure. Once the timer goes off, perform a natural pressure release for 10 minutes, then release any remaining pressure. Carefully open the lid.
4. Stir well and serve warm.

Spice-Stuffed Eggplants

Prep time: 15 minutes | Cook time: 9 minutes | Serves 4

1 tablespoon coriander seeds
½ teaspoon cumin seeds
½ teaspoon mustard seeds
2 to 3 tablespoons chickpea flour
2 tablespoons chopped peanuts
2 tablespoons coconut shreds
1-inch ginger, chopped
2 cloves garlic, chopped
1 hot green chili, chopped
½ teaspoon ground cardamom
Pinch of cinnamon
¹/₃ to ½ teaspoon cayenne
½ teaspoon turmeric
½ teaspoon raw sugar
½ to ¾ teaspoon salt
1 teaspoon lemon juice
1 cup water, plus more as needed
4 baby eggplants

1. Press the Sauté button on the Instant Pot. Add the coriander, mustard seeds and cumin to the pot. Roast for 2 minutes.
2. Add the chickpea flour, nuts and coconut shred to the pot, and roast for 2 minutes. Blend the mixture in a blender, then transfer to a medium-sized bowl.
3. Roughly blend the ginger, garlic, raw sugar, chili, and all the spices in the blender. Add the water and lemon juice to make a paste. Combine it with the dry flour mixture.
4. Cut the eggplants from one side and stuff with the spice mixture. Add 1 cup water to the Instant Pot and place the stuffed eggplants inside. Sprinkle some salt on top.
5. Set the lid in place. Select the Manual mode and set the cooking time for 5 minutes on High Pressure. When the timer goes off, do a quick pressure release. Carefully open the lid.
6. Serve hot.

Spaghetti Squash with Carrots

Prep time: 15 minutes | Cook time: 25 minutes | Serves 2

½ tablespoon olive oil
1 large spaghetti squash
¼ small yellow onion, chopped
1 jalapeño pepper, chopped
½ cup chopped green onions
½ cup chopped carrots
¼ cup chopped cabbage
1 garlic clove, minced
½ (6-ounce / 170-g) can sugar-free tomato sauce
½ tablespoon chili powder
½ tablespoon ground cumin
Salt and freshly ground black pepper, to taste
2 cups water
2 tablespoons chopped fresh parsley
¼ cup shredded cashew cheese

1. Pour the water into the Instant Pot and place the trivet inside.
2. Slice the squash into 2 halves and remove the seeds.
3. Place them over the trivet, skin side down, and sprinkle some salt and pepper over it.
4. Lock the lid. Select the Manual mode and set the cooking time for 15 minutes on High Pressure. Once the timer goes off, perform a natural pressure release for 10 minutes, then release any remaining pressure. Carefully open the lid. Empty the pot.
5. Shred the squash with a fork and keep the shredded pieces to one side.
6. Press the Sauté button on the Instant Pot and heat the oil. Add the onion, and garlic in the Instant Pot and sauté for 5 minutes.
7. Stir in the remaining vegetables and stir-fry for 3 minutes. Add the remaining ingredients.
8. Lock the lid. Select the Manual mode and set the cooking time for 2 minutes on High Pressure. Once the timer goes off, perform a natural pressure release for 10 minutes, then release any remaining pressure. Carefully open the lid.
9. Stir in the spaghetti squash shreds.
10. Garnish with the parsley and shredded cashew cheese. Serve warm.

Carrot and Broccoli Medley

Prep time: 10 minutes | Cook time: 20 minutes | Serves 3

1 tablespoon olive oil
½ white onion, diced
1½ cloves garlic, finely chopped
1 pound (454 g) potatoes, cut into chunks
1 pound (454 g) broccoli florets, diced

1 pound (454 g) baby carrots, cut into halves
¼ cup vegetable broth
½ teaspoon Italian seasoning
½ teaspoon Spike original seasoning
1 teaspoon fresh parsley

1. Press the Sauté button on the Instant Pot and heat the oil. Add the onion and sauté for 5 minutes. Stir in the carrots and garlic and stir-fry for 5 minutes. Add the remaining ingredients.
2. Set the lid in place. Select the Manual mode and set the cooking time for 10 minutes on High Pressure. When the timer goes off, do a quick pressure release. Carefully open the lid.
3. Stir gently and garnish with the fresh parsley, then serve.

Broccoli Florets with Cauliflower

Prep time: 5 minutes | Cook time: 7 minutes | Serves 3

½ medium onion, diced
2 teaspoons olive oil
1 garlic clove, minced
½ cup tomato paste
½ pound (227 g) frozen cauliflower

½ pound (227 g) broccoli florets
½ cup vegetable broth
½ teaspoon paprika
¼ teaspoon dried thyme
2 pinches sea salt

1. Press the Sauté button on the Instant Pot and heat the oil. Add the onion and garlic into the Instant Pot and sauté for 2 minutes.
2. Add the broth, tomato paste, cauliflower, broccoli and all the spices to the pot.
3. Set the lid in place. Select the Manual mode and set the cooking time for 5 minutes on High Pressure. When the timer goes off, do a quick pressure release. Carefully open the lid.
4. Stir well and serve hot.

Chapter 10 Side Dishes

Spicy Ratatouille

Prep time: 15 minutes | Cook time: 8 minutes | Serves 6

1 (1-pound / 454-g) globe eggplant, cut into 1-inch pieces
3 zucchinis, cut into 1-inch pieces
1 teaspoon fine sea salt
2 tablespoons extra-virgin olive oil, plus more for serving
1 large yellow onion, cut into 1-inch pieces
2 cloves garlic, minced
1 teaspoon dried basil
½ teaspoon freshly ground black pepper

½ teaspoon dried thyme
½ teaspoon red pepper flakes
1 bay leaf
3 red bell peppers, stemmed, deseeded and cut into 1-inch pieces
1 (14½-ounce / 411-g) can diced tomatoes
¼ cup dry white wine
Fresh basil leaves, for serving
Crusty bread, for serving

1. In a large bowl, toss together the eggplant and zucchini with the salt. Let stand for 15 minutes.
2. Select the Sauté setting on the Instant Pot, add the oil, and heat for 1 minute. Add the onion and garlic and sauté for about 4 minutes, or until the onion softens. Add the basil, black pepper, thyme, red pepper flakes, and bay leaf and sauté for about 1 minute. Add the eggplant-zucchini mixture and any liquid that has pooled in the bottom of the bowl, along with the bell peppers, tomatoes and their liquid, and wine. Stir to combine.
3. Set the lid in place. Select the Manual mode and set the cooking time for 2 minutes on Low Pressure. When the timer goes off, do a quick pressure release. Carefully open the lid.
4. Discard the bay leaf. Spoon the ratatouille into a serving bowl.
5. Drizzle the ratatouille with oil and sprinkle with fresh basil. Serve warm, with crusty bread.

Spiced Carrots

Prep time: 5 minutes | Cook time: 5 minutes | Serves 6

2 pounds (907 g) baby carrots, chopped
½ cup packed brown sugar
½ cup orange juice
2 tablespoons butter
¾ teaspoon ground

cinnamon
½ teaspoon salt
¼ teaspoon ground nutmeg
1 tablespoon cornstarch
¼ cup cold water

1. Add all the ingredients, except for the cornstarch and water, to the Instant Pot and stir to combine.
2. Set the lid in place. Select the Manual mode and set the cooking time for 3 minutes on Low Pressure. When the timer goes off, do a quick pressure release. Carefully open the lid.
3. Select the Sauté mode and bring it to a boil. Mix water and cornstarch in a bowl and add to the carrot mixture. Cook for 2 minutes.
4. Serve hot.

Deviled Potatoes

Prep time: 10 minutes | Cook time: 10 minutes | Serves 6

6 medium Yukon Gold potatoes, halved
1 cup water
5 tablespoons mayonnaise
1 teaspoon Dijon mustard
1 tablespoon sweet pickle relish
1 teaspoon sugar

½ teaspoon freshly squeezed lemon juice
½ teaspoon kosher salt
½ teaspoon freshly ground black pepper
1 tablespoon finely chopped fresh cilantro
1 teaspoon paprika

1. Place the halved potatoes in the steamer rack. Pour the water and insert the trivet in the Instant Pot. Place the steamer rack on the trivet.
2. Set the lid in place. Select the Manual mode and set the cooking time for 10 minutes on High Pressure. When the timer goes off, do a quick pressure release. Carefully open the lid.
3. Using tongs, carefully transfer the potatoes to a platter. Set aside to cool for 15 minutes.
4. In a medium bowl, stir together the mayonnaise, mustard, relish, sugar, lemon juice, salt and pepper.
5. Using a melon scooper or spoon, remove the middle part of the potatoes, creating a well. Spoon 1 to 1½ teaspoons of the mayonnaise mixture into each potato. Garnish each deviled potato with the cilantro and paprika before serving.

Smoky Carrots and Collard Greens

Prep time: 10 minutes | Cook time: 12 minutes | Serves 4 to 6

1 tablespoon extra-virgin olive oil
1 yellow onion, diced
8 ounces (227 g) carrots, peeled and diced
2 bunches collard greens, stems discarded and leaves sliced into 1-inch

ribbons
½ teaspoon smoked paprika
½ teaspoon fine sea salt, plus more as needed
¼ teaspoon freshly ground black pepper
½ cup water
1 tablespoon tomato paste

1. Select the Sauté setting on the Instant Pot, add the oil, and heat for 1 minute. Add the onion and carrots and sauté for about 4 minutes, or until the onion begins to soften. Stir in the collards and sauté for about 2 minutes, or until wilted. Stir in the smoked paprika, salt, pepper, and water. Dollop the tomato paste on top, but do not stir it in.
2. Set the lid in place. Select the Manual mode and set the cooking time for 5 minutes on High Pressure. When the timer goes off, do a quick pressure release. Carefully open the lid.
3. Stir to incorporate the tomato paste. Taste and adjust the seasoning with salt, if needed.
4. Spoon the collards into a serving bowl or onto serving plates. Serve warm.

Classic Succotash

Prep time: 5 minutes | Cook time: 10 minutes | Serves 6 to 8

2 tablespoons extra-virgin olive oil
1 clove garlic, minced
1 yellow onion, diced
1 (16-ounce / 454-g) bag frozen baby lima beans
1 (12-ounce / 340-g) bag frozen corn kernels
1 (14½-ounce / 411-g) can diced tomatoes
½ cup low-sodium vegetable broth
½ teaspoon dried thyme
½ teaspoon fine sea salt
¼ teaspoon freshly ground black pepper

1. Select the Sauté setting on the Instant Pot, add the oil and garlic, and heat for 2 minutes, or until the garlic is bubbling but not browned. Add the onion and sauté for about 5 minutes, or until the onion softens. Add the lima beans, corn, tomatoes and their liquid, broth, thyme, salt, and pepper, and vegetable broth. Stir to combine.
2. Set the lid in place. Select the Manual mode and set the cooking time for 3 minutes on High Pressure. When the timer goes off, do a quick pressure release. Carefully open the lid.
3. Stir the succotash, then transfer to a serving bowl. Serve warm.

Artichoke-Spinach Dip

Prep time: 10 minutes | Cook time: 10 to 11 minutes | Serves 8

2 teaspoons corn oil
¼ cup chopped onion
2 garlic cloves, finely chopped
8 ounces (227 g) fresh spinach, roughly chopped
½ teaspoon kosher salt
1 teaspoon freshly ground black pepper
5 ounces (142 g) cream cheese
1 (8½-ounce / 241-g) can water-packed artichoke hearts, drained and quartered
⅓ cup heavy cream
⅓ cup water
Chips or sliced veggies, for serving

1. Press the Sauté button on the Instant Pot and heat the oil. Add the onion and garlic and sauté for 1 minute. Add the spinach, salt, and pepper. Continue to sauté for 2 to 3 minutes, or until the spinach is wilted. Add the cream cheese, artichokes, cream, and water and mix thoroughly.
2. Set the lid in place. Select the Manual mode and set the cooking time for 7 minutes on High Pressure. When the timer goes off, do a quick pressure release. Carefully open the lid.
3. Stir the dip, then let cool for 5 minutes. Transfer to a serving bowl and serve with chips or sliced veggies.

Asparagus with Gribiche

Prep time: 10 minutes | Cook time: 5 minutes | Serves 4

2 large eggs
1½ cups water
1 pound (454 g) asparagus, trimmed and cut into 1-inch pieces
1 tablespoon Dijon mustard
¼ cup vegetable oil
1 tablespoon apple cider vinegar
2 to 3 tablespoons chopped dill pickle
1 tablespoon chopped fresh parsley
1 teaspoon granulated sugar
½ teaspoon kosher salt
½ teaspoon black pepper

1. Pour the water and insert the trivet in the Instant Pot. Place the eggs on one side of the trivet.
2. Tightly wrap the asparagus in foil and place on the trivet next to the eggs.
3. Set the lid in place. Select the Manual mode and set the cooking time for 5 minutes on High Pressure. When the timer goes off, do a quick pressure release. Carefully open the lid.
4. Meanwhile, fill a medium bowl with ice cubes and water.
5. Remove the eggs and place them in the ice water bath for 5 minutes. Peel and finely dice the eggs.
6. In a small bowl, combine the mustard, oil, vinegar, pickle, parsley, sugar, salt, and pepper. Stir in the chopped eggs.
7. Place the asparagus on a serving platter and spoon the gribiche on top. Serve.

Szechuan Honey-Glazed Asparagus

Prep time: 5 minutes | Cook time: 1 minute | Serves 4

2 bunches asparagus, woody ends removed
1 tablespoon extra-virgin olive oil
½ teaspoon kosher salt

½ teaspoon freshly ground black pepper
1 cup water
2 tablespoons honey
1 tablespoon Szechuan sauce

1. Place the asparagus in a large bowl. Drizzle with the olive oil, salt, and pepper, and toss to combine.
2. Place the asparagus in the steaming rack. Pour the water and insert the trivet in the Instant Pot. Place the steamer rack on the trivet. Lock the lid into place.
3. Set the lid in place. Select the Manual mode and set the cooking time for 1 minute on High Pressure. When the timer goes off, do a quick pressure release. Carefully open the lid.
4. Using tongs, transfer the asparagus to a serving bowl.
5. In a small bowl, combine the honey and Szechuan sauce. Drizzle over the asparagus and serve hot.

Sweet Potato Gratin

Prep time: 20 minutes | Cook time: 30 minutes | Serves 8

2 medium sweet potatoes, peeled and thinly sliced
2 tablespoons extra-virgin olive oil
1 teaspoon kosher salt
1 teaspoon freshly ground black pepper
1 tablespoon dried basil

1 tablespoon dried thyme
1 tablespoon butter, melted
½ cup heavy cream
1 cup Mexican-blend shredded cheese
2 tablespoons panko bread crumbs
1 cup water

1. In a large bowl, drizzle the olive oil over the sweet potato slices. Season with the salt, pepper, basil, and thyme. Mix thoroughly to coat the sweet potatoes. Set aside.

2. In a small bowl, mix the butter and cream.
3. In a springform pan, arrange a single layer of sweet potatoes. Spread about 2 tablespoons of the cream-butter mixture on top and sprinkle with 4 to 5 tablespoons of the cheese. Repeat these steps until all the sweet potato slices have been used, about three layers. After the last layer, sprinkle the bread crumbs on top. Cover the pan with aluminum foil.
4. Pour the water and insert the trivet in the Instant Pot. Place the springform pan on the trivet.
5. Lock the lid. Select the Manual mode and set the cooking time for 30 minutes on High Pressure. Once the timer goes off, perform a natural pressure release for 15 minutes, then release any remaining pressure. Carefully open the lid.
6. Carefully remove the pan. Let the sweet potatoes cool for at least 1 hour before serving so the cheese sets.

Grapefruit and Beet Salad

Prep time: 5 minutes | Cook time: 20 minutes | Serves 8

6 medium fresh beets
1½ cups water
¼ cup extra-virgin olive oil
3 tablespoons lemon juice
2 tablespoons cider vinegar

2 tablespoons honey
¼ teaspoon salt
¼ teaspoon black pepper
2 large grapefruits, peeled and sectioned
2 small red onions, halved and sliced

1. Scrub the beets, trimming the tops to 1 inch.
2. Pour the water and insert the trivet in the Instant Pot. Place the beets on the trivet.
3. Set the lid in place. Select the Manual mode and set the cooking time for 20 minutes on High Pressure. When the timer goes off, do a quick pressure release. Carefully open the lid.
4. Whisk together the remaining ingredients, except for the grapefruits and onion. Pour over beets. Stir in the grapefruits and onion and serve.

Beet Salad with Orange and Avocado

Prep time: 10 minutes | Cook time: 20 minutes | Serves 4

Salad:

1 pound (454 g) beets, each about 2½ inches in diameter

2 navel oranges, peeled and cut into segments

1 large avocados, pitted, peeled and

sliced

1 (5- to 6-ounce / 142- to 170-g) bag baby spinach

4 sprigs fresh mint, leaves removed and torn if large

¾ cup Feta cheese

1 cup water

Vinaigrette:

¼ cup extra-virgin olive oil

2 tablespoons fresh lemon juice

½ teaspoon dried oregano

¼ teaspoon fine sea salt

¼ teaspoon freshly ground black pepper

1 clove garlic, minced

1. Pour the water into the Instant Pot and place the wire metal steam rack in the pot. Arrange the beets in a single layer on the steam rack.
2. Set the lid in place. Select the Manual mode and set the cooking time for 20 minutes on High Pressure.
3. While the beets are cooking, prepare an ice bath.
4. To make the vinaigrette: In a widemouthed 1-pint jar, combine the oil, lemon juice, oregano, salt, pepper, and garlic. Using an immersion blender, blend until an emulsified vinaigrette forms. Set aside.
5. When the timer goes off, do a quick pressure release. Carefully open the lid. Using tongs, transfer the beets to the ice bath and let cool for 10 minutes.
6. Using a paring knife, remove the skins from the beets; they should peel off very easily. Trim and discard the ends of the beets, then slice them into wedges.
7. In a large bowl, toss the spinach with half of the vinaigrette. Arrange the spinach on a large serving plate or on individual salad plates, then top with the beets, oranges, avocado, and mint.
8. Using a pair of spoons, scoop bite-sized pieces of the feta out of its container and dollop it onto the salad. Spoon the rest of the vinaigrette over the salad and serve immediately.

Garlicky Boiled Bok Choy

Prep time: 5 minutes | Cook time: 7 minutes | Serves 2

1 garlic clove, smashed

1 bunch bok choy, trimmed

1 cup water

Salt and pepper, to taste

1. Add the water, garlic and bok choy to the Instant Pot.
2. Set the lid in place. Select the Manual mode and set the cooking time for 7 minutes on High Pressure. When the timer goes off, do a quick pressure release. Carefully open the lid.
3. Strain the cooked bok choy and transfer it to a platter.
4. Sprinkle some salt and pepper on top.
5. Serve.

Garlicky White Beets

Prep time: 10 minutes | Cook time: 13 minutes | Serves 4

6 whole white beets

4 cups water

2 teaspoons salt

2 tablespoons olive oil

4 cloves garlic, minced

2 tablespoons lime juice

1. Separate the white part of the beets from the green ones. Wash and rinse.
2. Cut the white parts into cubes and add them to the Instant Pot along with water.
3. Lock the lid. Select the Manual mode and set the cooking time for 10 minutes on High Pressure. Once the timer goes off, perform a natural pressure release for 15 minutes, then release any remaining pressure. Carefully open the lid.
4. Add the green parts of the beets to the Instant Pot and let it stay for 5 minutes. Strain the beets and set them aside.
5. Select the Sauté mode. Add the oil and garlic to the Instant Pot and sauté for 2 minutes.
6. Return the beets to the pot and sauté for 1 minute.
7. Drizzle with the lime juice and salt. Serve.

Spaghetti Squash with Pesto

Prep time: 5 minutes | Cook time: 12 minutes | Serves 6

1½ cups plus 3 tablespoons water, divided	spaghetti squash, pierced with a knife about 10 times
1 (3-pound / 1.4-kg)	¼ cup pesto

1. Pour 1½ cups of the water and insert the trivet in the Instant Pot. Put the pan on the trivet. Place the squash on the trivet.
2. Lock the lid. Select the Manual mode and set the cooking time for 12 minutes on High Pressure. Once the timer goes off, perform a natural pressure release for 10 minutes, then release any remaining pressure. Carefully open the lid.
3. Using tongs, carefully transfer the squash to a cutting board to cool for about 10 minutes.
4. Halve the spaghetti squash lengthwise. Using a spoon, scoop out and discard the seeds. Using a fork, scrape the flesh of the squash and shred into long "noodles". Place the noodles in a medium serving bowl.
5. In a small bowl, mix the pesto with the remaining 3 tablespoons of the water. Drizzle over the squash, toss to combine, and serve warm.

Adobo-Style Eggplant

Prep time: 10 minutes | Cook time: 6 minutes | Serves 4

1 (1-pound / 454-g) eggplant, cut into 1-inch pieces	1 large shallot, diced
1 teaspoon fine sea salt	1 red bell pepper, deseeded and cut into 1-inch squares
¼ cup low-sodium soy sauce	½ teaspoon freshly ground black pepper
2 tablespoons palm vinegar	2 tablespoons water
2 tablespoons avocado oil	Hot steamed rice, for serving
4 cloves garlic, minced	1 green onion, tender green part only, thinly sliced

1. In a colander, toss the eggplant with the salt. Let sit in the sink or on top of a dish for 30 minutes (some liquid will release from the eggplant as it sits), then rinse the eggplant well under running water. Pat the pieces dry with paper towels.
2. In a small bowl, combine the soy sauce and vinegar. Set aside.
3. Press the Sauté button on the Instant Pot and heat the oil for 1 minute. Add the garlic and shallot and sauté for 3 minutes, or until the shallot softens and the garlic begins to color.
4. Add the eggplant, bell pepper, and black pepper, and stir to coat the vegetables with the oil. Pour in the vinegar mixture and water.
5. Set the lid in place. Select the Manual mode and set the cooking time for 2 minutes on Low Pressure. When the timer goes off, do a quick pressure release. Carefully open the lid.
6. Give the vegetables a gentle stir to coat with the sauce, then let sit for a minute or two.
7. Spoon over bowls of steamed rice and sprinkle green onions on top. Serve hot.

Green Beans w`ith Tomatoes

Prep time: 5 minutes | Cook time: 7 minutes | Serves 8

2 tablespoons olive oil	tomatoes
2 garlic cloves, crushed	2 pounds (907 g) green beans
4 cups diced fresh	Salt, to taste

1. Press the Sauté button on the Instant Pot and heat the oil. Add the garlic to the pot and sauté for 1 minute. Stir in the tomatoes and sauté for another 1 minute.
2. Set the trivet in the pot and arrange the green beans over it.
3. Lock the lid. Select the Manual mode and set the cooking time for 5 minutes on High Pressure. Once the timer goes off, perform a natural pressure release for 5 minutes, then release any remaining pressure. Carefully open the lid.
4. Remove the trivet along with green beans. Add the beans to tomatoes in the pot.
5. Sprinkle salt and stir well. Serve hot.

Carrot and Mushroom Quinoa Salad

Prep time: 10 minutes | Cook time: 1 minute | Serves 4

½ cup quinoa, rinsed
¾ cup water
¼ teaspoon salt
½ carrot, peeled and shredded
½ cup green onions
½ cup diced cremini mushrooms
1 tablespoon lime juice
1 tablespoon vegetable oil
1 tablespoon freshly grated ginger
1 tablespoon sesame oil
Pinch of red pepper flakes

1. Add the quinoa, salt, and water to the Instant Pot.
2. Set the lid in place. Select the Manual mode and set the cooking time for 1 minute on High Pressure. When the timer goes off, do a quick pressure release. Carefully open the lid.
3. Add the remaining ingredients to a bowl and mix them well.
4. Add the cooked quinoa to the prepared mixture and mix well.
5. Serve.

Sweet Turnip Greens

Prep time: 5 minutes | Cook time: 5 minutes | Serves 10

2 pounds (907 g) turnips, peeled and chopped
12 ounces (340 g) fresh turnip greens
1 medium onion, chopped
2 tablespoons sugar
Salt and pepper, to taste
5 cups vegetable broth

1. Add all the ingredients to the Instant Pot and stir to combine.
2. Set the lid in place. Select the Manual mode and set the cooking time for 5 minutes on High Pressure. When the timer goes off, do a quick pressure release. Carefully open the lid.
3. Serve hot.

Citrus Corn and Beet Salad

Prep time: 10 minutes | Cook time: 8 minutes | Serves 6

2 medium red beets, peeled
1 corn on the cob, husks removed, washed
1½ cups water
¼ cup finely chopped onion
¼ cup finely chopped fresh cilantro
3 tablespoons mayonnaise
1 tablespoon extra-virgin olive oil
2 teaspoons freshly squeezed lemon juice
1 teaspoon grated lemon zest
1 teaspoon sugar
1 teaspoon kosher salt
1 teaspoon freshly ground black pepper

1. Place the whole beets and corn in the steamer rack. Pour the water and insert the trivet in the Instant Pot. Place the steamer rack on the trivet.
2. Set the lid in place. Select the Manual mode and set the cooking time for 4 minutes on High Pressure. When the timer goes off, do a quick pressure release. Carefully open the lid.
3. Using tongs, transfer the corn to a plate and set aside to cool.
4. Set the lid in place again. Select the Manual mode and set the cooking time for 4 minutes on High Pressure. When the timer goes off, do a quick pressure release. Carefully open the lid.
5. Using tongs, transfer the beets to the plate with the corn and set aside to cool.
6. Using a knife, carefully remove the corn kernels from the cob. Cut the beets into ½-inch cubes.
7. In a large bowl, combine the beets, corn, onion, cilantro, mayonnaise, olive oil, lemon juice and zest, sugar, salt, and pepper. Mix thoroughly and chill in the refrigerator for 1 hour.
8. Serve chilled.

Green Bean Stir-Fry

Prep time: 5 minutes | Cook time: 4 minutes | Serves 4

12 ounces (340 g) green beans, trimmed
1 cup water
2 tablespoons corn oil
2 garlic cloves, finely chopped
3 tablespoons crushed peanuts
2 tablespoons soy sauce
¼ teaspoon kosher salt
½ teaspoon cane sugar
2 teaspoons chili flakes

1. Place the beans in the steamer basket. Pour the water and insert the trivet in the Instant Pot. Place the basket on the trivet.
2. Set the lid in place. Select the Manual mode and set the cooking time for 1 minute on High Pressure. When the timer goes off, do a quick pressure release. Carefully open the lid.
3. Drain the beans and wipe the inner pot dry.
4. Press the Sauté button on the Instant Pot and heat the oil. Add the garlic and sauté for 1 minute. Add the peanuts and soy sauce and sauté for 2 more minutes.
5. In a large bowl, combine the green beans, garlic, peanuts, salt, and sugar. Mix until the sugar and salt are dissolved. Sprinkle with the chili flakes and serve hot.

Steamed Leeks with Tomato Sauce

Prep time: 10 minutes | Cook time: 2 minutes | Serves 6

1 large tomato, chopped
1 small navel orange, chopped
2 tablespoons minced fresh parsley
2 tablespoons sliced olives
1 teaspoon capers, drained
1 teaspoon red wine vinegar
1 teaspoon olive oil
½ teaspoon grated orange zest
½ teaspoon pepper
6 medium leeks, white portion only, halved lengthwise and cleaned
Crumbled Feta cheese, for serving
1 cup water, for the pot

1. In a bowl, stir together all the ingredients, except for the leeks, cheese and water. Set aside.
2. Pour the water and insert the trivet in the Instant Pot. Place the leeks on the trivet.
3. Set the lid in place. Select the Manual mode and set the cooking time for 2 minutes on High Pressure. When the timer goes off, do a quick pressure release. Carefully open the lid.
4. Transfer the leeks to a platter. Spoon the tomato mixture on top. Sprinkle with the cheese and serve.

Maple Brussels Sprouts with Walnuts

Prep time: 10 minutes | Cook time: 10 to 12 minutes | Serves 4

1 tablespoon olive oil
¼ cup minced shallots
4 cups halved Brussels sprouts
1 cup orange juice
¼ cup cranberry juice
2 tablespoons maple syrup
¼ cup chopped dried cranberries
¼ cup chopped walnuts

1. Combine the orange juice, cranberry juice and maple syrup in a small bowl. Whisk together until well blended.
2. Press the Sauté button on the Instant Pot and heat the oil. Add in the shallots and sauté them for 3 minutes. Add the sauce and the Brussels sprouts to the pot.
3. Set the lid in place. Select the Manual mode and set the cooking time for 4 minutes on High Pressure. When the timer goes off, do a quick pressure release. Carefully open the lid.
4. Use a slotted spoon to remove the Brussels sprouts from the pot and transfer them to a serving plate or bowl.
5. Press the Sauté button on the Instant Pot and cook the remaining sauce for 3 to 5 minutes, or until it thickens slightly and reduces.
6. Pour the sauce over the Brussels sprouts and toss to coat.
7. Garnish the Brussels sprouts with the dried cranberries and walnuts before serving.

Brussels Sprouts with Sesame Seeds

Prep time: 5 minutes | Cook time: 4 minutes | Serves 4

25 Brussels sprouts, halved lengthwise
1 cup water
1 tablespoon extra-virgin olive oil
2 garlic cloves, finely chopped
1 tablespoon

balsamic vinegar
1 teaspoon kosher salt
½ teaspoon freshly ground black pepper
1 tablespoon roasted sesame seeds

1. Place the Brussels sprouts in the steamer basket. Pour the water and insert the trivet in the Instant Pot. Place the basket on the trivet.
2. Set the lid in place. Select the Manual mode and set the cooking time for 1 minute on High Pressure. When the timer goes off, do a quick pressure release. Carefully open the lid.
3. Using tongs, carefully transfer the Brussels sprouts to a serving plate. Discard the water and wipe the inner pot dry.
4. Press the Sauté button on the Instant Pot and heat the oil. Add the garlic and sauté for 1 minute. Add the Brussels sprouts, vinegar, salt, and pepper, and sauté for 2 minutes. Sprinkle with the roasted sesame seeds and serve hot.

Balsamic Glazed Brussels Sprouts

Prep time: 5 minutes | Cook time: 9 to 14 minutes | Serves 4

14 ounces (397 g) whole medium-sized Brussels sprouts
1 cup water
1 tablespoon extra-virgin olive oil

Sea salt, to taste
Freshly ground black pepper, to taste
½ cup balsamic vinegar

1. Trim a thin slice off the bottom of the Brussels sprouts and remove a few outer leaves from each. Fit the pot with a steamer basket and add 1 cup water. Add the Brussels sprouts to the steamer basket.
2. Set the lid in place. Select the Manual mode and set the cooking time for 1 minute on High Pressure. When the timer goes off, do a quick pressure release. Carefully open the lid.
3. Remove the steamer basket. Discard the water in the pot.
4. Press the Sauté button on the Instant Pot and heat the oil. Add the steamed Brussels sprouts and season with salt and pepper. Turn occasionally with tongs or a spatula, until seared, about 3 minutes.
5. Meanwhile, make the balsamic glaze. Pour the balsamic vinegar into a small saucepan over medium-low heat. Simmer until the vinegar is reduced and syrupy and coats the back of a spoon, 5 to 10 minutes.
6. Serve the Brussels sprouts hot with a small bowl of the balsamic glaze on the side for drizzling.

Braised Kale with Garlic

Prep time: 5 minutes | Cook time: 5 minutes | Serves 4

1 large bunch kale
2 tablespoons extra-virgin olive oil
6 cloves garlic, thinly sliced crosswise

½ cup vegetable broth
¼ teaspoon sea salt
Freshly ground black pepper, to taste

1. Remove and discard the middle stems from the kale and roughly chop the leafy parts. Rinse and drain the kale.
2. Press the Sauté button on the Instant Pot and heat the oil. Add the garlic and sauté for about 2 minutes until tender and golden. Transfer the garlic and oil to a small bowl and set aside.
3. Add the broth to the inner pot. Place the kale on top and sprinkle with salt and pepper.
4. Set the lid in place. Select the Manual mode and set the cooking time for 3 minutes on Low Pressure. When the timer goes off, do a quick pressure release. Carefully open the lid.
5. Return the garlic and oil to the pot, and toss to combine.
6. Serve immediately.

BBQ Baked Beans

Prep time: 5 minutes | Cook time: 33 minutes | Serves 8

16 ounces (454 g) dried great northern beans, soaked overnight and drained
2 cups water
1 medium onion, chopped
2 teaspoons garlic powder, divided
2 teaspoons onion powder, divided
1 cup barbecue sauce
¾ cup packed brown sugar
½ teaspoon ground nutmeg
¼ teaspoon ground cloves
2 teaspoons hot pepper sauce

1. In the pot, combine the beans, water, onion, 1 teaspoon of the garlic powder and 1 teaspoon of the onion powder.
2. Set the lid in place. Select the Manual mode and set the cooking time for 30 minutes on High Pressure. When the timer goes off, do a quick pressure release. Carefully open the lid.
3. Stir in the barbecue sauce, sugar, nutmeg, cloves, hot pepper sauce, and the remaining garlic and onion powder.
4. Set the lid in place. Select the Manual mode and set the cooking time for 3 minutes on High Pressure. When the timer goes off, do a quick pressure release. Carefully open the lid.
5. Serve hot.

Steamed Artichoke with Aioli

Prep time: 10 minutes | Cook time: 15 minutes | Serves 2

1 large artichoke
1 cup water
Juice of ½ lemon
The Aioli Dipping Sauce:
½ cup raw cashews, soaked overnight or 2 hours in hot water
1½ tablespoons Dijon mustard
1 tablespoon apple cider vinegar
Juice of ½ lemon
2 cloves garlic
Pinch of ground turmeric
½ teaspoon sea salt
1/3 cup water

1. Fit the inner pot with the trivet and add 1 cup water. Trim the artichoke stem so that it is 1 to 2 inches long, and trim about 1 inch off the top. Squeeze the lemon juice over the top of the artichoke and add the lemon rind to the water. Place the artichoke, top-side down, on the trivet.
2. Set the lid in place. Select the Steam mode and set the cooking time for 15 minutes on High Pressure. When the timer goes off, do a quick pressure release. Carefully open the lid.
3. Check for doneness. Leaves should be easy to remove and the "meat" at the base of each leaf should be tender.
4. Meanwhile, make the aioli dipping sauce. Drain the cashews and place them in a blender. Add the Dijon, vinegar, lemon juice, garlic, turmeric, and sea salt. Add half the water and blend. Continue adding water as you blend until the sauce is smooth and creamy. Transfer the sauce to a small bowl or jar. Refrigerate until ready to use.
5. Use tongs to remove the hot artichoke and place on a serving dish. Serve the artichoke warm with the aioli.

Caramelized Sweet Potatoes

Prep time: 5 minutes | Cook time: 19 minutes | Serves 2

2 sweet potatoes, scrubbed
1 cup water
2 tablespoons coconut oil
Pinch of salt and black pepper
Pinch of chili powder

1. Pour the water and insert the trivet in the Instant Pot. Put the pan on the trivet.
2. Pour the water to the Instant Pot and place the steamer basket at the bottom. Add the sweet potatoes to the basket.
3. Set the lid in place. Select the Manual mode and set the cooking time for 15 minutes on High Pressure. When the timer goes off, do a quick pressure release. Carefully open the lid.
4. Remove and slice the potatoes. Clean the pot.
5. Press the Sauté button on the Instant Pot and heat the oil. Add the sliced sweet potatoes. Season with salt, pepper and chili powder and brown for 2 minutes on each side.
6. Serve hot.

Fresh Lemony Peas with Mint

Prep time: 5 minutes | Cook time: 2 minutes | Serves 4

4 cups fresh peas, not in pods
1 cup vegetable broth
1 tablespoon coconut oil, melted
¼ cup chopped fresh mint
¼ cup chopped fresh parsley
1 teaspoon lemon zest

1. Combine the peas and vegetable broth in the Instant Pot.
2. Set the lid in place. Select the Manual mode and set the cooking time for 2 minutes on High Pressure. When the timer goes off, do a quick pressure release. Carefully open the lid.
3. Drain off the excess liquid from the peas and place them in a bowl.
4. Drizzle the peas with the melted coconut oil and toss to coat.
5. Add the mint, parsley and lemon zest to the bowl and stir.
6. Serve immediately.

Sour and Sweet Beets and Kale

Prep time: 10 minutes | Cook time: 10 minutes | Serves 6

4 cups quartered beets
3 cups roughly chopped kale
1 cup sliced onion
1½ cups water
¼ cup walnut oil
¼ cup apple cider vinegar
1 tablespoon brown sugar
½ teaspoon salt
1 teaspoon black pepper

1. Combine the beets and the water in the Instant Pot.
2. Set the lid in place. Select the Manual mode and set the cooking time for 5 minutes on High Pressure. When the timer goes off, do a quick pressure release. Carefully open the lid.
3. Add in the kale and the onion.
4. Lock the lid again. Select the Manual mode and set the cooking time for 5 minutes on High Pressure. Once the timer goes off, perform a natural pressure release for 5 minutes, then release any remaining pressure.

5. While the steam is releasing, combine the walnut oil, apple cider vinegar, brown sugar, salt and black pepper. Whisk together until well blended.
6. Carefully open the lid. Remove the vegetables from the pot and thoroughly drain them.
7. Transfer the vegetables to a bowl and add in the dressing. Toss to coat.
8. Serve warm, or cover and refrigerate for several hours for a chilled side dish.

Maple Mashed Sweet Potato Casserole

Prep time: 5 minutes | Cook time: 30 to 35 minutes | Serves 6 to 8

3 pounds (1.4 kg) sweet potatoes, peeled and cut into 1-inch pieces
¼ cup coconut oil
¼ cup dark maple syrup
1 teaspoon fine sea
salt
½ teaspoon ground cinnamon
10 marshmallows, cut in half lengthwise
1 cup water

1. Pour the water into the Instant Pot and place a steamer basket in the pot. Add the sweet potatoes to the basket.
2. Set the lid in place. Select the Manual mode and set the cooking time for 5 minutes on High Pressure.
3. While the sweet potatoes are steaming, preheat the oven to 325ºF (163ºC). Grease a baking dish with coconut oil and line a baking sheet with aluminum foil.
4. When the timer goes off, do a quick pressure release. Carefully open the lid. Wearing heat-resistant mitts, lift out the steamer basket. Lift out the inner pot and discard the water.
5. Return the sweet potatoes to the still-warm inner pot. Add the coconut oil, maple syrup, salt, and cinnamon, then use a potato masher to mash the sweet potatoes until smooth.
6. Spoon the mashed potatoes into the baking dish. Top with a single layer of the marshmallows, cut side down. Place the dish on the prepared baking sheet. Bake for 25 to 30 minutes, until the marshmallows are puffed and golden brown on top. Serve warm.

Mushroom Rice Pilaf

Prep time: 5 minutes | Cook time: 9 minutes | Serves 6

¼ cup butter
1 cup medium-grain rice
2 garlic cloves, minced
6 green onions, chopped

½ pound (227 g) baby portobello mushrooms, sliced
1 cup water
4 teaspoons Better Than Bouillon

1. Press the Sauté button on the Instant Pot and melt the butter. Add the rice and cook for 5 minutes. Add the garlic, green onions, and mushrooms.
2. In a bowl, whisk together the water and bouillon. Pour over the rice mixture.
3. Set the lid in place. Select the Manual mode and set the cooking time for 4 minutes on High Pressure. When the timer goes off, do a quick pressure release. Carefully open the lid.
4. Serve hot.

Instant Pot Spanish Risotto

Prep time: 5 minutes | Cook time: 10 minutes | Serves 6

3 tablespoons olive oil
1 cup chopped yellow onion
2 garlic cloves, minced
2 cups white rice
2½ cups vegetable stock

¾ cup crushed tomatoes
½ teaspoon chili powder
¼ cup chopped cilantro
Salt and black pepper, to taste

1. Press the Sauté button on the Instant Pot and heat the oil. Add the onion and garlic and cook for 4 minutes. Add the rice and cook for 2 minutes. Stir in the stock, tomatoes, and chili powder.
2. Set the lid in place. Select the Manual mode and set the cooking time for 4 minutes on High Pressure. When the timer goes off, do a quick pressure release. Carefully open the lid.
3. Sprinkle with the cilantro and season with salt and pepper. Stir and serve.

Easy Braised Savoy Cabbage

Prep time: 5 minutes | Cook time: 7 to 8 minutes | Serves 4

1 tablespoon olive oil
¼ cup minced shallots
¼ cup white wine

4 cups savoy cabbage
1 cup vegetable broth

1. Press the Sauté button on the Instant Pot and heat the oil. Add in the shallots and sauté for 3 minutes. Add the white wine and cook for 1 to 2 minutes, or until the wine reduces. Add the savoy cabbage and the vegetable broth to the pot.
2. Lock the lid. Select the Manual mode and set the cooking time for 3 minutes on High Pressure. Once the timer goes off, perform a natural pressure release for 5 minutes, then release any remaining pressure. Carefully open the lid.
3. Serve immediately.

Spicy Ginger-Garlic Kale

Prep time: 5 minutes | Cook time: 6 minutes | Serves 4

1 tablespoon olive oil
5 cloves garlic
1 tablespoon fresh grated ginger
1 tablespoon crushed red pepper flakes

8 cups kale, stems removed and chopped
1½ cups vegetable broth
1 tablespoon garlic chili paste

1. Press the Sauté button on the Instant Pot and heat the oil. Add in the garlic, ginger and crushed red pepper flakes. Sauté the mixture for 2 minutes or until highly fragrant.
2. Add in the vegetable broth and garlic chili paste. Whisk until well blended. Add in the kale and stir.
3. Lock the lid. Select the Manual mode and set the cooking time for 4 minutes on High Pressure. Once the timer goes off, perform a natural pressure release for 5 minutes, then release any remaining pressure. Carefully open the lid.
4. Stir before serving.

Garlicky Steamed Broccoli

Prep time: 5 minutes | Cook time: 10 minutes | Serves 6

6 cups broccoli florets
1 cup water
½ garlic cloves, minced
2 tablespoons peanut oil
2 tablespoons Chinese rice wine
Sea salt, to taste

1. Pour the water and insert the trivet in the Instant Pot. Arrange the broccoli florets over the trivet.
2. Lock the lid. Select the Manual mode and set the cooking time for 5 minutes on High Pressure. Once the timer goes off, perform a natural pressure release for 5 minutes, then release any remaining pressure. Carefully open the lid.
3. Strain the florets and return them back to the pot. Add the remaining ingredients to the broccoli.
4. Select the Sauté mode and sauté for 5 minutes.
5. Serve.

Carrot Quinoa with Olives

Prep time: 10 minutes | Cook time: 1 minute | Serves 4

½ cup quinoa, rinsed
¾ cup water
¼ teaspoon salt
½ carrot, peeled and shredded
½ cup green onions
¼ cup sliced black olives
1 tablespoon lime juice
1 tablespoon olive oil
1 tablespoon freshly grated ginger
Pinch of red pepper flakes

1. Add the quinoa, salt, and water to the Instant Pot.
2. Set the lid in place. Select the Manual mode and set the cooking time for 1 minute on High Pressure. When the timer goes off, do a quick pressure release. Carefully open the lid.
3. Meanwhile, add the remaining ingredients to a bowl and mix them well.
4. Add the cooked quinoa to the prepared mixture and mix well.
5. Serve.

Balsamic Mushrooms

Prep time: 5 minutes | Cook time: 6 minutes | Serves 6

2 tablespoons olive oil
6 garlic cloves, minced
2 pounds (907 g) fresh mushrooms,
sliced
⅓ cup balsamic vinegar
⅓ cup white wine
Salt and black pepper, to taste

1. Press the Sauté button on the Instant Pot and heat the oil. Add the garlic to the pot and sauté for 1 minute. Add all the remaining ingredients to the pot.
2. Set the lid in place. Select the Manual mode and set the cooking time for 5 minutes on High Pressure. When the timer goes off, do a quick pressure release. Carefully open the lid.
3. Sprinkle the salt and black pepper and serve.

Sweet Potato Mash with Sage

Prep time: 5 minutes | Cook time: 5 minutes | Serves 4

4 cups peeled sweet potato chunks
1 cup water
3 tablespoon butter
4 sage leaves, thinly
sliced
Sea salt, to taste
Freshly ground black pepper, to taste

1. Fit the inner pot with a steamer basket and add 1 cup water. Place the sweet potato chunks into the basket.
2. Set the lid in place. Select the Manual mode and set the cooking time for 3 minutes on High Pressure. When the timer goes off, do a quick pressure release. Carefully open the lid.
3. Use tongs to carefully remove the steamer basket and potatoes. Discard the water and return the inner pot to the Instant Pot.
4. Press the Sauté button on the Instant Pot and melt the butter. Sauté the sage leaves until fragrant, about 2 minutes. Add the sweet potatoes to the pot and mash with a potato masher to the desired consistency. Season to taste with salt and pepper.
5. Serve immediately.

Lemony Corn Cobs

Prep time: 5 minutes | Cook time: 2 minutes | Serves 4

4 ears corn
2 cups water
Salt and pepper, to taste

1. 1 tablespoon lemon juice
2. 1 tablespoon melted butter
3.
4. Add the water and arrange the corn ears vertically in the Instant Pot.
5. Keep the larger end of the corn ears dipped in the water or arrange diagonally.
6. Lock the lid. Select the Manual mode and set the cooking time for 2 minutes on High Pressure. Once the timer goes off, perform a natural pressure release for 5 minutes, then release any remaining pressure. Carefully open the lid.
7. Strain the corn ears and transfer them to a platter.
8. Drizzle the lemon juice and melted butter on top.
9. Sprinkle salt and pepper and serve hot.

Balsamic Beet with Rosemary

Prep time: 10 minutes | Cook time: 20 minutes | Serves 4

4 beets
1 cup water
2 tablespoons balsamic vinegar
2 tablespoons chopped rosemary
2 tablespoons

capers, drained
Pinch of salt and black pepper
1 garlic clove, minced
1 tablespoon avocado oil

1. Put the water in the Instant Pot. Add the steamer basket. Place the beets in the basket.
2. Lock the lid. Select the Manual mode and set the cooking time for 20 minutes on High Pressure. Once the timer goes off, perform a natural pressure release for 10 minutes, then release any remaining pressure. Carefully open the lid.
3. Drain the beets, cool them down, peel and cut into cubes.
4. In a salad bowl, combine the beets with the remaining ingredients, toss and serve.

Chive and Garlic Home Fries

Prep time: 5 minutes | Cook time: 8 to 10 minutes | Serves 4

½ cup vegetable broth
4 cups cubed sweet potatoes
2 tablespoons butter
3 cloves garlic, minced

1 teaspoon paprika
1 teaspoon sea salt
½ teaspoon ground black pepper
1 tablespoon chopped fresh chives

1. Place a steamer basket into the Instant Pot. Pour in the broth. Add potatoes to the basket.
2. Lock the lid. Select the Manual mode and set the cooking time for 5 minutes on High Pressure. Once the timer goes off, perform a natural pressure release for 10 minutes, then release any remaining pressure. Carefully open the lid.
3. Remove the potatoes and basket from the pot. Set the potatoes aside. Discard the broth.
4. Press the Sauté button on the Instant Pot and melt the butter. Add the potatoes and stir-fry for 3 to 5 minutes until browned. Add garlic and heat an additional minute. Transfer the potatoes to a bowl and toss with the paprika, salt, and pepper.
5. Garnish with the chives and serve warm.

Citrus Brussels Sprouts

Prep time: 10 minutes | Cook time: 8 minutes | Serves 6

1½ pounds (680 g) Brussels sprouts, halved
Pinch of salt and black pepper
¼ cup orange juice

1 teaspoon grated orange zest
1 teaspoon grated lime zest
1 tablespoon olive oil

1. Add all the ingredients to the Instant Pot and stir to combine.
2. Lock the lid. Select the Manual mode and set the cooking time for 8 minutes on High Pressure. Once the timer goes off, perform a natural pressure release for 10 minutes, then release any remaining pressure. Carefully open the lid.
3. Divide the mix between plates and serve.

Vinegary Carrots

Prep time: 5 minutes | Cook time: 7 minutes | Serves 4

½ cup veggie stock
1 pound (454 g) baby carrots
1 teaspoon dried thyme
1 teaspoon dried

dill,
Pinch of salt and black pepper
2 tablespoons balsamic vinegar

1. Add all the ingredients to the Instant Pot and stir to combine.
2. Lock the lid. Select the Manual mode and set the cooking time for 7 minutes on High Pressure. Once the timer goes off, perform a natural pressure release for 10 minutes, then release any remaining pressure. Carefully open the lid.
3. Divide the mix between plates and serve as a side dish.

Chickpea and Tomato Bowl

Prep time: 15 minutes | Cook time: 25 minutes | Serves 3

½ tablespoon olive oil
½ onion, chopped
½ tablespoon minced fresh ginger
½ tablespoon minced garlic
½ teaspoons curry powder
½ teaspoon ground cumin
½ teaspoon ground coriander

1 medium tomato, chopped finely
½ cup dried chickpeas, rinsed, soaked and drained
½ cup water
Pinch of salt
Freshly ground black pepper, to taste
1 tablespoon chopped fresh parsley

1. Press the Sauté button on the Instant Pot and heat the oil for 3 minutes. Add the garlic, ginger, and all the spices and cook for another 2 minutes. Add the water and chickpeas to the pot.
2. Set the lid in place. Select the Manual mode and set the cooking time for 20 minutes on High Pressure. When the timer goes off, do a quick pressure release. Carefully open the lid.
3. Sprinkle the salt and black pepper on top and garnish with the parsley.
4. Serve hot.

Beets and Parsnips Mix

Prep time: 10 minutes | Cook time: 10 minutes | Serves 4

1 pound (454 g) parsnips, peeled and roughly cubed
2 beets, peeled and roughly cubed
Pinch of salt and

black pepper
1 cup veggie stock
½ teaspoon turmeric powder
1 tablespoon chopped chives

1. Add all the ingredients, except for the chives to the Instant Pot and stir to combine.
2. Lock the lid. Select the Manual mode and set the cooking time for 10 minutes on High Pressure. Once the timer goes off, perform a natural pressure release for 10 minutes, then release any remaining pressure. Carefully open the lid.
3. Divide the mix between plates and serve with the chives sprinkled on top.

Rosemary Carrots

Prep time: 10 minutes | Cook time: 15 minutes | Serves 4

2½ pounds (1.1 kg) carrots, sliced
3 tablespoons avocado oil
Salt and black pepper, to taste
1 cup veggie stock

1 teaspoon garam masala
½ teaspoon sweet chili powder
1 teaspoon dried rosemary

1. Press the Sauté button on the Instant Pot and heat the oil. Add the carrots and sauté for 5 minutes. Stir in the remaining ingredients.
2. Lock the lid. Select the Manual mode and set the cooking time for 10 minutes on High Pressure. Once the timer goes off, perform a natural pressure release for 10 minutes, then release any remaining pressure. Carefully open the lid.
3. Divide the mix between plates and serve as a side dish.

Smokey Garbanzo Mash

Prep time: 5 minutes | Cook time: 20 minutes | Serves 6

2 cups dried garbanzo beans
1 tablespoon liquid smoke
½ teaspoon salt
1 teaspoon black pepper
1 teaspoon smoked paprika
½ teaspoon cayenne powder
¼ cup fresh parsley
¼ cup coconut milk

1. Place the garbanzo beans in the Instant Pot and add enough water just to cover. Sprinkle in the liquid smoke and stir.
2. Lock the lid. Select the Bean/Chili mode and set the cooking time for 20 minutes on High Pressure. Once the timer goes off, perform a natural pressure release for 10 minutes, then release any remaining pressure. Carefully open the lid. Drain off any excess liquid.
3. Add the salt, black pepper, smoked paprika, cayenne powder, fresh parsley and coconut milk to the garbanzo beans.
4. Use an immersion blender or a potato masher to mash the garbanzo beans to a desired consistency.
5. Serve immediately.

Simple Mexican Corn

Prep time: 5 minutes | Cook time: 3 minutes | Serves 4

4 cups fresh corn kernels
1 cup water
½ teaspoon salt
1 tablespoon olive oil
1 teaspoon cumin
1 teaspoon smoked paprika
¼ cup fresh cilantro
1 tablespoon lime juice

1. Place the corn kernels, water and salt in the Instant Pot.
2. Lock the lid. Select the Manual mode and set the cooking time for 3 minutes on High Pressure.
3. While the corn is in the pot, combine the olive oil, cumin and paprika in a small saucepan or microwave-safe bowl. Heat just until warmed through and the oil is infused with the spices.

4. Once the timer goes off, perform a natural pressure release for 5 minutes, then release any remaining pressure. Carefully open the lid. Remove the corn from the pot and drain off any excess liquid.
5. Pour the spice-infused oil over the corn and toss to coat.
6. Add in the cilantro and lime juice and stir.
7. Serve immediately.

Creamy Spinach with Mushrooms

Prep time: 10 minutes | Cook time: 10 minutes | Serves 4

1 tablespoon olive oil
1 cup sliced fennel
2 cloves garlic, crushed and minced
¼ cup white wine
10 cups fresh spinach
2 cups sliced portabella
mushrooms,
1 cup coconut milk
½ cup vegetable broth
½ teaspoon salt
1 teaspoon coarse ground black pepper
1 teaspoon nutmeg
½ teaspoon thyme

1. Press the Sauté button on the Instant Pot and heat the oil. Add the fennel and garlic. Sauté the mixture for 3 minutes.
2. Add the white wine and sauté an additional 2 minutes, or until the wine reduces. Add the remaining ingredients and stir.
3. Lock the lid. Select the Manual mode and set the cooking time for 5 minutes on High Pressure. Once the timer goes off, perform a natural pressure release for 10 minutes, then release any remaining pressure. Carefully open the lid.
4. Stir before serving.

Easy Chickpea Hummus

Prep time: 10 minutes | Cook time: 20 minutes | Serves 4

½ cup dried chickpeas, soaked
3 cups water
1 bay leaf
1 tablespoon olive oil
2 garlic cloves
3 cups water
1 tablespoon tahini
½ lemon, juiced
¼ teaspoon powdered cumin
¼ teaspoon sea salt
¼ bunch parsley, chopped
¼ teaspoon paprika

1. Add the water, chickpeas, bay leaf and garlic cloves to the Instant Pot.
2. Lock the lid. Select the Manual mode and set the cooking time for 18 minutes on High Pressure. Once the timer goes off, perform a natural pressure release for 10 minutes, then release any remaining pressure. Carefully open the lid.
3. Strain and rinse the cooked chickpeas. Discard the bay leaf.
4. Select the Sauté mode. Add the oil and all the remaining ingredients to the Instant Pot and sauté for 2 minutes.
5. Return the chickpeas to the pot and use an immerse blender to form a smooth purée.
6. Stir and serve.

Chapter 11 Pasta and Noodles

Macaroni with Cashew Sauce

Prep time: 15 minutes | Cook time: 6 minutes | Serves 4 to 6

Macaroni:
1 pound (454 g) elbow macaroni
4 cups water
1 teaspoon fine sea salt

Sauce:
1 cup raw cashews, soaked in water for 2 hours, drained
⅓ cup water, plus more if needed
2 tablespoons nutritional yeast
1½ tablespoons fresh lemon juice
1 clove garlic, peeled
1 teaspoon prepared yellow mustard
1 teaspoon Tabasco sauce
½ teaspoon fine sea salt
¼ teaspoon cayenne pepper

1. Add the pasta, water, and salt to the Instant Pot. Use a spoon or spatula to spread the pasta in an even layer, making sure it is all submerged in the water.
2. Secure the lid. Select the Manual setting and set the cooking time for 6 minutes at High Pressure.
3. Meanwhile, combine the cashews, water, nutritional yeast, lemon juice, garlic, mustard, Tabasco, salt, and cayenne in a blender. Blend at high speed for 1 minute, until smooth.
4. When timer beeps, let the pressure release naturally for 5 minutes, then release any remaining pressure. Open the pot and stir in the sauce.
5. Spoon the macaroni into bowls and serve immediately.

Bolognese Spaghetti

Prep time: 15 minutes | Cook time: 10 minutes | Serves 6

Pasta:

5 cups water
8 ounces (227 g) spaghetti pasta
1 teaspoon extra-virgin olive oil
1 teaspoon kosher salt

Sauce:

1 tablespoon extra-virgin olive oil
1 onion, finely chopped
5 garlic cloves, finely chopped
2 cups canned crushed tomatoes
¼ cup finely chopped fresh basil leaves
½ cup dried green lentils
5 baby bella mushrooms, roughly chopped
1 teaspoon kosher salt
2 teaspoons freshly ground black pepper
1 cup vegetable broth
½ cup shredded Parmesan cheese

1. Pour the water into the Instant Pot, and add the spaghetti, olive oil, and salt. Stir gently.
2. Lock the lid. Select Manual mode and set the timer to 2 minutes on High Pressure.
3. When timer beeps, naturally release the pressure for 5 minutes, then quick release any remaining pressure. Unlock the lid. Drain the pasta.
4. Select Sauté and pour in the oil. Once hot, add the onion and garlic and cook until the onion is translucent, 3 minutes. Stir in the tomatoes, basil, lentils, mushrooms, salt, pepper, and broth. Mix thoroughly.
5. Lock the lid. Select Manual mode and set the timer to 5 minutes on High Pressure.
6. When timer beeps, naturally release the pressure for 5 minutes, then release any remaining pressure.
7. Unlock the lid. Using a potato masher, mash the lentils and tomatoes to get a chunky texture. Stir in the spaghetti, sprinkle with the cheese, and serve hot.

Mushroom Stroganoff with Fusilli Pasta

Prep time: 15 minutes | Cook time: 16 minutes | Serves 4

3 cups fusilli pasta
4 cups water
2 teaspoons kosher salt, divided
1 tablespoon plus 1 teaspoon corn oil, divided
2 tablespoons butter
1 yellow onion, roughly chopped
4 scallions, white parts only, finely chopped
2 garlic cloves, finely chopped
1 pound (454 g) baby bella mushrooms, halved
1 teaspoon freshly ground black pepper
1 cup vegetable stock
2 tablespoons all-purpose flour
2 teaspoons Dijon mustard
$1/_3$ cup sour cream
½ teaspoon sugar

1. Add the pasta and water to the Instant Pot. Stir in ½ teaspoon of salt and 1 teaspoon of oil. Lock the lid.
2. Select Manual mode and set the time for 3 minutes at High Pressure.
3. When timer beeps, quick release the pressure. Unlock the lid. Drain the pasta, reserving and setting aside 4 tablespoons of pasta water.
4. Select Sauté and add the butter and remaining 1 tablespoon of oil. Once hot, add the onion, scallions, and garlic. Sauté for 3 minutes. Add the mushrooms.
5. Season with the pepper and the remaining 1½ teaspoons of salt, and cook until the mushrooms are soft and tender, 5 minutes. Stir twice during cooking.
6. Add the stock and mix the ingredients thoroughly. Simmer for 2 minutes.
7. In a small bowl, mix together the flour and the reserved pasta water until smooth. Add the slurry and the mustard to the sauce and mix thoroughly. Thicken the sauce for 3 minutes. Select Keep Warm.
8. Stir in the sour cream and sugar until well incorporated. Cover with the lid and let the sauce rest for at least 5 minutes. Serve with the pasta.

Mushroom and Spinach Spaghetti

Prep time: 10 minutes | Cook time: 10 minutes | Serves 4

1 tablespoon canola oil
8 ounces (227 g) minced mushrooms
½ teaspoon kosher salt
½ teaspoon black ground pepper
8 ounces (227 g) uncooked spaghetti pasta
1¾ cups water
5 ounces (142 g) spinach
½ cup pesto
⅓ cup Mozzarella cheese

1. Set the Instant Pot to the Sauté function and heat the canola oil until shimmering.
2. Add the mushrooms, salt, and pepper. Sauté for 5 minutes and add the pasta and water.
3. Lock the lid, press the Manual button and set the timer to 5 minutes at High Pressure.
4. When timer beeps, quick release the pressure. Open the lid.
5. Stir in the spinach, pesto, and cheese. Serve warm.

Mushroom and Tofu Pennette

Prep time: 15 minutes | Cook time: 15 minutes | Serves 2

1 tablespoon butter
1 small diced onion
2 cup mushrooms, sliced
½ cup tofu, diced into chunks
1 tablespoon coconut oil
½ cup sun-dried tomatoes
½ teaspoon garlic powder
1 cup white wine
1½ cups vegetable broth
1 cup pennette pasta
¼ cup coconut cream
½ cup grated goat cheese

1. Put the butter in the Instant Pot and set on Sauté mode. Then add the onion and mushrooms and sauté for 4 minutes.
2. Add the tofu, coconut oil, and the sun-dried tomatoes and sauté for another 3 minutes.
3. Add the garlic powder and sauté for 1 more minute. Add the white wine and let simmer for 1 minute.

4. Pour in the vegetable broth and stir the mixture well. Pour in the pennette pasta.
5. Lock the lid and press Manual button. Set the timer for 6 minutes on High Pressure.
6. When timer beeps, quick release the pressure. Open the lid.
7. Add the coconut cream and goat cheese and let sit for 5 minutes
8. Transfer to a serving bowl, serve warm.

Penne Primavera

Prep time: 20 minutes | Cook time: 11 minutes | Serves 6

Pasta:
5 cups water
1 pound (454 g) penne pasta
1 teaspoon extra-
virgin olive oil
2 teaspoons kosher salt

Vegetables:
2 tablespoons extra-virgin olive oil
1 tablespoon butter
1 cup (1-inch pieces) chopped asparagus
1 cup (1-inch pieces) chopped carrots
1 zucchini, cut into bite-size pieces
1 teaspoon Italian
dried herb seasoning
2 tablespoons finely chopped fresh basil leaves
1 teaspoon kosher salt
1 teaspoon freshly ground black pepper
1 teaspoon grated lemon zest
½ cup grated Parmesan cheese

1. Pour the water into the Instant pot and add the pasta. Stir in the oil and salt. Lock the lid.
2. Select Manual setting and set the cooking time for 4 minutes on High Pressure.
3. When timer beeps, quick release the pressure. Unlock the lid. Drain the pasta, reserving 2 tablespoons of pasta water.
4. Select Sauté mode, pour in the olive oil, and add the butter. Once hot, add the asparagus, carrot, zucchini, Italian seasoning, basil, salt, and pepper.
5. Add the reserved pasta water, and mix well. Cook for 7 minutes or until the vegetables are tender.
6. Stir in the pasta, lemon zest, and cheese, and serve hot.

Spaghetti with Veggie Bolognese

Prep time: 10 minutes | Cook time: 10 minutes | Serves 6

Pasta:

1 teaspoon extra-virgin olive oil
1 teaspoon kosher salt

8 ounces (227 g) spaghetti pasta
5 cups water

Sauce:

1 tablespoon extra-virgin olive oil
1 onion, minced
5 garlic cloves, minced
5 mushrooms, roughly minced
2 cups canned crushed tomatoes
1 cup vegetable broth

½ cup dried green lentils
¼ cup finely minced basil leaves
1 teaspoon kosher salt
2 teaspoons freshly ground black pepper
½ cup shredded Parmesan cheese

1. Add all the ingredients for the pasta to the Instant Pot and stir to combine.
2. Lock the lid. Select the Manual mode and set the cooking time for 2 minutes on High Pressure. Once the timer goes off, perform a natural pressure release for 5 minutes, then release any remaining pressure. Carefully open the lid.
3. Drain the pasta and transfer to a bowl..
4. Press the Sauté button on the Instant Pot and heat the oil. Add the onion and garlic to the pot and sauté for 3 minutes. Stir in the remaining ingredients, except for the cheese.
5. Lock the lid. Select the Manual mode and set the cooking time for 5 minutes on High Pressure. Once the timer goes off, perform a natural pressure release for 10 minutes, then release any remaining pressure. Carefully open the lid.
6. Using a potato masher, mash the lentils and tomatoes until it reaches a chunky texture.
7. Stir in the spaghetti, sprinkle with the cheese and serve hot.

Cheesy Macaroni

Prep time: 5 minutes | Cook time: 5 minutes | Serves 6

16 ounces (454 g) elbow macaroni
4 cups vegetable broth
2 tablespoons butter
2 teaspoons Dijon mustard
1½ teaspoons garlic

powder
1 cup Cottage cheese
1 cup shredded Cheddar cheese
¼ cup Greek yogurt
Salt and black pepper, to taste

1. Add the macaroni noodles, broth, butter, Dijon mustard and garlic powder to the Instant Pot and stir to combine.
2. Set the lid in place. Select the Manual mode and set the cooking time for 5 minutes on High Pressure. When the timer goes off, do a quick pressure release. Carefully open the lid.
3. Stir in the cheeses, Greek yogurt, salt and pepper.
4. Serve immediately.

Penne Pasta with Tomato-Vodka Sauce

Prep time: 5 minutes | Cook time: 4 minutes | Serves 2

½ cup uncooked penne pasta
½ cup crushed tomatoes
1 cup water
⅛ cup coconut oil
1 tablespoon vodka
1 teaspoon garlic

powder
½ teaspoon salt
¼ teaspoon paprika
½ cup coconut cream
⅛ cup minced cilantro

1. Add all the ingredients, except for the coconut cream and cilantro, to the Instant Pot and stir to combine.
2. Set the lid in place. Select the Manual mode and set the cooking time for 4 minutes on High Pressure. When the timer goes off, do a quick pressure release. Carefully open the lid.
3. Stir in the coconut cream and fresh cilantro and serve hot.

Green Cabbage Egg Noodles

Prep time: 5 minutes | Cook time: 4 minutes | Serves 2

½ head green cabbage, shredded	1 cup water
1 small onion	1½ tablespoons butter
1 cup wide egg noodles	Salt and pepper, to taste

1. Add all the ingredients to the Instant Pot and stir to combine.
2. Set the lid in place. Select the Manual mode and set the cooking time for 4 minutes on High Pressure. When the timer goes off, do a quick pressure release. Carefully open the lid.
3. Serve immediately.

Veggie Noodles Stir Fry

Prep time: 5 minutes | Cook time: 17 minutes | Serves 2

1 tablespoon vegetable oil	garnish
½ teaspoon garlic powder	Sauce:
1 cup frozen stir-fry vegetables	1 cup hot water
2 ounces (57 g) soba noodles	¼ cup Hoisin sauce
½ cup water	¼ cup natural peanut butter
2 sliced leek, for	½ teaspoon ginger powder
	¼ teaspoon Sriracha hot sauce

1. In a bowl, whisk together all the ingredients for the sauce. Set aside.
2. Press the Sauté button on the Instant Pot and heat the oil. Add the garlic powder to the pot and sauté for 2 minutes. Add the vegetables and continue to sauté for 5 minutes. Stir in the soba noodles and water.
3. Lock the lid. Select the Manual mode and set the cooking time for 10 minutes on High Pressure. Once the timer goes off, perform a natural pressure release for 10 minutes, then release any remaining pressure. Carefully open the lid.
4. Stir until everything is combined, cover with the sauce and garnish with sliced leek.
5. Serve immediately.

Broccoli and Tofu Pasta

Prep time: 5 minutes | Cook time: 10 minutes | Serves 2

4 ounces (113 g) broccoli florets	broth
4 ounces (113 g) farfalle pasta	¼ cup basil pesto
½ cup tofu	½ tablespoon extra-virgin olive oil
¼ cup vegetable	2 ounces (57 g) heavy cream

1. Add all the ingredients, except for the heavy cream, to the Instant Pot and stir to combine.
2. Set the lid in place. Select the Manual mode and set the cooking time for 10 minutes on High Pressure. When the timer goes off, do a quick pressure release. Carefully open the lid.
3. Stir in the heavy cream and serve immediately.

Cabbage and Mushroom Pasta

Prep time: 10 minutes | Cook time: 5 minutes | Serves 4

4 cups chopped green cabbage	butter, melted
2 cups dried bowtie pasta	1 teaspoon ground marjoram
1½ cups water	1 teaspoon kosher salt
1 cup diced onion	1 teaspoon black pepper
1 cup sliced button mushrooms	1 cup frozen peas and carrots
2 tablespoons	

1. Add all the ingredients, except for the frozen peas and carrots, to the Instant Pot and stir to combine.
2. Scatter the peas and carrots on top of the mixture. Do not stir.
3. Lock the lid. Select the Manual mode and set the cooking time for 5 minutes on High Pressure. Once the timer goes off, perform a natural pressure release for 10 minutes, then release any remaining pressure. Carefully open the lid.
4. Spoon into individual bowls and serve.

Vinegary Brown Rice Noodles

Prep time: 5 minutes | Cook time: 3 minutes | Serves 6

8 ounces (227 g) uncooked brown rice noodles
2 cups water
½ cup soy sauce
2 tablespoons brown sugar
2 tablespoons white vinegar

2 tablespoons butter
1 tablespoon chili garlic paste
2 red bell peppers, thinly sliced
Topping:
Green onions
Peanuts
Sesame seeds

1. Add all the ingredients, except for the red bell peppers, to the Instant Pot and stir to combine.
2. Set the lid in place. Select the Manual mode and set the cooking time for 3 minutes on High Pressure. When the timer goes off, do a quick pressure release. Carefully open the lid.
3. Stir in the red bell peppers. Sprinkle with the green onions, peanuts and sesame seeds. Serve immediately.

Creamy Broccoli Fettucine Pasta

Prep time: 10 minutes | Cook time: 8 to 9 minutes | Serves 8

1 teaspoon olive oil
3 garlic cloves, minced
2 cups minced broccoli
4¼ cups water, divided
1 pound (454 g) fettucine pasta

1 tablespoon butter
Salt, to taste
1 cup heavy cream
½ cup shredded Parmesan cheese
Ground black pepper, to taste
2 tablespoons minced parsley

1. Press the Sauté button on the Instant Pot and heat the oil. Add the garlic to the pot and sauté for 1 minute, or until fragrant. Stir in the broccoli and ¼ cup of the water.
2. Set the lid in place. Select the Manual mode and set the cooking time for 3 minutes on High Pressure. When the timer goes off, do a quick pressure release. Carefully open the lid.
3. Drain the broccoli and transfer to a bowl.

4. Add the remaining 4 cups of the water, pasta, butter and salt to the Instant Pot and stir to combine.
5. Set the lid in place. Select the Manual mode and set the cooking time for 3 minutes on High Pressure. When the timer goes off, do a quick pressure release. Carefully open the lid. Drain any excess liquid from the pot.
6. Select the Sauté mode and stir in the cooked broccoli, heavy cream, Parmesan, salt and black pepper. Cook for 1 to 2 minutes.
7. Serve garnished with the parsley.

Penne Pasta with Zucchini

Prep time: 10 minutes | Cook time: 10 minutes | Serves 5

1 tablespoon butter
1 yellow onion, thinly sliced
1 shallot, finely chopped
Salt and black pepper, to taste
2 garlic cloves, minced
12 mushrooms, thinly sliced
1 zucchini, thinly sliced
Pinch of dried

oregano
Pinch of dried basil
2 cups water
1 cup vegetable stock
2 tablespoons soy sauce
Splash of sherry wine
15 ounces (425 g) penne pasta
5 ounces (142 g) tomato paste

1. Press the Sauté button on the Instant Pot and melt the butter. Add the onion, shallot, salt and pepper to the pot and sauté for 3 minutes. Add the garlic and continue to sauté for 1 minute.
2. Stir in the mushrooms, zucchini, oregano and basil. Cook for 1 minute more. Pour in the water, stock, soy sauce and wine. Add the penne, tomato paste, salt and pepper.
3. Set the lid in place. Select the Manual mode and set the cooking time for 5 minutes on High Pressure. When the timer goes off, do a quick pressure release. Carefully open the lid.
4. Serve hot.

Simple Tomato Pasta

Prep time: 5 minutes | Cook time: 8 to 10 minutes | Serves 6

1 tablespoon olive oil
¼ cup minced shallots
¼ cup dry red wine
1 pound (454 g) spaghetti pasta, broken in half
4 cups vegetable broth
3 cups chopped tomatoes
½ cup chopped fresh basil
½ teaspoon salt
1 teaspoon black pepper

1. Press the Sauté button on the Instant Pot and heat the oil. Add the scallions to the pot and sauté for 1 to 2 minutes, or until tender. Pour in the red wine and continue to cook for 2 to 3 minutes, or until the wine reduces. Stir in the remaining ingredients.
2. Set the lid in place. Select the Manual mode and set the cooking time for 5 minutes on High Pressure. When the timer goes off, do a quick pressure release. Carefully open the lid.
3. Stir before serving.

Baked Eggplant Parmesan Pasta

Prep time: 10 minutes | Cook time: 9 to 10 minutes | Serves 6 to 8

1 (14-ounce / 397-g) can diced tomatoes
3 cloves garlic, minced
4 cups peeled, chopped eggplant
1½ cups water
1 cup diced onion
3 tablespoons unsalted butter, divided
1 tablespoon dried
Italian seasoning
1 tablespoon tomato paste
1½ teaspoons kosher salt
1 teaspoon red pepper flakes
9 ounces (255 g) penne pasta
½ cup bread crumbs
⅓ cup shredded Parmesan cheese
1½ cups bocconcini

1. In the Instant Pot, stir together the tomatoes, garlic, eggplant, water, onion, 2 tablespoons of the butter, Italian seasoning, tomato paste, salt and red pepper flakes. Stir in the pasta.

2. Lock the lid. Select the Manual mode and set the cooking time for 7 minutes on High Pressure. Once the timer goes off, perform a natural pressure release for 10 minutes, then release any remaining pressure. Carefully open the lid.
3. Meanwhile, in a small skillet, melt the remaining 1 tablespoon of the butter over medium heat. Add the bread crumbs and mix well. Remove from the heat and let cool. Mix with the Parmesan cheese and set aside.
4. Preheat the broiler to 500ºF (260ºC).
5. Add the bocconcini to the pasta and transfer the pasta to a casserole dish. Sprinkle with the bread crumb mixture and broil for 2 to 3 minutes.
6. Serve hot.

Tomato and Black Bean Rotini

Prep time: 5 minutes | Cook time: 9 to 10 minutes | Serves 4

1 red onion, diced
1 to 2 teaspoons olive oil
1 to 2 teaspoons ground chipotle pepper
1 (28-ounce / 794-g) can crushed tomatoes
8 ounces (227 g) rotini
1 cup water
1½ cups fresh corn
1½ cups cooked black beans
Salt and freshly ground black pepper, to taste

1. Press the Sauté button on the Instant Pot and heat the oil. Add the red onion and cook for 5 to 6 minutes, stirring occasionally, or until the onion is lightly browned.
2. Stir in the chipotle pepper, tomatoes, rotini and water.
3. Lock the lid. Select the Manual mode and set the cooking time for 4 minutes on High Pressure. Once the timer goes off, perform a natural pressure release for 4 minutes, then release any remaining pressure. Carefully open the lid.
4. Stir in the corn and black beans. Taste and season with salt and pepper.
5. Serve immediately.

Mascarpone-Mushroom Pasta

Prep time: 10 minutes | Cook time: 5 minutes | Serves 4

2 tablespoons butter
3 cloves garlic, minced
1 teaspoon dried thyme
½ teaspoon red pepper flakes
8 ounces (227 g) cremini mushrooms, trimmed and sliced
1 cup chopped onion
1¾ cups water
1 teaspoon kosher
salt
1 teaspoon black pepper
8 ounces (227 g) fettuccine, broken in half
8 ounces (227 g) Mascarpone cheese
1 cup shredded Parmesan cheese
2 teaspoons fresh thyme leaves, for garnish

1. Press the Sauté button on the Instant Pot and melt the butter. Add the garlic, thyme, and red pepper flakes to the pot and sauté for 30 seconds. Stir in the mushrooms, onion, water, salt and pepper.
2. Add the fettuccine, pushing it down into the liquid. Add the Mascarpone on top of the pasta. Do not stir.
3. Lock the lid. Select the Manual mode and set the cooking time for 5 minutes on High Pressure. Once the timer goes off, perform a natural pressure release for 5 minutes, then release any remaining pressure. Carefully open the lid.
4. Stir in the Parmesan cheese.
5. Divide the pasta among four dishes, garnish with the thyme and serve.

Fusilli Pasta with Spinach and Pine Nuts

Prep time: 5 minutes | Cook time: 12 minutes | Serves 4

1 tablespoon butter
2 garlic cloves, crushed
1 pound (454 g) spinach
1 pound (454 g) fusilli pasta
Salt and black
pepper, to taste
Water, as needed
2 garlic cloves, chopped
¼ cup chopped pine nuts
Grated cheese, for serving

1. Press the Sauté button on the Instant Pot and melt the butter. Add the crushed garlic and spinach to the pot and sauté for 6 minutes. Add the pasta, salt and pepper. Pour in the water to cover the pasta and mix.
2. Set the lid in place. Select the Manual mode and set the cooking time for 6 minutes on Low Pressure. When the timer goes off, do a quick pressure release. Carefully open the lid.
3. Stir in the chopped garlic and nuts. Garnish with the cheese and serve.

Sumptuous One-Pot Garden Pasta

Prep time: 10 minutes | Cook time: 11 minutes | Serves 6

1 tablespoon olive oil
1 cup leeks, sliced thin
3 cloves garlic, crushed and minced
2 cups sliced portabella mushrooms
¼ cup dry red wine
2 cups sliced summer squash
1 teaspoon oregano
1 teaspoon rosemary
1 teaspoon sea salt
1 teaspoon coarse ground black pepper
1 pound (454 g) small pasta of choice
2 cups chopped tomatoes
2 cups vegetable broth
1 cup water
1 tablespoon tomato paste
½ cup chopped fresh basil

1. Press the Sauté button on the Instant Pot and heat the oil. Add the leeks and garlic to the pot and sauté for 3 minutes. Add the mushrooms and red wine and continue to sauté for 3 minutes, or until the wine reduces.
2. Add the summer squash and season with the oregano, rosemary, sea salt and black pepper. Stir in the remaining ingredients, except for the fresh basil.
3. Set the lid in place. Select the Manual mode and set the cooking time for 5 minutes on High Pressure. When the timer goes off, do a quick pressure release. Carefully open the lid.
4. Serve garnished with the fresh basil.

Creamy Marsala Tofu Pasta

Prep time: 5 minutes | Cook time: 15 minutes | Serves 2

1 tablespoon butter
2 cups sliced mushrooms
1 small onion, diced
½ cup sun-dried tomatoes
½ cup tofu, diced into chunks
½ teaspoon garlic powder

1 cup white Marsala wine
1½ cups vegetable broth
1 cup Pennette pasta
½ cup grated goat cheese
¼ cup cream

1. Press the Sauté button on the Instant Pot and melt the butter. Add the mushrooms and onion to the pot and cook for 4 minutes. Add the tomatoes and tofu and cook for 3 minutes.
2. Add the garlic powder and cook for 1 minute. Pour in the white wine and cook for 1 minute. Stir in the broth. Add the pasta and don't stir.
3. Set the lid in place. Select the Manual mode and set the cooking time for 6 minutes on High Pressure. When the timer goes off, do a quick pressure release. Carefully open the lid.
4. Add the cheese and cream and let sit for 5 minutes. Serve hot.

Lemony Spinach Pasta

Prep time: 5 minutes | Cook time: 4 minutes | Serves 6

1 pound (454 g) fusilli pasta
4 cups chopped fresh spinach
4 cups vegetable broth
2 cloves garlic, crushed and minced
1 cup plain coconut milk
1 teaspoon lemon

zest
1 teaspoon lemon juice
¼ cup chopped fresh parsley
1 tablespoon chopped fresh mint
½ teaspoon sea salt
½ teaspoon coarse ground black pepper

1. Stir together the fusilli pasta, spinach, vegetable broth and garlic in the Instant Pot.

2. Set the lid in place. Select the Manual mode and set the cooking time for 4 minutes on High Pressure.
3. Meanwhile, whisk together the coconut milk, lemon zest and lemon juice in a bowl.
4. When the timer goes off, do a quick pressure release. Carefully open the lid. Drain off any excess liquid that might remain.
5. Add the coconut milk mixture to the pasta, along with the parsley and mint. Season with salt and pepper.
6. Stir gently and let sit for 5 minutes before serving.

Creamy Tomato Pasta

Prep time: 5 minutes | Cook time: 9 minutes | Serves 4

1 (28-ounce / 794-g) can crushed tomatoes
10 ounces (284 g) penne, rotini, or fusilli (about 3 cups)
1 tablespoon dried basil
½ teaspoon garlic powder

½ teaspoon salt, plus more as needed
1½ cups water
1 cup unsweetened coconut milk
2 cups chopped fresh spinach (optional)
Freshly ground black pepper, to taste

1. Combine the tomatoes, pasta, basil, garlic powder, salt, and water in the Instant Pot.
2. Secure the lid. Select the Manual mode and set the cooking time for 4 minutes at High Pressure.
3. Once cooking is complete, do a natural pressure release for 5 minutes, then release any remaining pressure. Carefully open the lid.
4. Stir in the milk and spinach (if desired). Taste and season with more salt and pepper, as needed.
5. Set your Instant Pot to Sauté and let cook for 4 to 5 minutes, or until the sauce is thickened and the greens are wilt. Serve warm.

Parmesan Mushroom-Spinach Pasta

Prep time: 5 minutes | Cook time: 10 minutes | Serves 4

1 tablespoon oil
8 ounces (227 g) mushrooms, minced
½ teaspoon kosher salt
½ teaspoon black ground pepper
8 ounces (227 g) uncooked spaghetti pasta
1¾ cups water
5 ounces (142 g) spinach
½ cup pesto
1/3 cup grated Parmesan cheese

1. Press the Sauté button on the Instant Pot and heat the oil. Add the mushrooms, salt and pepper to the pot and sauté for 5 minutes. Add the pasta and water.
2. Set the lid in place. Select the Manual mode and set the cooking time for 5 minutes on High Pressure. When the timer goes off, do a quick pressure release. Carefully open the lid.
3. Stir in the spinach, pesto, and cheese. Serve immediately.

Tomato Basil Campanelle Pasta

Prep time: 5 minutes | Cook time: 2 minutes | Serves 2

2 cups dried campanelle pasta
1¾ cups vegetable stock
½ teaspoon salt
2 tomatoes, cut into large dices
1 or 2 pinches red pepper flakes
½ teaspoon dried oregano
½ teaspoon garlic powder
10 to 12 fresh sweet basil leaves, finely chopped
Freshly ground black pepper, to taste

1. In the Instant Pot, stir together the pasta, stock, and salt. Spread the tomatoes on top.
2. Set the lid in place. Select the Manual mode and set the cooking time for 2 minutes on High Pressure. When the timer goes off, do a quick pressure release. Carefully open the lid.
3. Stir in the red pepper flakes, oregano and garlic powder.
4. Sprinkle the basil and pepper. Serve immediately.

Asian Peanut Noodles

Prep time: 10 minutes | Cook time: 2 minutes | Serves 3 to 4

½ cup smooth peanut butter
¼ cup rice vinegar or apple cider vinegar
¼ cup soy sauce
1 to 2 tablespoons toasted sesame oil (optional)
1 teaspoon ground ginger (optional)
Pinch of red pepper
flakes or cayenne (optional)
2½ cups water, plus more as needed
8 ounces (227 g) thick udon noodles or soba noodles
4 carrots, scrubbed or peeled and cut into matchsticks
½ head broccoli, cut into 1-inch pieces

1. Stir together the peanut butter, vinegar, soy sauce, sesame oil (if desired), ginger (if desired), and red pepper flakes (if desired) in a bowl until smooth and well incorporated.
2. Pour the peanut sauce into the Instant Pot and add the water.
3. Add the noodles to the Instant Pot, breaking them into shorter strands if they're too long to lie flat on the bottom and making sure the liquid covers them. Add another ¼ cup of water, if needed. Stir the noodles a bit to make sure they don't stick together. Top with the carrots and broccoli.
4. Secure the lid. Select the Manual mode and set the cooking time for 2 minutes at Low Pressure.
5. Once cooking is complete, do a quick pressure release. Carefully open the lid.
6. Toss everything together, breaking up any noodles that may have stuck together, and serve hot.

Creamy Kimchi Pasta

Prep time: 5 minutes | Cook time: 4 to 5 minutes | Serves 4 to 6

8 ounces (227 g) dried small pasta
2⅓ cups vegetable stock
2 garlic cloves, minced
½ red onion, sliced
½ to 1 teaspoon salt
1¼ cups kimchi, with any larger pieces chopped
½ cup coconut cream

1. In the Instant Pot, combine the pasta, stock, garlic, red onion and salt.
2. Set the lid in place. Select the Manual mode and set the cooking time for 1 minute on High Pressure. When the timer goes off, do a quick pressure release. Carefully open the lid.
3. Select Sauté mode. Stir in the kimchi. Simmer for 3 to 4 minutes. Stir in the coconut cream and serve.

Lemony Bow Tie Pasta

Prep time: 5 minutes | Cook time: 11 to 12 minutes | Serves 4 to 5

1 Vidalia onion, diced
2 garlic cloves, minced
1 tablespoon olive oil
3½ cups water
10 ounces (284 g)
bow tie pasta
Grated zest and juice of 1 lemon
¼ cup black olives, pitted and chopped
Salt and freshly ground black pepper, to taste

1. Press the Sauté button on the Instant Pot and heat the oil. Add the onion and garlic to the pot. Cook for 7 to 8 minutes, stirring occasionally, or until the onion is lightly browned.
2. Add the water and pasta.
3. Set the lid in place. Select the Manual mode and set the cooking time for 4 minutes on High Pressure. When the timer goes off, do a quick pressure release. Carefully open the lid.
4. Stir the pasta and drain any excess water. Stir in the lemon zest and juice and the olives. Season with salt and pepper.
5. Serve immediately.

Basil Tomato Pasta

Prep time: 10 minutes | Cook time: 10 minutes | Serves 4

1 teaspoon olive oil, plus more for drizzling
1 large Vidalia onion, diced
10 ounces (284 g) penne, rotini, or fusilli
2 cups water
¼ cup sun-dried tomatoes, chopped
½ teaspoon salt, plus more as needed
1 cup cherry tomatoes, halved or quartered
2 tablespoons finely chopped fresh basil
½ teaspoon garlic powder (optional)
Freshly ground black pepper, to taste

1. Set your Instant Pot to Sauté and heat 1 teaspoon of olive oil.
2. Add the onion and sauté for 4 to 5 minutes, stirring occasionally, until the onion is tender.
3. Add the pasta, water, tomatoes, and a pinch of salt. Stir well.
4. Secure the lid. Select the Manual mode and set the cooking time for 4 minutes at High Pressure.
5. Once cooking is complete, do a natural pressure release for 5 minutes, then release any remaining pressure. Carefully open the lid.
6. Set your Instant Pot to Sauté again and stir in the cherry tomatoes, basil, garlic powder (if desired), and another drizzle of olive oil.
7. Taste and season with more salt and pepper, as needed. Serve warm.

Thai Red Curry Noodles

Prep time: 5 minutes | Cook time: 1 minute | Serves 4

1 (13.5-ounce / 383-g) can coconut milk
2 cups water
¼ cup red curry paste
1 tablespoon soy sauce

1 tablespoon freshly squeezed lime juice
1 to 2 teaspoons toasted sesame oil
8 ounces (227 g) thick ramen noodles or wide brown rice noodles

1. Combine all the ingredients except the noodles in the Instant Pot
2. Add the noodles to the pot, breaking them into shorter strands if they're too long to lie flat on the bottom.
3. Secure the lid. Select the Manual mode and set the cooking time for 1 minute at High Pressure.
4. Once cooking is complete, do a quick pressure release. Carefully open the lid.
5. Toss everything together, breaking up any noodles that may have stuck together. Serve warm.

Easy Instant Pot Pasta

Prep time: 5 minutes | Cook time: 5 minutes | Serves 4

4 cups pasta sauce
3 cups water
4 cups dried,

uncooked gluten-free pasta (spirals or penne)

1. Combine the sauce and water in the Instant Pot. Stir in the pasta and press under the sauce.
2. Secure the lid. Select the Manual mode and set the cooking time for 5 minutes at Low Pressure.
3. Once cooking is complete, do a quick pressure release. Carefully open the lid.
4. Cool for 5 minutes and serve on a plate.

Pasta Puttanesca

Prep time: 15 minutes | Cook time: 5 minutes | Serves 4

1 pound (454 g) thin spaghetti
3½ cups water
1 pint (300 g) grape tomatoes, cut in half
¾ cup pitted Castelvetrano olives, cut in half
½ cup pitted black olives, cut in half
2 tablespoon chopped fresh

parsley
2 tablespoon capers
2 tablespoon extra-virgin olive oil
1 tablespoon chopped fresh basil
1 teaspoon salt, plus more as needed
½ teaspoon freshly ground black pepper, plus more as needed

1. Crack the spaghetti noodles in half to ensure they fit inside the pot.
2. Toss all the ingredients in the Instant Pot.
3. Secure the lid. Select the Manual mode and set the cooking time for 5 minutes at High Pressure.
4. Once cooking is complete, do a quick pressure release. Carefully open the lid and use the tongs to toss and mix the pasta together.
5. Taste and season with more salt and pepper, as needed. Serve warm.

Chapter 12 Beans, Lentils, and Peas

Super Bean and Grain Burgers

Prep time: 25 minutes | Cook time: 1 hour 15 minutes | Makes 12 patties

1 tablespoon olive oil
½ cup chopped onion
8 cloves garlic, minced

1 cup dried black beans
½ cup quinoa, rinsed
½ cup brown rice
4 cups water

Patties:
½ cup ground flaxseed
1 tablespoon dried marjoram
2 teaspoons smoked paprika

2 teaspoons salt
1 teaspoon ground black pepper
1 teaspoon dried thyme

1. Select the Sauté setting of the Instant Pot and heat the oil until shimmering.
2. Add the onion and sauté for 5 minutes or until transparent.
3. Add the garlic and sauté a minute more or until fragrant.
4. Add the black beans, quinoa, rice and water to the onion mixture and stir to combine.
5. Put the lid on. Set to Manual mode. Set cooking time for 34 minutes on High Pressure.
6. When timer beeps, release the pressure naturally for 15 minutes, then release any remaining pressure. Open the lid.
7. Preheat the oven to 350°F (180°C) and line 2 baking sheets with parchment paper.
8. Mash the beans in the pot, then mix in the ground flaxseed, marjoram, paprika, salt, pepper and thyme.
9. Divide and shape the mixture into 12 patties and put on the baking sheet.
10. Cook in the preheated oven for 35 minutes or until firmed up. Flip the patties halfway through the cooking time.
11. Serve immediately.

Kidney Beans with Ajwain Sauce

Prep time: 15 minutes | Cook time: 40 minutes | Serves 6

Bean:
2 cups dried kidney beans, soaked for at least 8 hours and drained

6 cups water
1 tablespoon grated ginger
1 teaspoon salt

Sauce:
1 onion, minced
½ teaspoon ajwain seeds
1 teaspoon minced garlic
2 cups finely diced tomatoes
¼ cup yogurt
1 teaspoon ground

fenugreek
1 teaspoon garam masala
¾ teaspoon turmeric
2 tablespoons ground coriander
⅛ teaspoon ground red chile pepper

1. Pour the water in the Instant Pot and sprinkle with ginger and salt. Add soak the beans in the water.
2. Set the Manual mode of the pot and set the cooking time for 10 minutes on High Pressure.
3. When timer beeps, allow the pressure to release naturally for 5 minutes, then release any remaining pressure. Open the lid.
4. Carefully pour the beans into a bowl. Let them sit. Clean the Instant Pot.
5. Set the Sauté setting of the pot. Sauté the onion for 4 minutes or until lightly browned.
6. Add the ajwain and garlic and sauté for 1 minute or until fragrant.
7. Mix in the tomatoes and cook until their liquid has evaporated, 5 minutes. Stir in the yogurt, fenugreek, garam masala, turmeric, coriander, and red chile pepper.
8. Drain 2 cups of liquid from the beans and stir 1 cup into the sauce. Add the beans to the sauce and mix well.
9. Simmer on the Sauté setting for 20 minutes or until thickened, stirring occasionally.
10. Transfer to a serving dish and serve.

Black Chickpea Curry

Prep time: 15 minutes | Cook time: 15 minutes | Serves 6

1 tablespoon olive oil
2 cups minced onion
2 teaspoons garam masala
½ teaspoon ground coriander
2 teaspoons cumin seeds
3 teaspoons minced garlic
½ teaspoon ground turmeric
½ teaspoon ground chile
1 cup black chickpeas, soaked in water for at least 8 hours, drained
1½ cups diced tomatoes
1½ cups water
2 tablespoons grated ginger
2 teaspoons crushed curry leaves
Salt, to taste

1. Select the Sauté setting on the Instant Pot, and heat the oil until shimmering.
2. Add the onion and sauté for 5 minutes or until transparent.
3. Add the garam masala, coriander, cumin seeds, garlic, turmeric and chile and sauté for 2 minutes.
4. Add the chickpeas, tomatoes, water, ginger and curry leaves, and stir to combine.
5. Put the lid on. Select the Manual setting and set the timer for 8 minutes on High Pressure.
6. When timer beeps, allow the pressure to release naturally for 5 minutes, then release any remaining pressure. Open the lid.
7. Sprinkle with salt and serve.

Green Pea and Asparagus Risotto

Prep time: 10 minutes | Cook time: 10 minutes | Serves 4

1½ cups Arborio rice
4 cups water, divided
1 tablespoon vegetable bouillon
1 cup fresh sweet green peas
1½ cups chopped asparagus
2 tablespoons nutritional yeast
1 tablespoon lemon juice
Fresh chopped thyme, for garnish
Salt and ground black pepper, to taste

1. Add the rice, 3½ cups of water, and vegetable bouillon to the Instant Pot. Put the lid on.
2. Select Manual setting and set a timer for 5 minutes on High Pressure.
3. When timer beeps, perform a natural pressure release for 5 minutes, then release any remaining pressure. Open the lid.
4. Stir in the peas, asparagus, nutritional yeast, remaining water, and lemon juice.
5. Set to Sauté function. Sauté for 5 minutes or until the asparagus and peas are soft.
6. Spread the thyme on top and sprinkle with salt and pepper before serving.

White Beans with Poblano and Tomatillos

Prep time: 15 minutes | Cook time: 39 minutes | Serves 6

1 cup chopped poblano, deseeded and stem removed
2 cups chopped tomatillos
1 cup chopped onion
½ jalapeño, deseeded
1½ teaspoons ground cumin
1½ cups dried white beans, soaked for 8 hours, drained
2 teaspoons dried oregano
1½ cups water
Salt and ground black pepper, to taste

1. Add the poblano, tomatillos, onion and jalapeño to a food processor. Pulse to break them into tiny pieces.
2. Set the Sauté setting of the Instant Pot and pour in the blended mixture.
3. Fold in the cumin. Sauté for 4 minutes or until the onion is translucent.
4. Stir in the beans, oregano, and water. Put the lid on.
5. Select the Manual setting and set cooking time for 35 minutes at High Pressure.
6. When timer beeps, allow the pressure to release naturally for 15 minutes, then release any remaining pressure. Open the lid.
7. Sprinkle with salt and pepper before serving.

Lentils with Spinach

Prep time: 15 minutes | Cook time: 15 minutes | Serves 2

1 tablespoon olive oil
½ teaspoon cumin seeds
¼ teaspoon mustard seeds
3 cloves garlic, finely chopped
1 green chili, finely chopped
1 large tomato, chopped
1½ cups spinach, finely chopped
¼ teaspoon turmeric powder
½ teaspoon salt
¼ cup split pigeon peas, rinsed
¼ cup split red lentil, rinsed
1½ cups water
¼ teaspoon garam masala
2 teaspoons lemon juice
Cilantro, for garnish

1. Press the Sauté button on the Instant Pot. Add the oil and then the cumin seeds and mustard seeds.
2. Let the seeds sizzle for a few seconds and then add the garlic and green chili. Sauté for 1 minute or until fragrant.
3. Add the tomato and cook for 1 minute. Add the chopped spinach, turmeric powder and salt, and cook for 2 minutes.
4. Add the rinsed peas and lentils and stir. Pour in the water and put the lid on.
5. Press the Manual button and set the cooking time for 10 minutes on High Pressure.
6. When timer beeps, let the pressure release naturally for 5 minutes, then release any remaining pressure.
7. Open the pot and add the garam masala, lemon juice and cilantro. Serve immediately.

Kidney Bean Punjabi Rajma

Prep time: 10 minutes | Cook time: 35 minutes | Serves 6

1 tablespoon peanut oil
1 cup diced tomato
1½ cups diced onion
1 tablespoon minced ginger
1 teaspoon garam masala
1 teaspoon ground cumin
1 tablespoon minced garlic
1 teaspoon ground cayenne pepper
1 teaspoon ground turmeric
1 teaspoon salt
1 teaspoon ground coriander
1 cup dried red kidney beans
2 cups water

1. Put the oil into the Instant Pot, and add the tomato, onion, ginger, garam masala, cumin, garlic, cayenne, turmeric, salt, and coriander. Stir to combine.
2. Place a trivet on top of the onion mixture.
3. Put the beans and water into a heatproof bowl. Cover the bowl with foil. Place the covered bowl on top of the trivet.
4. Lock the lid. Select the Bean/Chili setting and set the time for 30 minutes on High Pressure.
5. When timer beeps, let the pressure release naturally for 10 minutes, then quick release any remaining pressure.
6. Unlock the lid. Carefully remove the bowl of red kidney beans and the trivet.
7. Slightly mash about half the beans with the back of a spoon.
8. Select Sauté mode. Pour the beans and any remaining liquid into the onion masala and mix well. Bring to a boil before serving.

Kongbap

Prep time: 5 minutes | Cook time: 22 minutes | Serves 6

½ cup dried whole peas
½ cup brown rice
½ cup dried black soybeans
½ cup pearl barley
7 cups water, divided
1 tablespoon sesame oil

1. Combine the peas, brown rice, soybeans, and pearl barley to a large bowl and add 4 cups of the water. Soak overnight.
2. Rinse, drain, and add to the Instant Pot. Add the remaining 3 cups water. Drizzle the oil over the water. Stir to combine.
3. Secure the lid. Select Manual mode and set cooking time for 22 minutes on High Pressure.
4. When timer beeps, use a natural pressure release for 10 minutes, then release any remaining pressure.
5. Open the lid. Serve immediately.

Kidney Bean Vegetarian Étouffée

Prep time: 20 minutes | Cook time: 28 minutes | Serves 4

1 tablespoon olive oil
1 cup minced onion
2 cups minced bell pepper
2 teaspoons minced garlic
1 cup dried kidney beans, soaked in water for 8 hours, drained
1½ teaspoons dried thyme
3 bay leaves
2 teaspoons smoked paprika
1 cup water
2 teaspoons dried marjoram
½ teaspoon ground cayenne pepper
1 (14.5-ounce / 411-g) can crushed tomatoes
1 teaspoon dried oregano
Salt and ground black pepper, to taste

1. Select the Sauté setting of the Instant Pot and heat the oil until shimmering.
2. Add the onion and sauté for 5 minutes or until transparent.
3. Add the bell pepper and garlic. Sauté for 5 more minutes or until the bell peppers are tender.
4. Add the beans, thyme, bay leaves, smoked paprika, water, marjoram and cayenne to the pot. Stir to combine.
5. Put the lid on. Select the Manual setting and set the timer for 15 minutes at High Pressure.
6. When timer beeps, use a natural pressure release for 5 minutes, then release any remaining pressure. Open the lid. Remove the bay leaves.
7. Mix in the crushed tomatoes and oregano. Sprinkle with salt and pepper. Set the cooking time for 3 minutes on High Pressure.
8. When timer beeps, release the pressure naturally for 5 minutes, then release any remaining pressure. Open the lid.
9. Serve immediately.

Black-Eyed Pea and Kale Curry

Prep time: 15 minutes | Cook time: 30 minutes | Serves 4

1 tablespoon olive oil
½ teaspoon cumin seeds
1 medium red onion, chopped
4 cloves garlic, finely chopped
1-inch piece ginger, finely chopped
1 green chili, finely chopped
2 large tomatoes, chopped
½ teaspoon turmeric powder
1 teaspoon coriander powder
¼ teaspoon garam masala
1 teaspoon salt
1 cup dried black-eyed peas, soaked in water for 3 hours, drained
2 cups water
3 cups kale, chopped
2 teaspoons lime juice

1. Press the Sauté button on the Instant Pot. Add the oil and the cumin seeds and let them sizzle for a few seconds.
2. Add the onion and sauté for 2 minutes or until soft.
3. Add the garlic, ginger and green chili and sauté for 1 minute or until golden brown.
4. Add the tomatoes and cook for 3 minutes, or until soft.
5. Add the turmeric powder, coriander powder, garam masala and salt. Cook for 1 minute.
6. Fold in the black-eyed peas and water. Lock the lid.
7. Press the Manual button and set the timer for 20 minutes on High Pressure.
8. When timer beeps, let the pressure release naturally for 10 minutes, then release any remaining pressure.
9. Open the pot and press the Sauté button. Add the kale and simmer for 3 minutes.
10. Stir in the lime juice and serve.

Black-Eyed Peas with Swiss Chard

Prep time: 15 minutes | Cook time: 10 minutes | Serves 6

1 teaspoon olive oil
1 medium large onion, thinly sliced
1 small jalapeño, minced
1 cup diced red bell pepper
3 cloves garlic, minced
1½ cups dried black-eyed peas, soaked overnight, drained
1 teaspoon chili powder
2 teaspoons smoked paprika
4 dates, finely chopped
1½ cups water
1 (15-ounce / 425-g) can fire-roasted tomatoes with green chiles
2 cups chopped Swiss chard
Salt, to taste

1. Select the Sauté setting of the Instant Pot and heat the oil until shimmering.
2. Add the onion and sauté for 5 minutes or until transparent.
3. Add the peppers and garlic. Sauté for a minute more or until fragrant.
4. Add the black-eyed peas, chili powder, and smoked paprika, and stir. Add the dates and water.
5. Put the lid on. Set to Manual mode and set cooking time for 3 minutes at High Pressure.
6. When timer beeps, let the pressure release naturally for 5 minutes, then release any remaining pressure. Open the lid.
7. Add the tomatoes and Swiss chard. Set cooking time for 1 minute on High Pressure.
8. When cooking is complete, quick release the pressure and open the lid.
9. Sprinkle with salt and serve.

On Pot Black-Eyed Peas with Rice

Prep time: 15 minutes | Cook time: 14 minutes | Serves 4

1 teaspoon extra-virgin olive oil
1 large onion, diced
2 carrots, diced
3 celery stalks, diced
3 cloves garlic, minced
1 cup dried black-eyed peas
½ cup white rice
1 medium tomato, diced
1 teaspoon dried oregano
1 teaspoon dried parsley
¼ teaspoon ground cumin
1 teaspoon crushed red pepper
¼ teaspoon ground black pepper
¼ cup tomato paste
2½ cups vegetable broth
2 tablespoons lemon juice
Salt, to taste

1. Select the Sauté setting of the Instant Pot and heat the oil until shimmering.
2. Add the onion, carrots, celery and garlic and sauté for 6 minutes or until tender.
3. Add the black-eyed peas, rice, tomato, oregano, parsley, cumin red and black peppers, tomato paste and broth to the onion mixture and stir to combine.
4. Put the lid on. Select the Manual setting and set the timer for 8 minutes at High Pressure.
5. When timer beeps, let the pressure release naturally for 5 minutes, then release any remaining pressure. Open the lid.
6. Mix in the lemon juice and salt before serving.

Pinto Bean and Beet Hummus

Prep time: 5 minutes | Cook time: 13 minutes | Serves 4

2 large beets, peeled and chopped
2 cups canned pinto beans, rinsed
2 cups vegetable stock
1 teaspoon garlic powder
Salt, to taste
½ lemon, juiced
¼ cup olive oil

1. Combine pinto beans, beets, stock, garlic powder, and salt into Instant Pot.
2. Seal the lid, select Manual mode, and set cooking time for 13 minutes on High Pressure.
3. When timer beeps, do a quick pressure release, and unlock the lid.
4. Transfer mixture to a blender and process until smooth. Add lemon juice and olive oil and blend again to combine. Pour mixture into bowls and serve.

Lentils with Rutabaga and Rice

Prep time: 15 minutes | Cook time: 30 minutes | Serves 4

1 tablespoon olive oil
½ cup chopped onion
2 cloves garlic, minced
3½ cups water
1 cup brown lentils
1 cup peeled and diced rutabaga
1½ cups brown rice
2-inch sprig fresh rosemary
1 tablespoon dried marjoram
Salt and ground black pepper, to taste

1. Select the Sauté setting of the Instant Pot and heat the oil until shimmering.
2. Add the onion and sauté for 5 minutes or until transparent.
3. Add the garlic and sauté a minute more or until fragrant.
4. Add the lentils, rutabaga, brown rice, rosemary, water, and marjoram to the pot and stir to combine.
5. Put the lid on. Set the Manual mode and set cooking time for 23 minutes at High Pressure.
6. When timer beeps, let the pressure release naturally for 10 minutes, then release any remaining pressure. Open the lid.
7. Sprinkle with salt and pepper before serving.

Triple Beans and Kombu Bowls

Prep time: 5 minutes | Cook time: 25 minutes | Serves 6

1 teaspoon olive oil
½ cup diced sweet onion
2 cloves garlic, minced
2 cups mixed dried pinto, red kidney, and adzuki beans
1-inch strip kombu
4 cups water
½ to 1 teaspoon dulse flakes

1. In the Instant Pot, heat the oil on Sauté mode. Add the onion and garlic and sauté for 3 minutes, or until the onions are translucent. Stir in the beans, kombu, and water.
2. Secure the lid. Select Manual mode and set cooking time for 25 minutes on High Pressure.

3. When timer beeps, use a natural pressure release for 15 minutes, then release any remaining pressure.
4. Remove the lid. Stir in the dulse flakes. Serve immediately.

Chickpeas with Jackfruit

Prep time: 20 minutes | Cook time: 15 minutes | Serves 2 to 3

2 teaspoons olive oil
½ teaspoon cumin seeds
½-inch piece cinnamon stick
2 bay leaves
4 cloves, crushed
2 black cardamoms, crushed
4 green cardamoms, crushed
8 black peppercorns, crushed
2 dried red chilies
4 cloves garlic, chopped
2 medium tomatoes, chopped
½ cup split chickpeas, soaked in water for 40 minutes, drained
1 (20-ounce / 567-g) can jackfruit, drained, rinsed and diced
1 teaspoon coriander powder
¾ teaspoon salt
¾ cup water
2 teaspoons lemon juice
Cilantro, for garnish

1. Press the Sauté button on the Instant Pot. Add the oil and then add the cumin seeds, cinnamon stick, bay leaves, crushed spices, and dried red chilies. Sauté for a few seconds until fragrant.
2. Add the chopped garlic and cook for 1 minute or until golden brown and then add the tomato.
3. Cook the tomato for 2 minutes and then add the chickpeas, jackfruit, coriander powder, and salt and mix to combine. Cook for 1 minute and then pour in the water.
4. Lock the lid. Press the Manual button and set the timer for 10 minutes on High Pressure.
5. When timer beeps, let the pressure release naturally for 5 minutes, then release any remaining pressure.
6. Open the pot and press the Sauté button. Stir in the lemon juice, garnish with cilantro and serve.

Moong Bean with Cabbage

Prep time: 10 minutes | Cook time: 8 minutes | Serves 2

2 teaspoons olive oil
½ teaspoon mustard seeds
1 small red onion, chopped
2 green chilies, sliced
5 cups cabbage, shredded
½ cup split moong

bean, rinsed
½ teaspoon turmeric powder
½ teaspoon salt
⅓ cup water
¼ cup fresh dill, chopped
Garam masala, for topping

1. Press the Sauté button on the Instant Pot. Add the oil and the mustard seeds. Heat for a few seconds until the mustard seeds pop.
2. Add the onion and sliced green chilies. Sauté for 2 minutes or until softened.
3. Add the shredded cabbage and sauté for 1 minute.
4. Add the moong bean, turmeric powder, and salt and mix well.
5. Pour in the water and close the pot. Press the Manual button and set the timer for 5 minutes on High Pressure.
6. When timer beeps, let the pressure release naturally for 5 minutes, then release any remaining pressure.
7. Open the pot, add the chopped dill, and sprinkle with garam masala. Stir to mix well. Serve hot.

Lemony Black Bean Curry

Prep time: 15 minutes | Cook time: 35 minutes | Serves 6

1 tablespoon butter
1 teaspoon cumin seeds
1 onion, minced
1 tablespoon ginger paste
1 tablespoon garlic paste
1 teaspoon chili powder
½ teaspoon garam masala

½ teaspoon ground turmeric
2 teaspoons ground coriander
1 cup black beans, rinsed, soaked in water overnight, drained
2 cups water
1 teaspoon fresh lemon juice
Salt, to taste

1. Add the butter to the Instant Pot and select Sauté mode. Add the cumin seeds

and cook for 30 seconds or until pops.
2. Add the onion, ginger paste, garlic paste, chili powder, garam masala, turmeric, and coriander, and cook for 4 minutes.
3. Stir in the chickpeas and water. Secure the lid. Select the Bean/Chili mode and set the timer for 30 minutes on High Pressure.
4. When timer beeps, use a natural pressure release for 15 minutes, then release any remaining pressure.
5. Remove the lid and stir in the lemon juice. Sprinkle with salt and serve.

Sumptuous Navy Beans

Prep time: 20 minutes | Cook time: 50 minutes | Serves 10

2 tablespoons extra-virgin olive oil
1 green bell pepper, deseeded and chopped
1 onion, minced
1 jalapeño pepper, minced
3 garlic cloves, minced
6 ounces (170 g) tomato paste
¼ cup molasses
1 teaspoon balsamic vinegar

2 cups vegetable broth
1 tablespoon mustard
¼ teaspoon smoked paprika
¼ cup sugar
¼ teaspoon ground black pepper
1 pound (454 g) navy beans, soaked in water for at least 4 hours, drained
2 cups water
Salt, to taste

1. Add the butter to the Instant Pot and select Sauté setting.
2. Add the bell pepper and onion and cook for 4 minutes or until the onion is translucent.
3. Add the jalapeño and garlic and cook for 1 minute or until fragrant.
4. Meanwhile, combine remaining ingredients in a bowl, except the beans and water, and beat until smooth to make the sauce.
5. Stir the beans, water and sauce mixture in the pot. Secure the lid.
6. Set on Manual mode and set cooking time for 45 minutes on High Pressure.
7. When timer beeps, allow a natural pressure release for 15 minutes, then release any remaining pressure.
8. Remove the lid and stir in the salt before serving.

Ritzy Bean, Pea, and Lentils Mix

Prep time: 20 minutes | Cook time: 11 minutes | Serves 4

1 tablespoon plus 1 teaspoon butter, divided
4 green cardamoms
1 bay leaf
3 cloves
1 teaspoon cumin seeds
2 dried red chilies
¼ teaspoon asafetida
2-inch piece ginger, finely chopped
1 green chili, chopped
1 large tomato, chopped
¼ cup split pigeon peas, rinsed and soaked for 30 minutes, drained
¼ cup split chickpeas, rinsed and soaked for 30 minutes, drained
¼ cup split black beans, rinsed and soaked for 30 minutes, drained
¼ cup split mung beans, rinsed and soaked for 30 minutes, drained
¼ cup split red lentils, rinsed and soaked for 30 minutes, drained
½ teaspoon turmeric powder
1 teaspoon salt
3 cups water
2 tablespoons cilantro, chopped
2 teaspoons lemon juice

1. Press the Sauté button on the Instant Pot. Add 1 tablespoon of butter to the pot and then add the green cardamoms, bay leaf, cloves and cumin seeds. Sauté for a few seconds, until fragrant.
2. Add the dried red chilies and asafetida and sauté for a few seconds.
3. Add the chopped ginger and green chili and cook for a minute.
4. Stir in the tomato and cook for 2 minutes, or until tender.
5. Add the soaked peas, beans, and lentils. Sprinkle with turmeric powder and salt. Mix well.
6. Pour in the water and close the lid. Press the Manual button and set the timer for 7 minutes on High Pressure.
7. When timer beeps, let the pressure release naturally for 10 minutes, then release any remaining pressure.
8. Open the pot, stir and add the remaining 1 teaspoon of butter, cilantro and lemon juice. Serve hot.

Red Lentils with Butternut Squash

Prep time: 15 minutes | Cook time: 12 minutes | Serves 4

2 teaspoons olive oil
½ teaspoon mustard seeds
½ teaspoon cumin seeds
⅛ teaspoon asafetida
1 green chili, sliced
2 dried red chilies, broken
1½ teaspoons ginger, finely chopped
12 curry leaves
2 medium tomatoes, chopped
2 cups butternut squash, diced into 1-inch pieces
¾ cup split red lentils
2½ cups water, divided
½ teaspoon turmeric powder
1 teaspoon salt
1 tablespoon cilantro, chopped
1½ teaspoons lemon juice

1. Press the Sauté button of the Instant Pot. Add the oil, mustard seeds and cumin seeds. Let the mustard seeds pop for a few seconds.
2. Add the asafetida, green chili and broken dried red chilies. Sauté for a few seconds.
3. Add the ginger and curry leaves and cook for a minute or until the ginger is golden brown.
4. Stir in the tomatoes and squash. Cook for 2 minutes. Add the lentils and mix well. Pour in 1 cup of the water, turmeric powder and salt and mix well.
5. Secure the lid, press the Manual button. Set cooking time for 6 minutes on High Pressure.
6. When timer beeps, naturally release the pressure for 5 minutes, then release any remaining pressure.
7. Open the pot, press the Sauté button and add the remaining 1½ cups of water, cilantro and lemon juice. Simmer for 2 minutes.
8. Serve warm.

Green Beans with Beetroot

Prep time: 15 minutes | Cook time: 5 minutes | Serves 2 to 3

1 cup water
1 cup green beans, cut into ½-inch pieces
1 large beetroot, diced small, around ½-inch pieces
1½ tablespoons olive oil
½ teaspoon mustard seeds
2 teaspoons split and dehusked black gram lentils
2 teaspoons chickpeas
2 dried red chilies, broken
⅛ teaspoon asafetida
12 curry leaves
⅛ teaspoon turmeric powder
½ teaspoon salt
$^1/_3$ cup fresh grated coconut

1. Pour the water in the Instant Pot. Put the chopped green beans and beetroot in a steamer basket and then put the steamer basket in the pot.
2. Close the lid. Press the Steam button and set the time to 2 minutes on High Pressure.
3. When timer beeps, do a quick pressure release. Open the lid. Remove the steamer basket from the pot and transfer the steamed vegetables to a bowl. Set aside.
4. Press the Sauté button, add the oil and mustard seeds. Heat for a few seconds until pop.
5. Add the lentils and chickpeas and cook for 2 minutes, or until golden.
6. Add the dried red chilies and asafetida and sauté for a few seconds.
7. Add the curry leaves, stir, then add the steamed vegetables, turmeric powder and salt.
8. Toss to combine well, then fold in the fresh grated coconut. Transfer to a serving dish and serve.

Lentils and Fried Onion Dal

Prep time: 15 minutes | Cook time: 26 minutes | Serves 4

2¾ cups water, divided
½ cup chana dal
2 teaspoons avocado oil
2 dried red chiles
¼ teaspoon cumin seeds
4 garlic cloves, minced
1 cup thinly sliced red onion
1 large tomato, chopped
½ teaspoon ground turmeric
1 teaspoon salt
½ teaspoon ground cumin
¼ cup chopped fresh cilantro

1. Pour 1 cup of water into the Instant Pot, then place a trivet in the pot.
2. In a heatproof bowl, combine the dal and 1 cup of water. Place the bowl on the trivet.
3. Lock the lid. Select Manual mode and set cooking time for 6 minutes on High Pressure.
4. When cooking is complete, let the pressure release naturally for 5 minutes, then release any remaining pressure. Unlock the lid.
5. Meanwhile, heat a medium saucepan over medium-high heat. Add the oil. When it shimmers, add the red chiles, cumin seeds, and garlic and cook for 1 minute.
6. Add the onion slices and cook, stirring occasionally, until the onions are crisp and lightly browned, 5 to 8 minutes.
7. Add the tomato and mash with the back of a spoon. Sprinkle with the turmeric, salt, and cumin, mixing well.
8. When the dal is finished, carefully remove the bowl from the Instant Pot. Transfer the dal to the saucepan and add the remaining ¾ cup of water. Stir to combine.
9. Turn the heat to low and let it simmer for 5 to 10 minutes, or until the flavors meld. Garnish with the cilantro and serve.

Bean Tagine with Ras el Hanout

Prep time: 20 minutes | Cook time: 37 minutes | Serves 8

2½ cups (about 1 pound / 454 g) dried Northern beans, soaked in salted water overnight, rinsed and drained
¼ cup olive oil, plus more for serving
4 cloves garlic, minced
1 yellow onion, sliced
3 cups vegetable broth
8 medium carrots (about 1 pound / 454 g in total), peeled and cut into

½-inch rounds
1 tablespoon tomato paste
1 tablespoon fresh lemon juice
Salt, to taste
2 tablespoons chopped fresh mint
Ras el Hanout:
2 teaspoons paprika
½ teaspoon ground cinnamon
½ teaspoon ground coriander
½ teaspoon ground cumin
¼ teaspoon cayenne pepper.

1. Select the Sauté setting on the Instant Pot, add the oil and garlic, and heat for 2 minutes, until the garlic is bubbling but not browned.
2. Add the onion and sauté for 5 minutes until the onion is softened and the garlic is toasty and brown.
3. Stir in the broth and use a wooden spoon to nudge loose any browned bits from the bottom of the pot.
4. Stir in the carrots, ingredients for the ras el hanout, and salt. Stir in the beans, making sure all of the beans are submerged in the cooking liquid.
5. Secure the lid. Select Bean/Chili setting and set the cooking time for 30 minutes at High Pressure.
6. When timer beeps, let the pressure release naturally for 20 minutes, then release any remaining pressure.
7. Open the pot and stir in the tomato paste and lemon juice.
8. Ladle the tagine into bowls. Drizzle with oil and sprinkle with mint. Serve hot.

Black-Eyed Peas with Spinach

Prep time: 10 minutes | Cook time: 13 minutes | Serves 6

1 tablespoon peanut oil
⅛ teaspoon cumin seeds
⅛ teaspoon black mustard seeds
1 tablespoon minced garlic
1 tablespoon minced ginger
1 cup diced tomato
½ teaspoon ground

turmeric
½ teaspoon ground cumin
½ teaspoon ground coriander
¼ teaspoon ground cayenne pepper
1 teaspoon salt
1 cup dried black-eyed peas
2 cups water
4 cups raw spinach

1. Set the Instant Pot to Sauté mode. When the Instant Pot is hot, add the oil and heat until shimmering.
2. Add the cumin seeds and mustard seeds and cook for 1 minute or until they sputter like popcorn popping. Add the garlic and ginger and sauté for 30 seconds.
3. Add the tomato and cook for 1 to 2 minutes until the tomato has softened.
4. Add the turmeric, cumin, coriander, cayenne, and salt, and mix well.
5. Add the black-eyed peas and water, and mix. Place the spinach on top.
6. Lock the lid. Select Manual mode. Set cooking time for 10 minutes on High Pressure.
7. When timer beeps, allow 10 minutes of natural pressure release, then release any remaining pressure. Unlock the lid.
8. Serve immediately.

Beluga Lentils with Lacinato Kale

Prep time: 15 minutes | Cook time: 40 minutes | Serves 6

¼ cup olive oil, plus more for serving
2 shallots, diced
5 cloves garlic, minced
½ teaspoon red pepper flakes
½ teaspoon ground nutmeg
1 teaspoon fine sea salt

2 bunches (about 1 pound / 454 g) lacinato kale, stems discarded and leaves chopped into 1-inch pieces
2 large carrots, peeled and diced
2½ cups water
1 cup beluga lentils, rinsed

1. Select the Sauté setting on the Instant Pot, add the oil, and heat for 1 minute.
2. Add the shallots and garlic and sauté for about 4 minutes until the shallots soften.
3. Add the red pepper flakes, nutmeg, and salt and sauté for 1 minute more.
4. Stir in the kale and carrots and sauté for about 3 minutes, until the kale fully wilts. Stir in the water and lentils.
5. Secure the lid. Select Bean/Chili setting and set the cooking time for 30 minutes at High Pressure.
6. When timer beeps, let the pressure release naturally for 10 minutes, then release any remaining pressure.
7. Open the pot and give the mixture a stir.
8. Ladle the lentils into serving dishes and drizzle with oil. Serve warm.

Indian Green Pea Matar

Prep time: 10 minutes | Cook time: 15 minutes | Serves 2

½ tablespoon avocado oil
¼ teaspoon cumin seeds
½ yellow onion, chopped
1 cup green peas
1 tomato, puréed
½ teaspoon garam masala
½ tablespoon coriander

2 curry leaves
½ teaspoon chili powder
Sea salt and ground black pepper, to taste
1½ cups vegetable broth
1 tablespoon chickpea flour
½ cup coconut yogurt

1. Press the Sauté button on the Instant Pot and heat the oil. Once hot, cook the cumin seeds for about 1 minute or until fragrant.
2. Add the onion and continue sautéing for an additional 3 minutes.
3. Stir in the green peas, tomatoes, garam masala, coriander, curry leaves, chili powder, salt, black pepper, and broth.
4. Secure the lid. Choose the Manual mode and set cooking time for 12 minutes at High Pressure.
5. Once cooking is complete, use a quick pressure release. Carefully remove the lid.
6. Stir in the chickpea flour and let it simmer on the Sauté mode until thickened. Serve in soup bowls with yogurt on the side.

Japan Anasazi Beans and Mushrooms

Prep time: 10 minutes | Cook time: 16 minutes | Serves 4

1 cup dried anasazi beans, soaked in water overnight, rinsed and drained
1 tablespoon olive oil
2 cups half-moon slices onion
½ teaspoon sugar
½ cup finely diced

mushrooms
¼ teaspoon liquid smoke
1 teaspoon smoked paprika
2 cups vegetable broth
¼ cup water
2 teaspoons red miso

1. In the Instant Pot, heat the olive oil on Sauté mode. Add the onion and sugar and cook for 10 minutes or until soft and brown.
2. Add the beans, mushrooms, liquid smoke, paprika, broth, and water. Stir to combine.
3. Secure the lid. Select Manual mode and set cooking time for 6 minutes on High Pressure.
4. When timer beeps, use a natural pressure release for 5 minutes, then release any remaining pressure.
5. Remove the lid and stir in the miso. Serve immediately.

Red Lentil Coconut Curry 10

Prep time: 5 minutes | Cook time: 15 minutes | Serves 4

1 teaspoon sesame oil
2 cubes frozen glazed onions
2 large cloves garlic, minced
1 large sweet potato, diced (about 3½ cups)
¼ cup water
¼ cup dried red lentils
½ cup sushi rice
1 (13.5-ounce / 383-g) can coconut milk
2 tablespoons gochujang
1 teaspoon curry powder
½ cup vegetable broth
1 teaspoon tamari or soy sauce
½ cup chopped unsalted roasted peanuts for garnish
¼ cup chopped fresh cilantro, for garnish

1. Heat the sesame oil in the Instant Pot on the Sauté function with the onions, garlic, sweet potatoes, and water for 5 minutes.
2. Add the lentils, sushi rice, coconut milk, gochujang, curry powder, and vegetable broth. Stir well.
3. Cover the pot, select Manual mode, and set cooking time for 7 minutes on High Pressure.
4. When timer beeps, use a natural pressure release for 5 minutes, then release any remaining pressure.
5. Remove the lid. Stir until potatoes have disappeared, turning into a bright cream clinging to the rice. Stir in the tamari.
6. Spoon into bowls and garnish each serving with peanuts and cilantro.

Barbecue Northern Bean Bake

Prep time: 20 minutes | Cook time: 54 minutes | Serves 8

2½ cups (about 1 pound / 454 g) dried great Northern beans, soaked in water for at least 8 hours, rinsed and drained
1 cup barbecue sauce
¼ cup yellow mustard
2 tablespoons maple syrup
1¾ cups water
1½ teaspoons freshly ground black pepper
1½ teaspoons smoked paprika
3 tablespoons avocado oil
1 large yellow onion, diced
2 cloves garlic, minced
1 bay leaf

1. In a small bowl, stir together the barbecue sauce, mustard, maple syrup, water, pepper, and smoked paprika.
2. Select the Sauté setting on the Instant Pot, add the oil, and heat for 2 minutes.
3. Add the onion and sauté for about 10 minutes, stirring often, until it begins to caramelize.
4. Add the garlic and sauté for about 2 minutes more until the garlic is no longer raw.
5. Add the barbecue sauce mixture, beans, and bay leaf. Stir to combine, using a wooden spoon to nudge loose any browned bits from the bottom of the pot.
6. Secure the lid. Select Bean/Chili setting and set the cooking time for 40 minutes at High Pressure.
7. When timer beeps, let the pressure release naturally for 20 minutes, then release any remaining pressure. Open the pot, stir the beans, and discard the bay leaf.
8. Ladle the beans into bowls and serve hot.

Refried Pinto Beans with Jalapeños

Prep time: 5 minutes | Cook time: 10 minutes | Serves 6

1 cup dried pinto beans, soaked in water overnight, rinsed and drained
1 tablespoon olive oil
4 cloves garlic, minced
½ cup diced yellow onion
1 fresh jalapeños, deseeded and diced
3 cups water
1 teaspoon chili powder
½ teaspoon cumin
¼ teaspoon cayenne pepper
½ teaspoon salt

1. In the Instant Pot, heat the oil on Sauté mode.
2. Add the garlic, onion, and jalapeño and sauté for 3 minutes, until the onion is soft.
3. Add the pinto beans and enough water to cover the beans plus another 1 inch of liquid. Add the chili powder, cumin, and cayenne pepper. Stir to combine.
4. Secure the lid. Select Manual mode and set cooking time for 6 minutes at High Pressure.
5. When timer beeps, use a natural pressure release for 5 minutes, then release any remaining pressure.
6. Remove the lid, drain the beans and return the beans to the Instant Pot. Add salt. Mash the beans with a hand masher. Serve immediately.

Ritzy Chickpea Veggie Burritos

Prep time: 15 minutes | Cook time: 14 minutes | Serves 3

1 tablespoon coconut oil
1 medium red onion, finely chopped
1 red bell pepper, deseeded and chopped
1 garlic clove, minced
1 teaspoon cumin powder
1 cup canned chickpeas, drained
1 cup vegetable broth
Salt and ground black pepper, to taste
3 corn tortillas
1 large avocado, chopped
½ cup shredded red cabbage
3 tablespoons chopped cilantro
3 tablespoons tomato salsa
½ cup coconut cream

1. Set the Instant Pot to Sauté mode. Heat coconut oil and sauté onion and bell pepper until softened, 4 minutes.
2. Add garlic, cumin, and cook for 1 minute or until fragrant.
3. Mix in chickpeas, heat through for 1 minute with frequent stirring, and pour in the broth. Season with salt and pepper.
4. Seal the lid. Select Manual mode and set cooking time for 8 minutes on High Pressure.
5. When timer beeps, do a natural release for 5 minutes, then release any remaining pressure. Open the lid.
6. Lay tortillas on a flat surface and divide chickpea filling at the center. Top with avocados, cabbage, cilantro, salsa, and coconut cream. Wrap, tuck ends, and slice in halves. Serve immediately.

Sautéed Beluga Lentil and Zucchinis

Prep time: 15 minutes | Cook time: 10 minutes | Serves 4

2 tablespoons olive oil
2 large zucchinis, chopped
4 garlic cloves, minced
½ tablespoon dried oregano
½ tablespoon curry powder
Salt and ground black pepper, to taste

2 cups canned beluga lentils, drained
¼ cup chopped parsley, divided
½ cup chopped basil
1 small red onion, diced
2 tablespoons balsamic vinegar
1 teaspoon Dijon mustard

1. Set the Instant Pot to Sauté mode. Heat the oil and sauté the zucchinis until tender.
2. Mix in the garlic and cook until fragrant, 30 seconds. Top with oregano, curry, salt, and pepper. Allow to combine for 1 minute, stirring frequently.
3. Pour in lentils, cook for 3 minutes, and stir in half of parsley, basil, and onion. Sauté until onion softens, about 5 minutes.
4. Meanwhile, in a bowl, combine vinegar with mustard and pour mixture over lentils. Plate and garnish with remaining parsley.

Scarlet Runner Bean and Potato Hash

Prep time: 5 minutes | Cook time: 20 minutes | Serves 4

1 tablespoon avocado oil
3 cups diced potatoes
2 cups diced red and yellow pepper
4 cloves garlic, minced
1 cup diced celery
1 cup Scarlet Runner

beans, soaked in water overnight, rinsed and drained
2 vegetable broth
1 tablespoon dried oregano
1 teaspoon chili powder
Salt, to taste

1. Heat the oil in the Instant Pot on the Sauté function.
2. Add the potatoes, peppers, garlic, and celery, and sauté for 4 minutes.
3. Add the beans. Begin adding broth until cover the beans. Stir in the dried oregano and chili powder.
4. Cover the pot. Select Manual mode and set cooking time for 12 minutes on High Pressure.
5. When timer beeps, use a natural pressure release for 5 minutes, then release any remaining pressure.
6. Remove the cover. Sprinkle with salt and serve.

Adzuki Beans and Vegetable Bowl

Prep time: 5 minutes | Cook time: 25 minutes | Serves 4

1 teaspoon sesame oil
2 cloves garlic, minced
1 teaspoon grated ginger
1 cup dried adzuki beans
½ cup brown rice
½ cup sliced shiitake

mushrooms
2 cups shredded collard greens
1-inch strip kombu
3 cups water
3 umeboshi plums, mashed
1 tablespoon lemon juice
1 tablespoon tamari

1. In the Instant Pot, heat the oil on Sauté mode.
2. Add the garlic and ginger and sauté for 2 minutes until the garlic is softened
3. Stir in the adzuki beans, brown rice, mushrooms, greens, kombu, and water.
4. Secure the lid. Select Manual mode and set cooking time for 22 minutes on High Pressure.
5. When timer beeps, use a natural pressure release for 15 minutes, then release any remaining pressure.
6. Remove the cover and stir. Return to the pot, and simmer while stirring in the mashed umeboshi plums, lemon juice, and tamari on Sauté mode for 3 minutes.
7. Serve immediately.

Balsamic Black Beans with Parsnip

Prep time: 5 minutes | Cook time: 11 minutes | Serves 6

1 cup dried black beans, soaked in water overnight, rinsed and drained
1 teaspoon olive oil
2 cloves garlic, minced
1 cup diced parsnip

½ teaspoon ground coriander
½ teaspoon ground cardamom
2 cups water
2 tablespoons balsamic vinegar

1. In the Instant Pot, heat the oil on Sauté mode. Add the garlic and sauté for a minute or until soft, but not brown.
2. Add the parsnip, coriander, and cardamom and sauté for 5 minutes.
3. Add the black beans and water. Stir to combine.
4. Secure the lid. Select Manual mode and set cooking time for 5 minutes on High Pressure.
5. When timer beeps, use a natural pressure release for 5 minutes, then release any remaining pressure.
6. Remove the lid and stir in 2 tablespoons of the balsamic vinegar. Serve immediately.

Black Bean and Pepper Tacos

Prep time: 10 minutes | Cook time: 23 minutes | Serves 2

1 tablespoon sesame oil
½ onion, chopped
1 teaspoon garlic, minced
1 sweet pepper, deseeded and sliced
1 jalapeño pepper, deseeded and minced
1 teaspoon ground cumin

½ teaspoon ground coriander
8 ounces (227 g) black beans, rinsed
2 (8-inch) whole wheat tortillas, warmed
½ cup cherry tomatoes, halved
⅓ cup coconut cream

1. Press the Sauté button and heat the oil. Cook the onion, garlic, and peppers for 3 minutes or until tender and fragrant.
2. Add the ground cumin, coriander, and beans to the Instant Pot.

3. Secure the lid. Choose the Manual mode and cook for 20 minutes at High Pressure.
4. Once cooking is complete, use a natural pressure release for 10 minutes, then release any remaining pressure. Carefully remove the lid.
5. Serve the bean mixture in the tortillas, then garnish with the cherry tomatoes and coconut cream.

Black Beans with Crumbled Tofu

Prep time: 15 minutes | Cook time: 23 minutes | Serves 2

1 cup canned black beans
2 cups vegetable broth
1 tablespoon avocado oil
1 small red onion, finely chopped
3 garlic cloves, minced
3 tomatoes, chopped

1 (14-ounce / 397-g) extra-firm tofu, crumbled
1 teaspoon turmeric powder
1 teaspoon cumin powder
1 teaspoon smoked paprika
Salt and ground black pepper, to taste

1. Pour the beans and broth in Instant Pot. Seal the lid, select Manual mode, and set cooking time for 10 minutes on High Pressure.
2. When timer beeps, do a quick pressure release. Transfer the beans to a medium bowl. Drain excess liquid and wipe Instant Pot clean.
3. Select Sauté mode. Heat the avocado oil and sauté onion, garlic, and tomatoes until softened, 4 minutes.
4. Crumble the tofu into the pan and cook for 5 minutes.
5. Season with turmeric, cumin, paprika, salt, and black pepper. Cook for 1 minute. Add black beans, stir, and allow heating for 3 minutes.
6. Serve immediately.

Cinnamon Chickpeas Curry

Prep time: 15 minutes | Cook time: 35 minutes | Serves 4

1 cup dried chickpeas
1 tablespoon baking soda
4 cups water, divided
1 teaspoon olive oil
1 clove garlic, minced
¼ cup diced onion
½ teaspoon hot curry powder
¼ teaspoon ground cinnamon
1 bay leaf
½ teaspoon sea salt

1. Add the chickpeas, baking soda, and 2 cups of the water to a large bowl and soak for 1 hour. Rinse the chickpeas and drain.
2. In the Instant Pot, heat the oil on Sauté mode. Add the garlic and onion and sauté for 3 minutes.
3. Add the curry, cinnamon, and bay leaf and stir well. Stir in the chickpeas and 2 cups of the water.
4. Cover the lid. Select Manual mode and set cooking time for 32 minutes on High Pressure.
5. When timer beeps, use a natural pressure release for 15 minutes, then release any remaining pressure.
6. Remove the lid and stir in the sea salt. Remove the bay leaf before serving.

Hearty Black-Eyed Peas with Collard

Prep time: 5 minutes | Cook time: 3 to 4 minutes | Serves 4 to 6

1 yellow onion, diced
1 tablespoon olive oil
1 cup dried black-eyed peas
¼ cup chopped sun-dried tomatoes
¼ cup tomato paste
1 teaspoon smoked paprika
2 cups water
4 large collard green leaves
Salt and freshly ground black pepper, to taste

1. In the Instant Pot, select Sauté mode. Add the onion and olive oil and cook for 3 to 4 minutes, stirring occasionally, until the onion is softened.
2. Add the black-eyed peas, tomatoes, tomato paste, paprika, water, and stir to combine.
3. Close the lid, then select Manual mode and set cooking time for 30 minutes on High Pressure.
4. Once the cook time is complete, let the pressure release naturally for about 15 minutes, then release any remaining pressure.
5. Trim off the thick parts of the collard green stems, then slice the leaves lengthwise in half or quarters. Roll them up together, then finely slice into ribbons.
6. Sprinkle the sliced collard greens with salt and massage it into them with hands to soften.
7. Open the lid. Add the collard greens and ½ teaspoon of salt to the pot, stirring to combine and letting the greens wilt in the heat.
8. Serve immediately.

Simple Amaranth Lentils

Prep time: 5 minutes | Cook time: 12 minutes | Serves 4

1 teaspoon butter
2 cloves garlic, minced
¼ cup diced yellow onion
½ cup amaranth
½ cup dried brown lentils
2 cups shredded Swiss chard
2 cups water
¼ teaspoon ground coriander
½ teaspoon sea salt
¼ cup chopped scallion

1. In the Instant Pot, melt the butter on Sauté mode.
2. Add the garlic and onion and sauté until the onion is soft, about 3 minutes.
3. Add the amaranth, lentils, and Swiss chard and stir to combine.
4. Add enough water to cover everything. Stir to combine.
5. Secure the lid. Select Manual mode and set cooking time for 9 minutes on High Pressure.
6. When timer beeps, use a natural pressure release for 5 minutes, then release any remaining pressure.
7. Remove the cover and stir in the coriander and salt. Garnish with the scallion. Serve immediately.

Sloppy Lentils Joes

Prep time: 20 minutes | Cook time: 40 minutes | Serves 8

¼ cup olive oil
1 green bell pepper, deseeded and diced
1 large carrot, peeled and diced
2 stalks celery, diced
1 yellow onion, diced
3 cloves garlic minced
1 tablespoon chili powder
1 teaspoon fine sea salt
½ teaspoon freshly ground black pepper
½ teaspoon ground cumin
½ teaspoon smoked paprika

2 tablespoons Worcestershire sauce
1 tablespoon cider vinegar
4 cups vegetable broth
2¼ cups (about 1 pound / 454 g) green lentils, rinsed
¼ cup sugar
1 (15-ounce / 425-g) can tomato sauce
¼ cup tomato paste
8 whole-wheat hamburger buns, split and toasted
8 sweet yellow onion slices

1. Select the Sauté setting on the Instant Pot, add the oil, and heat for 2 minutes.
2. Add the bell pepper, carrot, celery, onion, and garlic and sauté for about 10 minutes, until the onion is translucent but not yet beginning to brown.
3. Add the chili powder, salt, pepper, cumin, and smoked paprika, and sauté for 1 minute.
4. Add the Worcestershire, vinegar, broth, and lentils and stir well.
5. Add the sugar, tomato sauce, and tomato paste on top.
6. Secure the lid. Select Bean/Chili setting and set the cooking time for 25 minutes at High Pressure.
7. When timer beeps, let the pressure release naturally for at least 10 minutes, then release any remaining pressure.
8. Open the pot and stir to incorporate the tomato paste.
9. Place the bun bottoms, cut side up, on individual plates and ladle the Sloppy Joe mixture onto the buns. Serve hot.

Spiced Sprouted Beans

Prep time: 10 minutes | Cook time: 6 minutes | Serves 6

1 tablespoon peanut oil
1 teaspoon cumin seeds
½ cup chopped tomato
3 garlic cloves, minced
½ cup chopped onion
1 teaspoon minced ginger
1 cup sprouted beans

¼ cup unsweetened shredded coconut
½ teaspoon ground turmeric
¼ teaspoon ground cayenne pepper
1 teaspoon ground coriander
½ teaspoon ground cumin
1 teaspoon salt
½ cup water
¼ cup chopped fresh cilantro

1. Set the Instant Pot to Sauté. When the pot is hot, add the oil and heat until shimmering. Add the cumin seeds and cook for 1 minute or until sputter like popcorn popping.
2. Add the tomato, garlic, onion, and ginger, and sauté for 2 minutes or until the onion is soft and translucent.
3. Add the sprouted beans, coconut, turmeric, cayenne, coriander, cumin, salt, and water, and stir to combine.
4. Lock the lid. Select Manual mode and set cooking time for 4 minutes on High Pressure.
5. When cooking is complete, quick release the pressure.
6. Unlock the lid. Garnish with cilantro and serve.

Tempeh Chops with White Beans

Prep time: 15 minutes | Cook time: 16 minutes | Serves 4

2 tablespoons olive oil
2 pounds (907 g) tempeh, chopped
1 large yellow onion, chopped
1 small fennel bulb, chopped
3 carrots, cubed
3 large garlic cloves, roughly chopped
1 cinnamon stick
1 bay leaf

1½ teaspoons ground allspice
1 teaspoon ras el hanout
½ teaspoon ginger paste
6 large tomatoes, chopped
4 cups vegetable broth
1 (15-ounce / 425-g) can white beans

1. Add the oil to the Instant Pot and select Sauté mode.
2. Pour in the tempeh and fry for 3 minutes or until golden brown on all sides.
3. Remove to a plate. Put onion, fennel, carrots, and garlic into the pot and sauté for 6 minutes.
4. Drop in cinnamon stick, bay leaf, allspice, ras el hanout, and ginger paste. Sauté for 2 minutes. Pour in tomatoes and broth and stir.
5. Seal the lid. Select Manual mode and set cooking time for 2 minutes on High Pressure.
6. When timer beeps, do a natural release for 1 minutes, then release any remaining pressure and open the lid.
7. Select Sauté mode. Stir in the tempeh and beans; cook for 3 minutes to warm through. Serve warm.

Yellow Mung Bean with Spinach Bowls

Prep time: 15 minutes | Cook time: 15 minutes | Serves 4

1 cup yellow mung beans, rinsed
3½ cups water
1½ teaspoons fine sea salt
3 tablespoons coconut oil
1 teaspoon cumin seeds
1 yellow onion, thinly sliced
1 jalapeño chile, deseeded and diced
3 cloves garlic,

thinly sliced
1 Roma tomato, diced
½ teaspoon ground turmeric
1 teaspoon ground coriander
¼ teaspoon cayenne pepper
¼ cup chopped fresh cilantro
1 (5- to 6-ounce / 142- to 170-g) bag baby spinach

1. Add the mung beans, water, and salt to the Instant Pot.
2. Secure the lid. Select Bean/Chili setting and set the cooking time for 5 minutes at High Pressure.
3. Meanwhile, in a large skillet over medium-high heat, melt the coconut oil.
4. Add the cumin seeds and cook, stirring, until toasty and fragrant, about 1 minute.
5. Add the onion and jalapeño and sauté for about 4 minutes until the onion softens.
6. Nudge the mixture to the sides of the skillet. Add the garlic to the center of the skillet and sauté for about 2 minutes until the garlic is browned but not burnt.
7. Add the tomato and sauté for about 3 minutes, mixing in the ingredients from the sides of the skillet.
8. Remove the skillet from the heat and stir in the turmeric, coriander, and cayenne. Set aside.
9. When timer beeps, let the pressure release naturally for 5 minutes, then release any remaining pressure.
10. Open the pot and add the mixture from the skillet along with the cilantro and the spinach, then stir to combine.
11. Ladle them into bowls and serve hot.

Chickpea Tagine with Pickled Raisins

Prep time: 30 minutes | Cook time: 25 minutes | Serves 4

1 cup dried chickpeas, soaked in salted water for 8 hours, rinsed and drained
2 teaspoons kosher salt
Spicy Pickled Raisins:

Tagine:
2 tablespoons olive oil
1 large yellow onion, diced
2 medium carrots, diced
5 garlic cloves, minced
2 teaspoons ground cinnamon
2 teaspoons ground coriander
1 teaspoon cumin seeds or ground cumin
1 teaspoon sweet paprika
2 bay leaves
1½ teaspoons kosher salt, plus more to taste
1¼ cups vegetable broth or water

⅓ cup golden raisins
⅓ cup apple cider vinegar
2½ tablespoons organic cane sugar
¼ teaspoon crushed red pepper flakes, to taste

3 cups peeled and finely diced peeled butternut squash (from one 1½-pound / 680-g butternut squash)
¼ cup finely diced dried apricots (about 8 apricots)
1 (14.5-ounce / 411-g) can crushed tomatoes
4 ounces (113 g) Tuscan kale, stems and midribs removed, roughly chopped
¼ cup roughly chopped fresh cilantro
Zest and juice of 1 small lemon

1. Place the raisins in a bowl. In a small saucepan, combine the vinegar, sugar, and pepper flakes and bring to a boil over medium-high heat, whisking until the sugar is dissolved.
2. Remove the vinegar mixture from the heat and carefully pour the hot vinegar mixture over the raisins. Leave the bowl uncovered and allow the mixture to come to room temperature. Set aside.
3. Select the Sauté setting on the Instant Pot and let the pot heat for a few minutes before adding the olive oil.
4. Once the oil is hot, add the onion and carrots. Cook until the vegetables have softened, 4 to 5 minutes.
5. Add the garlic and cook for 1 minute, stirring frequently.
6. Add the cinnamon, coriander, cumin seeds, paprika, bay leaves, and salt. Stir the spices into the vegetables for 30 seconds until the mixture is fragrant.
7. Pour in the broth, drained chickpeas, butternut squash, and dried apricots. Stir to combine all the ingredients. Pour the crushed tomatoes on top, but do not stir, allowing the tomatoes to sit on top.
8. Secure the lid. Select the Manual mode and set the cook time for 12 minutes on High Pressure.
9. When timer beeps, use a natural pressure release for 5 minutes, then release any remaining pressure.
10. Open the pot, discard the bay leaves, and stir in the kale. Select the Sauté setting and cook for 2 to 3 minutes to wilt the kale.
11. Add the cilantro and lemon zest and half of the lemon juice.
12. Transfer the tagine to bowls and add a few spoons of the spicy pickled raisins to each bowl. Serve immediately.

Chapter 13 Desserts

Hearty Prune Cake

Prep time: 15 minutes | Cook time: 50 minutes | Serves 2

¼ cup vegetable oil
2 cups chopped prunes, divided
2 cups coconut flour
1 cup coconut milk
¼ cup honey
1 teaspoon baking powder
1 tablespoon lemon juice
1 teaspoon vanilla extract
¼ teaspoon almond extract
½ teaspoon salt
¼ cup water
1 egg

1. Spray the vegetable oil on 2 round baking pans.
2. Whisk together baking powder, salt and coconut flour in a bowl. Set aside.
3. Take a large bowl to make the cream and add the vegetable oil with the honey. Add the egg and beat well.
4. Take the coconut milk flour mixture. Stir in vanilla and almond extracts and 1 cup of chopped prunes.
5. Pour water into Instant Pot, put in the trivet and set the pan on top.
6. Lock the lid and set Manual mode. Set the timer for 30 minutes on High Pressure.
7. When timer beeps, use a quick pressure release and open the lid. Set the cake aside.
8. For the Filling:
9. Combine reaming chopped prunes, honey, water and lemon juice in the Instant Pot.
10. Lock the lid and set Manual mode. Set cooking time for 20 minutes on High Pressure.
11. When timer beeps, quick release the pressure and spread the filling on top of the cake.
12. Serve immediately.

Basmati Zarda

Prep time: 15 minutes | Cook time: 11 minutes | Serves 4

1 cup sella basmati rice, rinsed, soaked in water for 30 minutes, drained
½ cup whole milk
Pinch of saffron strands
2 teaspoons butter
15 cashews, chopped in half
15 almonds, chopped in half
1 to 2 tablespoons golden raisins
6 green cardamoms
6 cloves
¾ cup granulated white sugar
¾ cup water
2 teaspoons rose water
3 teaspoons desiccated coconut

1. Heat the milk in a small saucepan over medium heat, do not bring it to a boil. Add the saffron strands and set aside.
2. Press the Sauté button and add the butter and then the cashews, almonds and raisins. Sauté for 4 minutes or until the nuts turn light golden brown and then remove the nuts and raisins from the pot and set them aside.
3. Add the cardamoms and cloves and sauté for a few seconds until fragrant.
4. Add the soaked and drained basmati rice and sauté for 30 seconds.
5. Add the sugar, ¾ cup of water and the saffron milk. Stir for 1 minute until the sugar dissolves.
6. Add the rose water and close the lid. Press the Manual button. Set cooking time for 6 minutes at High Pressure.
7. When timer beeps, let the pressure release naturally for 5 minutes, then release any remaining pressure.
8. Open the lid, let the rice cool down a bit and then fluff with a fork. Add the fried nuts and raisins to the rice. Sprinkle with desiccated coconut and serve.

Super Lemon Bundt Cake

Prep time: 15 minutes | Cook time: 30 minutes | Serves 8

1 cup plain Greek yogurt
¾ cup sugar
1¼ teaspoons baking powder
½ teaspoon baking soda
½ teaspoon kosher salt
½ cup corn oil, plus more to grease the

pan
1½ cups all-purpose flour
1 tablespoon plus ½ teaspoon freshly squeezed lemon juice, divided
1½ teaspoons grated lemon zest
2 cups water
¼ cup sugar

1. In a large bowl, whisk together the yogurt and sugar until the sugar is well dissolved. Stir in the baking soda, baking powder, salt and set aside for 5 minutes or until the mixture begins to bubble.
2. Meanwhile, sift the flour into a medium bowl.
3. Whisk the yogurt mixture, then slowly whisk in the oil until fully incorporated. Stir in teaspoon of lemon juice and the lemon zest then add the sifted flour, and gently mix to form a smooth batter.
4. Grease a Bundt cake pan with corn oil, and pour in the batter. Tap the pan twice on the counter to break any air pockets, and tightly cover with aluminum foil.
5. Pour the water into the inner pot, and put the trivet inside. Put the pan on the trivet and lock the lid.
6. Select Manual mode of the pot and set the timer for 30 minutes on High Pressure.
7. When timer beeps, naturally release the pressure for 15 minutes, then release any remaining pressure.
8. Unlock the lid. Remove the pan, slowly remove the foil and let the cake cool for at least 30 minutes.
9. Run the knife along the edge of the pan and invert the cake onto a plate.
10. In a small bowl, add the remaining tablespoon of lemon juice to the sugar and mix thoroughly.
11. Drizzle the glaze on top of the cake and serve.

Hearty Orange Cake

Prep time: 20 minutes | Cook time: 35 minutes | Serves 6

Dry:

1¼ cups whole wheat pastry flour
1½ teaspoons ground cinnamon
1 teaspoon ground allspice

½ teaspoon baking soda
½ teaspoon baking powder
¼ teaspoon ground cloves

Wet:

½ cup orange juice with pulp (1 medium orange)
⅓ cup maple syrup or agave nectar

2 tablespoons ground flaxseed
3 tablespoons melted coconut oil

Mix-Ins:

2 tablespoons orange zest
¾ cup dried cranberries or diced

dried dates
½ cup chopped walnuts or pecans

1. Oil a Bundt pan and set aside.
2. For the dry ingredients, mix the flour, cinnamon, allspice, baking soda, baking powder and cloves in a medium-size mixing bowl.
3. For the wet ingredients, combine the juice, syrup, flaxseed and oil in a large measuring cup. Add the wet ingredients to the dry and mix well. Fold in the mix-ins.
4. Spread the cake mixture into the prepared pan and cover with foil.
5. Put the steel insert into the Instant Pot, pour in 1½ cups water and add the stainless steel steam rack with handles that came with the Instant Pot.
6. Tear off two pieces of foil 3 feet long, fold each one lengthwise two times. Lay the foil handles out on the counter in a plus sign near the pot. Put the pan in the center, where the two pieces cross. Pull the handles up and carefully lift the pan into the Instant Pot.
7. Put the lid on. Select Manual mode of the pot and set the cooking time for 35 minutes on High Pressure.
8. When timer beeps, let the pressure release naturally for 15 minutes, then release any remaining pressure.
9. Remove the lid. Let cool before serving.

Banana Cake

Prep time: 15 minutes | Cook time: 30 minutes | Serves 6

¼ cup corn oil, plus more to grease the pan
1 cup vanilla cream cheese frosting
1½ teaspoons baking powder
1½ cups all-purpose flour

½ teaspoon baking soda
2 medium ripe bananas, mashed
10 crushed pecans
10 crushed walnuts
2 cups water
½ cup sugar
¼ cup milk

1. In a bowl, combine the baking powder, baking soda and the flour.
2. In a large pot, mix the banana purée, milk, sugar and oil.
3. Mix the wet and dry mixture to form a smooth batter and fold in 5 pecans and 5 walnuts.
4. Grease a cake pan with some corn oil, pour the batter and take care not to create air pockets. Then cover with aluminum foil.
5. Pour the water into the Instant Pot, put the cake on the trivet and lock the lid.
6. Select Manual mode and set the cooking time to 30 minutes on High Pressure.
7. When timer beeps, naturally release the pressure for 15 minutes, then release any remaining pressure.
8. Remove the lid, the cake pan and the aluminum foil. Let the cake cool for at least 30 minutes.
9. Glaze the cake and sprinkle the remaining pecans and walnuts on top.
10. Slice and serve.

Oat Stuffed Apples

Prep time: 10 minutes | Cook time: 30 minutes | Serves 4

1 cup rolled oats
1 tablespoon ground flaxseeds
1 teaspoon pure vanilla extract
1 teaspoon ground cinnamon
¼ cup maple syrup

Pinch of ground cloves
Pinch of salt
1½ cups water
4 medium apples, cored and cut in half vertically

1. Combine the oats, flaxseeds, vanilla, cinnamon, maple syrup, cloves and salt in a bowl.
2. Put a rack in the Instant Pot and pour in the water.
3. Spread 2 tablespoons of the oat mixture on the cut side of each apple half and press the mixture down into the cavity of the core.
4. Put the apples in a baking pan that fits in the Instant Pot. Cover the dish with foil and put in the Instant Pot.
5. Set the Manual mode of the Instant Pot. Set the timer for 30 minutes on High Pressure.
6. When timer beeps, let the pressure release naturally for 15 minutes, then release any remaining pressure.
7. Open the lid and serve.

Quinoa and Almond Pudding

Prep time: 10 minutes | Cook time: 42 minutes | Serves 2

2 teaspoons butter
½ cup quinoa
2½ cups milk
⅛ cup ground almonds

¼ cup condensed milk
Ground cardamom, to taste

1. Select Sauté setting of the Instant Pot and add the butter. Then, add the quinoa and sauté for 2 minutes.
2. Pour in the milk and bring to a boil, keep stirring.
3. Lock the lid. Set on Manual mode and set the timer for 10 minutes on High Pressure.
4. When cooking is complete, perform a natural pressure release for 5 minutes, then release any remaining pressure.
5. Remove the lid and mix in the ground almonds, condensed milk, and cardamom.
6. Lock the lid, turn to Slow Cook mode and set the timer for 30 minutes on Low Pressure.
7. When timer beeps, perform a natural pressure release, then release any remaining pressure.
8. Remove the lid and serve.

Chocolate and Coconut Fondue

Prep time: 5 minutes | Cook time: 3 minutes | Serves 4

1 cup bittersweet chocolate
1 cup coconut cream
2 teaspoons sugar
2 cups water
2 teaspoons coconut essence
2 teaspoons coconut milk powder

1. Combine the chocolate, coconut cream, and sugar in a large heat-proof bowl.
2. Put the trivet in the Instant Pot and pour in the water. Put the bowl on the trivet and lock the lid.
3. Select Manual setting and set cooking time for 3 minutes at High Pressure.
4. When timer beeps, release the pressure naturally for 5 minutes, then release any remaining pressure.
5. Open the lid and mix in the coconut essence and coconut milk powder.
6. Serve warm.

Tapioca Pearl and Mango Pudding

Prep time: 15 minutes | Cook time: 17 minutes | Serves 4

½ cup tapioca pearls, rinsed, soaked for at least 15 minutes, drained
1½ cups water, divided
1 (14-ounce / 397-g) can coconut milk
¼ teaspoon cardamom powder
1 teaspoon rose water
½ cup plus 1 tablespoon fresh mango purée
3 tablespoons brown sugar
2 tablespoons crushed cashews
1 tablespoon golden raisins
Sliced pistachios, for serving

1. Press the Sauté button on the Instant Pot. Put the tapioca pearls in the pot and simmer for 5 minutes or until translucent.
2. Add the coconut milk and ½ cup of water. Stir and close the pot with the lid.
3. Press the Manual button and set the cooking time for 10 minutes on Low Pressure.

4. When timer beeps, let the pressure release naturally for 5 minutes, then release any remaining pressure.
5. Open the pot and press the Sauté button. Add the cardamom powder, rose water and mango purée and mix well.
6. Then add the brown sugar, cashews and raisins and mix well. Let the pudding simmer for 2 minutes.
7. Chill the pudding before serving. Garnish with sliced pistachios and serve.

Super Easy Poached Figs

Prep time: 5 minutes | Cook time: 4 minutes | Serves 4

1 cup red wine
1 pound (454 g) figs
½ cup pine nuts
Sugar, to taste

1. Put the wine and sugar in the Instant Pot. Mix and put the figs.
2. Set the Instant Pot on Manual mode. Cover and set the timer for 4 minutes on High Pressure.
3. When timer beeps, perform a quick pressure release. Open and sprinkle with pine nuts. Serve.

Lemony Raspberry Curd

Prep time: 5 minutes | Cook time: 2 minutes | Serves 4

12 ounces (340 g) raspberries
2 tablespoons flax meal mixed with 4 tablespoons water
2 tablespoons lemon juice
2 tablespoons butter
Sugar to taste

1. Combine all the ingredients in the Instant Pot and mix until sugar dissolves.
2. Set the pot to Manual mode. Cover and set the cooking time for 2 minutes on High Pressure.
3. When timer beeps, use a quick pressure release. Open the lid.
4. Serve chilled.

Lush Mango Cheesecake

Prep time: 25 minutes | Cook time: 50 minutes | Serves 8

½ cup unsalted butter and 1 tablespoon unsalted butter at room temperature
2 chopped mangos and 1 thinly sliced mango
1 pound (454 g) cream cheese

½ cup sugar and 2 tablespoons sugar, divided
2 cups water and 2 tablespoons water, divided
1½ cups graham cracker crumbs
2 tablespoons cornstarch

1. Mix the graham cracker crumbs, melted butter, and 2 tablespoons of sugar in a bowl. Reserve 2 tablespoons of the mixture for garnish.
2. Butter a springform pan. Add the crumb mixture to the pan and evenly press it down. Put in the freezer for 15 minutes.
3. Meanwhile, in a blender, combine the 2 chopped mangos and 2 tablespoons of water. Purée until smooth.
4. Take a large bowl, use a hand mixer to beat the cream cheese until light and fluffy and add the remaining 2 cup of sugar. Stir until well combined.
5. Add the cornstarch and mango purée and gently fold the mixture until well combined.
6. Remove the pan from the freezer and pour the filling on top of the crust. Cover the pan with aluminum foil.
7. Pour the remaining 2 cups of water into the inner pot and put the trivet inside. Put the pan on top of the trivet and lock the lid.
8. Set the Manual mode and set the timer for 50 minutes at High Pressure.
9. When cooking is complete, naturally release the pressure for 25 minutes, then release any remaining pressure.
10. Remove the lid, the cake and the aluminum foil and let it cool at room temperature for 1 hour. Then cover the cheesecake again with foil and refrigerate for at least 6 hours.
11. Sprinkle with the reserved crumb mixture and decorate with the sliced mangos. Serve immediately.

Cinnamon Glaze Apple Cake

Prep time: 20 minutes | Cook time: 30 minutes | Serves 4

Apple Cake:
2 tablespoons flaxseed meal plus 6 tablespoons water
1½ cups all-purpose flour
½ tablespoon baking powder
½ teaspoon salt
3 cups apples
½ tablespoon

cinnamon powder
¾ cup beet sugar
½ cup butter, melted
2 tablespoons orange juice
1 teaspoon vanilla extract
Cooking spray
1 cup water

Cinnamon Glaze:
1 cup beet powdered sugar
½ teaspoon

cinnamon powder
1 tablespoon coconut milk

1. In a bowl, mix the flaxseed meal with the water and set aside. Allow to sit for 15 minutes to thicken.
2. In a separate bowl, combine the flour, baking powder, and salt.
3. In a third bowl, mix the apples, cinnamon, and beet sugar.
4. When the flax egg is ready, whisk in the butter, orange juice, and vanilla. Stir together all three ingredients until well mixed.
5. Lightly spray a springform pan with cooking spray and pour the batter into the pan.
6. Add the water to the Instant Pot and insert a trivet. Place the springform pan on the trivet.
7. Lock the lid. Select the Manual mode and set the cooking time for 30 minutes at High Pressure.
8. When the timer beeps, perform a natural pressure release for 15 minutes, then release any remaining pressure. Carefully remove the lid.
9. Remove the cake pan, the trivet and discard the water. Leave the cake cool for 5 to 10 minutes in the pan.
10. Meanwhile, in a bowl, make the cinnamon glaze by whisking the sugar, cinnamon powder, and coconut milk until mixed.
11. Remove the cake from the pan and cut into slices. Serve drizzled with the cinnamon glaze.

Easy Hazelnut Flan

Prep time: 15 minutes | Cook time: 8 minutes | Serves 8

8 tablespoons hazelnut syrup
2 teaspoons vanilla extract
¼ teaspoon salt
½ cups granulated sugar

1 cup whipping cream
4 cups whole milk
½ cup caramel
2 cups water
3 egg yolks
5 eggs

1. Whisk together eggs, egg yolks, salt and sugar in a bowl.
2. Boil milk and add gradually to the egg mixture.
3. Add vanilla extract, whipping cream and hazelnut syrup to this mixture.
4. Put the caramel in the custard cups and add the hazelnut mixture in them.
5. Arrange the trivet in the Instant Pot and add water.
6. Put the custard cups on the trivet and lock the lid.
7. Set the Instant Pot to Manual mode and set cooking time for 8 minutes at High Pressure.
8. When timer beeps, release the pressure naturally for 5 minutes, then release any remaining pressure.
9. Open the lid and serve after refrigerating for 3 hours.

Caramel Peanut Butter Custard

Prep time: 15 minutes | Cook time: 10 minutes | Serves 10

1 cup caramel
4 whole eggs
4 egg yolks
¼ teaspoon salt
2 teaspoons vanilla extract
8 tablespoons

peanut butter
½ cup granulated sugar
1 cup whipping cream
4 cups whole milk
2 cups water

1. Take a bowl and whisk together egg yolks, eggs, salt and sugar. Then boil milk and add gradually to the egg mixture.
2. Add vanilla extract, peanut butter and whipping cream to the mixture.

3. Put the caramel in the custard cups and add the peanut butter mixture in them.
4. Arrange the trivet in the Instant Pot, add water put the custard cups on the trivet and lock the lid.
5. Set to Manual mode and set cooking time for 10 minutes at High Pressure.
6. When timer beeps, release the pressure naturally for 5 minutes, then release any remaining pressure. Open the lid.
7. Serve after refrigerating for 3 hours.

Beer Poached Pears

Prep time: 5 minutes | Cook time: 10 minutes | Serves 2

3 peeled (stem on) firm pears
1½ cups (1 bottle) stout beer
½ cup packed brown

sugar
1 vanilla bean, split lengthwise and seeds scraped

1. Slice a thin layer from the bottom of each pear so they can stand upright. Use a melon baller to scoop out the seeds and core from the bottom.
2. Stir together the beer, brown sugar, and vanilla bean and seeds in the Instant Pot until combined. Place the pears upright in the pot.
3. Lock the lid. Select the Manual mode and set the cooking time for 9 minutes at High Pressure.
4. When the timer beeps, perform a quick pressure release. Carefully remove the lid.
5. Using tongs, carefully remove the pears by their stems and transfer to a plate and set aside.
6. Set the Instant Pot to Sauté and simmer until the liquid in the Instant Pot is reduced by half.
7. Strain the liquid into a bowl through a fine-mesh sieve, then pour over the pears.
8. Serve at room temperature or chilled.

Pumpkin Pudding

Prep time: 5 minutes | Cook time: 20 minutes | Serves 4

15 ounces (425 g) pumpkin purée
2 medium eggs, whisked
½ cup heavy
whipping cream
1 teaspoon pumpkin pie spice
1 teaspoon vanilla
¾ cup Erythritol

1. Whisk together all the ingredients in a large bowl.
2. Pour 1½ cups of water into the Instant Pot and put a trivet in the pot.
3. Grease a baking pan. Pour the mixture into it.
4. Cover the pan with foil and put the pan with the pumpkin mixture on the trivet.
5. Lock the lid and set the cooking time for 20 minutes at High Pressure.
6. When timer beeps, release the pressure naturally, then release any remaining pressure. Remove the lid.
7. Let cool and slice to serve.

Corn and Chile Pudding

Prep time: 5 minutes | Cook time: 25 minutes | Serves 8

2 tablespoons vegetable oil
1 (8-ounce / 227-g) package corn bread mix
1 (14-ounce / 397-g) can creamed corn
1 (4.5-ounce / 128-g) can chopped mild green chiles
½ cup whole milk
2 large eggs, lightly beaten
¼ cup water

1. Grease a round springform pan with vegetable oil. Set aside.
2. In a large bowl, combine the corn bread mix, creamed corn, chiles, milk, eggs, and water. Mix well. Transfer the corn mixture to the pan; cover with foil.
3. Pour 2 cups water into the Instant Pot. Put a trivet in the pot. Put the pan on the trivet.
4. Lock the lid. Select Manual mode and set the timer for 25 minutes at High Pressure.
5. When timer beeps, use a natural pressure release for 15 minutes, then

release any remaining pressure. Open the lid.
6. Let the pudding cool to room temperature, and then run a knife along the edges to separate the pudding from the sides of the pan.
7. Carefully unclasp the springform ring and remove it. Serve immediately.

Apple Pie

Prep time: 20 minutes | Cook time: 30 minutes | Serves 8

2 apples, chopped
Juice of 1 lemon
3 tablespoons sugar
1 teaspoon vanilla extract
1 teaspoon
cornstarch
1 (2-crust) box refrigerated pie crusts
1 cup water

1. In a mixing bowl, combine the apples, lemon juice, sugar, and vanilla. Allow the mixture to stand for 10 minutes, then drain and reserve 1 tablespoon of the liquid.
2. In another bowl, whisk the cornstarch into the reserved liquid and mix with the apple mixture.
3. Put the pie crusts on a lightly floured surface and cut into 8 circles. Spoon a tablespoon of apple mixture in the center of the circle. Brush the edges with some water and fold the dough over the filling.
4. Press the edges with a fork to seal. Cut 3 small slits on top of each pie and grease with cooking spray.
5. Arrange the cakes in a single layer in a greased baking pan. Pour the water into the Instant Pot. Fit in a trivet and place the pan on top.
6. Seal the lid, select Manual mode and set the cooking time for 30 minutes on High Pressure.
7. When timer beeps, perform a natural pressure release for 10 minutes, then release the remaining pressure, and unlock the lid.
8. Serve immediately.

Apple and Pear Clafoutis

Prep time: 10 minutes | Cook time: 20 minutes | Serves 8

2 eggs
1 cup apples, chopped
1 cup pears, chopped
¾ cup sugar
2 cups all-purpose flour
1 cup milk
1 tablespoon vanilla extract
2 tablespoons powdered sugar
2 cups water
Butter, for greasing

1. Grease a baking pan with butter. Mix the eggs, vanilla, and sugar in a bowl. Add milk, and flour gradually and pour in the pan.
2. Top with chopped fruits and cover tightly with foil. Arrange the trivet in the Instant Pot and add water. Put the pan on the trivet and cover the pot.
3. Select Manual mode on the Instant Pot. Set the timer for 20 minutes on High Pressure.
4. When timer beeps, use a quick pressure release. Open and serve.

Coconut Pineapple Pudding

Prep time: 10 minutes | Cook time: 5 minutes | Serves 4

1 tablespoon coconut oil
1½ cups water
1 cup whole rice
14 ounces (397 g) coconut milk
2 tablespoons flax meal mixed with 3
tablespoons water
Stevia, to taste
½ teaspoon vanilla extract
8 ounces (227 g) canned pineapple, chopped

1. In the Instant Pot, mix the rice, oil, and water.
2. Set the pot to Manual mode. Cover and set the cooking time for 3 minutes on Low Pressure.
3. When timer beeps, quick release the pressure. Open the lid.
4. Add stevia, milk, vanilla, flax meal, and pineapple. Stir and cover. Set cooking time for 2 minutes on Low Pressure.
5. When timer beeps, quick release the pressure.
6. Open the lid and serve.

Hearty Giant Chocolate Cookies

Prep time: 5 minutes | Cook time: 6 minutes | Serves 8

2 cups blanched almond flour
3 tablespoons arrowroot starch
1 teaspoon baking soda
¼ teaspoon sea salt
4 tablespoons melted coconut oil
2 tablespoons pure maple syrup
1 teaspoon pure vanilla extract
⅓ cup chopped dairy-free dark chocolate
1 cup water

1. In a medium bowl, whisk together the almond flour, arrowroot, baking soda, and salt.
2. Make a well in the middle of the dry ingredients. Pour the coconut oil, maple syrup, and vanilla into the well, and whisk to combine.
3. Stir in the dark chocolate. The mixture may be a little crumbly but should hold together when pressed.
4. Cut out a piece of parchment paper to fit the bottom of a springform pan. Press the dough firmly on top of the parchment. Cover the pan with foil.
5. Fit the Instant Pot with a trivet and add the water. Place the foil-covered springform pan onto the trivet.
6. Lock the lid. Select Manual mode and set the cook time for 6 minutes on High Pressure.
7. Once the cook time is complete, allow the pressure to release naturally for 6 minutes, then quick release any remaining pressure.
8. Preheat the oven broiler.
9. Carefully remove the lid and take the pan out of the Instant Pot. Remove the sides of the springform pan.
10. Transfer the cookie under the broiler for 1 minute, or just until golden on top. Let the cookie cool for 10 minutes, then cut into 8 wedges and serve.

Blue and Black Berries Cobbler

Prep time: 15 minutes | Cook time: 15 minutes | Serves 6

1¾ cups water, divided
1 cup all-purpose flour
1½ cups sugar, divided
1 teaspoon baking powder
¼ teaspoon salt
¼ teaspoon ground cinnamon
¼ teaspoon ground nutmeg

2 eggs, lightly beaten
2 tablespoons whole milk
2 tablespoons oil
2 cups fresh blackberries
2 cups fresh blueberries
1 teaspoon grated orange zest
Whipped cream, for serving

1. Add 1 cup of water in the pot and put in a trivet.
2. In a bowl, combine flour, ¾ cup sugar, baking powder, salt, cinnamon, and nutmeg.
3. In another bowl, combine the eggs, milk, and oil. Stir into dry ingredients just until moistened. Pour batter in a greased baking dish.
4. In a pan, combine the berries, remaining water, orange zest, and remaining sugar and bring to a boil. Immediately pour over batter.
5. Cover the baking pan with foil and put it on the trivet. Cover the pot.
6. Set to Manual mode and set cooking time for 15 minutes on High Pressure.
7. When timer beeps, use a quick pressure release. Open the lid.
8. Cool for 30 minutes and serve with whipped cream.

Black Bean and Oat Brownies

Prep time: 5 minutes | Cook time: 25 minutes | Serves 4

1½ cups canned black beans, drained
½ cup steel-cut oats
½ teaspoon salt
3 tablespoons unsweetened cocoa powder
½ cup maple syrup

¼ cup coconut oil
¾ teaspoon baking powder
½ cup chocolate chips
Cooking spray
1½ cups water

1. Pulse the black beans, oats, salt, cocoa powder, maple syrup, coconut oil, and baking powder in a food processor until very smooth.
2. Pour the batter into a medium bowl and fold in the chocolate chips.
3. Spray a 7-inch springform pan with cooking spray and pour in the batter. Cover the pan with aluminum foil.
4. Pour the water into the Instant Pot and insert a trivet. Place the pan on the trivet.
5. Lock the lid. Select the Manual mode and set the cooking time for 25 minutes at High Pressure.
6. When the timer beeps, perform a natural pressure release for 10 minutes, then release any remaining pressure. Carefully remove the lid.
7. Let cool for 5 minutes, then transfer to the fridge to chill for 1 to 2 hours.
8. Cut the brownies into squares and serve.

Vanilla Rice Pudding with Cherries

Prep time: 5 minutes | Cook time: 30 minutes | Serves 6

1 cup short-grain brown rice
1¾ cups coconut milk, plus more as needed
1½ cups water
4 tablespoons unrefined sugar or pure maple syrup,

plus more as needed
1 teaspoon vanilla extract
Salt, to taste
¼ cup dried cherries or ½ cup fresh or frozen pitted cherries

1. Combine the rice, milk, water, sugar, vanilla, and salt in the Instant Pot.
2. Lock the lid. Select the Manual mode and set the cooking time for 30 minutes at High Pressure.
3. When the timer beeps, perform a natural pressure release for 20 minutes, then release any remaining pressure. Carefully remove the lid.
4. Stir in the cherries and rest the lid back on (no need to lock it), and let sit for about 10 minutes.
5. Serve with more milk or sugar, as needed.

Cardamom Rice Pudding with Pistachios

Prep time: 15 minutes | Cook time: 10 minutes | Makes 4 cups

½ cup long-grain basmati rice
1½ cups water
1 (13.5-ounce / 383-g) can coconut milk
1 small (5¼-ounce / 149-g) can coconut cream
½ cup brown rice
syrup or agave nectar
½ teaspoon ground cardamom
¼ teaspoon fine sea salt
¼ cup currants
¼ cup chopped pistachios

1. Combine the rice and water in the Instant Pot. Secure the lid. Select Manual mode and set the cooking time for 5 minutes at High Pressure.
2. Meanwhile, in a blender, combine the coconut milk, coconut cream, brown rice syrup, cardamom, and salt. Blend at medium speed for about 30 seconds, until smooth. Set aside.
3. When timer beeps, let the pressure release naturally for 10 minutes, then release any remaining pressure. Open the pot and use a whisk to break up the cooked rice. Whisking constantly, pour the coconut milk mixture in a thin stream into the rice.
4. Select the Sauté setting. Cook the pudding for about 5 minutes, whisking constantly, until it is thickened and bubbling.
5. Sit the pudding until set. Remove the pudding from the pot. Stir in the currants.
6. Pour the pudding into a glass or ceramic dish or into individual serving bowls. Cover and refrigerate the pudding for at least 4 hours.
7. Sprinkle the pudding with chopped pistachios. Serve chilled.

Chocolate Pudding with Raspberry Sauce

Prep time: 20 minutes | Cook time: 15 minutes | Serves 4

Chocolate Pudding:
5 tablespoons flaxseed meal plus 1 cup water
6 tablespoons unsweetened cocoa powder
1/3 cup cornstarch
Salt, to taste
4½ cups almond milk
4 ounces (113 g) butter
2 teaspoons vanilla extract

Raspberry Sauce:
1 pound (454 g) fresh raspberries
2 tablespoons freshly squeezed
lemon juice
¼ cup beet sugar
1 tablespoon water

1. In a bowl, mix the flaxseed meal with the water until evenly combined and allow to sit for 15 minutes to thicken.
2. In a separate bowl, combine the cocoa powder, cornstarch, and salt.
3. Press the Sauté button on the Instant Pot and pour in the almond milk. Let simmer for a few seconds, but not to boil.
4. Fetch a tablespoon of the milk into the cocoa powder mixture and stir. Pour the mix into the milk and stir in the flaxseed mixture (flax egg), butter, and vanilla extract. Allow to simmer for 6 minutes, stirring frequently, and spoon into dessert bowls. Turn the pot off and wash the Instant Pot clean.
5. Select the Sauté mode and add the raspberries, lemon juice, sugar, and water. Allow to simmer for 6 minutes.
6. Drain the sauce through a strainer into a bowl. Allow to cool for 5 minutes and spoon the raspberry sauce over the chocolate pudding. Serve immediately.

Crunchy Mini Cinnamon Monkey Breads

Prep time: 10 minutes | Cook time: 20 minutes | Serves 4

1 (1-pound / 454-g) can buttermilk biscuits, cut into 6 pieces
1/3 cup granulated sugar
Salt, to taste
1/2 cup crushed cinnamon crunch cereal, divided, plus more for sprinkling
1/4 cup melted unsalted butter
1 cup water
1 cup maple syrup
2 tablespoons almond milk

1. In a bowl, combine the sugar, salt and half of the crushed cereal. Add the cut biscuit pieces to the bowl. Toss to evenly coat.
2. Place 2 tablespoons of the coated biscuits, along with a spoonful of the cereal mixture, in each well of a silicone egg bite mold. Top each pile of coated dough with melted butter.
3. Pour the water into the Instant Pot and insert a trivet. Place the filled mold on top of the trivet.
4. Secure the lid. Press the Manual button and set cooking time for 20 minutes on High Pressure.
5. When timer beeps, quick release the pressure. Remove the lid and take out the silicone mold. Let the monkey breads cool in the mold.
6. Meanwhile, in a medium bowl, mix the milk and maple syrup until smooth.
7. Remove the monkey breads from the mold. Drizzle each monkey bread with milk mixture. Top with a sprinkle of crushed cereal.

Chocolate Cake with Ganache

Prep time: 10 minutes | Cook time: 30 minutes | Serves 10

1 cup water
1 cup whole wheat pastry flour
1/2 cup unsweetened cocoa powder
1/2 cup raw turbinado sugar
1 teaspoon baking soda
1/2 teaspoon baking powder
1/2 teaspoon instant coffee
1/4 teaspoon salt
3/4 cup unsweetened almond milk
1 teaspoon pure vanilla extract
1 tablespoon apple cider vinegar
1/4 cup melted coconut oil
1/4 cup chopped, toasted hazelnuts, for garnish
1 cup fresh raspberries, for garnish
Fresh mint leaves, for garnish
For the Ganache:
3/4 cup chopped dairy-free dark chocolate
1/4 canned coconut milk

1. Fit the Instant Pot with a trivet and add the water. Coat a springform pan with cooking spray.
2. In a medium bowl, whisk together the flour, cocoa powder, sugar, baking soda, baking powder, instant coffee, and salt.
3. In another medium bowl, whisk together the almond milk, vanilla, vinegar, and oil. Stir the wet mixture into the dry mixture to form a batter.
4. Transfer the batter into the prepared pan and smooth into an even layer with the back of a spoon.
5. Cover the pan with foil and place on the trivet. Lock the lid. Select Manual mode and set the cook time for 30 minutes on High Pressure.
6. Once the cook time is complete, allow the pressure to release naturally for 10 minutes, then quick release any remaining pressure.
7. Carefully remove the lid and the cake pan. Remove the foil and let the cake cool on a cooling rack.
8. Meanwhile, make the ganache: Place the chocolate in a small glass bowl. Heat the coconut milk in a small saucepan, until it just begins to simmer.
9. Carefully pour the coconut milk over the chocolate and stir until all the chocolate has melted and the mixture is smooth.
10. Pour the ganache over the top of the cooled cake, letting it drip down the sides. Serve with the hazelnuts, berries, and mint on top.

Carrot Raisin Halwa

Prep time: 10 minutes | Cook time: 14 minutes | Serves 6

2 tablespoons coconut oil
2 tablespoons raw cashews
2 tablespoons raisins
2 cups shredded carrots
1 cup almond milk

¼ cup sugar
2 tablespoons ground cashews
¼ teaspoon ground cardamom
Chopped pistachios, for garnish

1. Set the Instant Pot to Sauté and melt the coconut oil until it shimmers.
2. Add the cashews and raisins and cook them until the cashews are golden brown, about 4 minutes.
3. Add the carrots, milk, sugar, and ground cashews, and stir to incorporate.
4. Lock the lid. Select the Manual mode and set the cooking time for 10 minutes at High Pressure.
5. When the timer beeps, perform a natural pressure release for 10 minutes, then release any remaining pressure. Carefully remove the lid.
6. Stir well, mashing the carrots together a bit. Set the Instant Pot to Sauté again and cook, stirring, for about 2 to 3 minutes, until thickened.
7. Turn off the Instant Pot. Stir in the cardamom and let the mixture sit for 10 minutes to thicken up.
8. Garnish with the pistachios and serve.

Cinnamon Balls

Prep time: 15 minutes | Cook time: 20 minutes | Serves 8

¼ cup whole-wheat flour
½ cup all-purpose flour
½ teaspoon baking powder
3 tablespoons sugar, divided

¼ teaspoon plus ½ tablespoon cinnamon
¼ teaspoon sea salt
2 tablespoons cold butter, cubed
$1/_3$ cup almond milk
1 cup water

1. Mix the whole-wheat flour, all-purpose flour, baking powder, 1 tablespoon of sugar, ¼ teaspoon of cinnamon, and salt in a medium bowl.
2. Add the butter and use a pastry cutter to cut into butter, breaking it into little pieces until resembling cornmeal. Pour in the milk and mix until the dough forms into a ball.
3. Knead the dough on a flat surface. Divide the dough into 8 pieces and roll each piece into a ball. Put the balls in a greased baking pan with space in between each ball and oil the balls.
4. Pour the water into the Instant Pot. Put in a trivet and place the pan on top.
5. Seal the lid, select Manual mode and set the time for 20 minutes on High Pressure.
6. When timer beeps, perform a natural pressure release for 5 minutes, then release any remaining pressure.
7. In a mixing bowl, combine the remaining sugar and cinnamon. Toss the dough balls in the cinnamon and sugar mixture to serve.

Simple Peppermint Hot Chocolate

Prep time: 2 minutes | Cook time: 9 minutes | Serves 4

4 cups coconut milk
¼ cup cocoa powder
¾ teaspoon peppermint extract

6 tablespoons turbinado sugar
¼ teaspoon fine sea salt

1. Combine the milk, cocoa powder, peppermint extract, sugar, and salt in the Instant Pot and whisk to mix well.
2. Select the Sauté setting and set the cooking time for 9 minutes. Cover the pot.
3. After 4 minutes, open the pot, whisk the mixture for 1 minute, then cover and keep cooking.
4. When the timer goes off, give the hot chocolate a final whisk.
5. Ladle the hot chocolate into mugs and serve.

Citrus Apple Crisps with Oat Topping

Prep time: 10 minutes | Cook time: 9 minutes | Serves 4

1 cup water

For the Filling:

3½ cups peeled and diced apples (1-inch chunks)
1 tablespoon fresh lemon juice
1 tablespoon fresh

orange juice
½ teaspoon ground cinnamon
2 teaspoons coconut sugar

For the Topping:

½ cup old-fashioned rolled oats
½ cup almond flour
3 tablespoons almond butter

1 tablespoon pure maple syrup
¼ cup coconut sugar
¼ teaspoon sea salt

1. To make the filling: In a medium bowl, toss together all the ingredients. Portion the filling into 4 ramekins, filling all the way to the top. Cover the ramekins with foil.
2. Fit the Instant Pot with a trivet and add the water. Place the ramekins on the trivet.
3. Lock the lid. Select Manual mode and set the cook time for 9 minutes on High Pressure.
4. Once the cook time is complete, quick release the pressure.
5. Meanwhile, make the topping: Place all the ingredients for the topping in the food processor, and pulse to combine. Preheat the oven to 500°F (260°C).
6. Carefully remove the lid and the ramekins. Remove the foil.
7. Spoon the topping evenly over the apple mixture. Transfer the ramekins to the oven, and bake until the topping is golden brown, about 4 minutes.
8. Serve warm.

Fresh Lemon Mousse

Prep time: 5 minutes | Cook time: 10 minutes | Serves 4

2 tablespoons butter, room temperature
$1/_3$ cup beet sugar
½ cup plus ¼ cup plus ¼ cup plus ¼ cup coconut cream, whipped

2 lemons, zested and juiced
Pinch of salt
1 cup water
Extra lemon zest, for garnish

1. Whisk the butter with the beet sugar with a hand mixer in a bowl. Beat in ½ cup of coconut cream, lemon zest and juice, and salt. Cover the bowl with aluminum foil.
2. Pour the water into the Instant Pot and insert a trivet. Put the bowl on the trivet.
3. Secure the lid. Select the Manual mode and set the cooking time for 10 minutes at High Pressure.
4. Once cooking is complete, do a natural pressure release for 10 minutes, then release any remaining pressure. Carefully open the lid.
5. Take out the bowl and remove the foil. The mixture will be curdy and clumpy, so whisk until smooth, and strain through a fine mesh into a bowl.
6. Cover the mixture itself with plastic wrap, making sure to press onto the curd. Place in the refrigerator for 2 hours.
7. When ready, remove the wrap and whisk the cream until stiff peak forms. Gently fold in the second portion (¼ cup) of coconut cream, then the third portion, and the last portion. Spoon the mousse into serving bowls.
8. Garnish with the extra lemon zest and serve.

Rhubarb and Strawberry Compote

Prep time: 10 minutes | Cook time: 5 minutes | Makes 4 cups

1 pound (454 g) rhubarb (about 4 large stalks), trimmed and cut into 1-inch pieces
1 pound (454 g) strawberries, hulled and quartered lengthwise
½ cup turbinado sugar
½ teaspoon ground cardamom

1. Combine the rhubarb, strawberries, sugar, and cardamom in the Instant Pot and stir well, making sure to coat the rhubarb and strawberries evenly with the sugar. Let the mixture sit for 15 minutes. Stir.
2. Secure the lid. Select Manual mode and set the cooking time for 5 minutes at Low Pressure.
3. When timer beeps, let the pressure release naturally for about 15 minutes, then release any remaining pressure. Open the pot and stir the compote to break down the rhubarb.
4. Serve the compote warm.

Creamy Lemon Custard Pie

Prep time: 10 minutes | Cook time: 15 minutes | Serves 6

½ cup coconut oil, melted, plus more for greasing the pan
¾ cup coconut flour
½ cup plus 2 tablespoons unrefined sugar, divided
1 (13.5-ounce / 383-g) can full-fat coconut milk
½ cup freshly squeezed lemon juice (from 4 lemons)
¼ cup cornstarch or arrowroot powder
2 cups water

1.
2. Grease a 6-inch springform pan or pie dish with melted coconut oil.
3. Stir together ½ cup of coconut oil, coconut flour, and 2 tablespoons of sugar in a small bowl. Press the crust into the greased pan.
4. In a medium bowl, whisk together the coconut milk, lemon juice, cornstarch, and remaining ½ cup of sugar until the starch is dissolved. Pour this mixture over the crust. Cover the pan with aluminum foil.
5. Pour the water into the Instant Pot and insert a trivet. Using a foil sling or silicone helper handles, lower the pan onto the trivet.
6. Lock the lid. Select the Manual mode and set the cooking time for 15 minutes at High Pressure.
7. When the timer beeps, perform a quick pressure release. Carefully remove the lid.
8. Serve at room temperature or chilled.

Fast Pear and Cranberry Crisps

Prep time: 10 minutes | Cook time: 5 minutes | Serves 6

3 large pears, peeled, cored and diced
1 cup fresh cranberries
1 tablespoon granulated sugar
2 teaspoons ground cinnamon
½ teaspoon ground nutmeg
½ cup water
1 tablespoon pure maple syrup
6 tablespoons almond butter
1 cup old-fashioned rolled oats
⅓ cup dark brown sugar
¼ cup all-purpose flour
½ teaspoon sea salt
½ cup pecans, toasted

1. In the Instant Pot, combine the pears and cranberries and sprinkle with the granulated sugar. Let sit for a few minutes, then sprinkle with the cinnamon and nutmeg. Pour the water and maple syrup on top.
2. In a medium bowl, stir together the almond butter, oats, brown sugar, flour and salt.
3. Spoon the mixture on the fruit in the Instant Pot.
4. Secure the lid. Select Manual mode, and set cooking time for 5 minutes on High Pressure.
5. When timer beeps, use a quick pressure release. Open the lid.
6. Spoon into bowls. Top with pecans and serve.

Fudgy Chocolate Brownies

Prep time: 10 minutes | Cook time: 5 minutes | Makes 3 brownies

2 cups water
3 ounces (85 g) dairy-free dark chocolate
1 tablespoon coconut oil
½ cup applesauce
2 tablespoons unrefined sugar
⅓ cup all-purpose flour
½ teaspoon baking powder
Salt, to taste

1. Pour the water into the Instant Pot and insert a trivet. Set the Instant Pot to Sauté.
2. Stir together the chocolate and coconut oil in a large bowl. Place the bowl on the trivet. Stir occasionally until the chocolate is melted, then turn off the Instant Pot.
3. Stir the applesauce and sugar into the chocolate mixture. Add the flour, baking powder, and salt and stir just until combined. Pour the batter into 3 ramekins. Cover each ramekin with aluminum foil. Using a foil sling or silicone helper handles, lower the ramekins onto the trivet.
4. Lock the lid. Select the Manual mode and set the cooking time for 5 minutes at High Pressure.
5. When the timer beeps, perform a quick pressure release. Carefully remove the lid.
6. Cool for 5 to 10 minutes before serving.

Hearty Apricot Cobbler

Prep time: 15 minutes | Cook time: 25 minutes | Serves 4

4 cups sliced apricots
½ cup plus ¼ cup brown sugar, divided
2 tablespoons plus ¾ cup plain flour, divided
½ teaspoon cinnamon powder
¼ teaspoon nutmeg powder
1½ teaspoons salt, divided
1 teaspoon vanilla extract
¼ cup water
½ teaspoon baking powder
½ teaspoon baking soda
3 tablespoons butter, melted
1 cup water

1. In a heatproof bowl, mix the apricots, ½ cup of brown sugar, 2 tablespoons of flour, cinnamon, nutmeg, ½ teaspoon of salt, vanilla, and water; set aside.
2. In another bowl, mix the remaining flour, salt and brown sugar, baking powder and soda, and butter. Spoon mixture over apricot mixture and spread to cover.
3. Pour the water in the pot, fit in a trivet and place heatproof bowl on top.
4. Seal the lid, select Manual mode, and set cooking time for 25 minutes on High Pressure.
5. When timer beeps, allow a natural release for 10 minutes, then release any remaining pressure. Open the lid.
6. Remove bowl and serve.

Raspberry and Oat Crumble

Prep time: 10 minutes | Cook time: 20 minutes | Serves 4

2 tablespoons arrowroot starch
½ cup plus 1 tablespoon water, divided
1 teaspoon lemon juice
5 tablespoons sugar, divided
2 cups raspberries
½ cup flour
¼ cup brown sugar
½ cup rolled oats
1 teaspoon cinnamon powder
¼ cup cold butter, cut into pieces

1. In a small bowl, combine the arrowroot starch, lemon juice, 1 tablespoon of water, and 3 tablespoons of sugar. Mix in the raspberries, and toss well. Pour the mixture in a baking pan.
2. In a separate bowl, mix the flour, brown sugar, oats, cinnamon, butter, and remaining sugar, and form crumble. Spread the crumble evenly on the raspberries.
3. Put a trivet in the pot. Cover the pan with foil and pour half cup of water into the pot. Put the pan on the trivet.
4. Seal the lid, select Manual mode, and set cooking time for 20 minutes on High Pressure.
5. When timer beeps, do a quick pressure release. Open the lid.
6. Remove foil and serve.

White Chocolate and Blackberry Muffins

Prep time: 20 minutes | Cook time: 8 minutes | Serves 6

1 tablespoon flaxseed meal plus 3 tablespoons water
2⅓ cups all-purpose flour
1½ cup beet sugar
1 tablespoon baking soda
¾ cup butter, melted
2 teaspoons vanilla extract
1 cup almond milk
1 cup blackberries
¾ white chocolate chips, divided
2 cups water

1. In a small bowl, whisk the flaxseed meal with water until combined. Allow to sit for 15 minutes to thicken.
2. In a larger bowl, combine the flour, beet sugar, and baking soda. Stir in the melted butter, and then beat in the flax egg, vanilla extract, and almond milk until well incorporated. Fold in the blackberries and half of the white chocolate chips.
3. Spoon the mixture into a 12-holed silicon egg bites mold and scatter the remaining white chocolate chips on top.
4. Pour the water into the Instant Pot and insert a trivet. Place the egg bites mold on the trivet. Cover with aluminum foil.
5. Lock the lid. Select the Manual mode and set the cooking time for 8 minutes at High Pressure.
6. When the timer beeps, perform a natural pressure release for 10 minutes, then release any remaining pressure. Carefully remove the lid.
7. Transfer to a wire rack to cool completely before serving.

Lemon Blueberry Cheesecake

Prep time: 10 minutes | Cook time: 6 minutes | Serves 6

1 tablespoon coconut oil, melted, for greasing the pan
1¼ cups soft pitted Medjool dates, divided
1 cup gluten-free rolled oats
2 cups cashews
1 cup fresh blueberries
3 tablespoons freshly squeezed lemon juice or lime juice
1¾ cups water
Salt, to taste

1. Grease a 6-inch springform pan or pie dish with melted coconut oil.
2. In a food processor, combine 1 cup of dates and the oats. Processor until they form a sticky mixture. Press this mixture into the prepared pan.
3. In a blender, combine the remaining ¼ cup of dates, cashews, blueberries, lemon juice, ¾ cup of water, and a pinch of salt. Blend on high speed for about 1 minute, until smooth and creamy, stopping a couple of times to scrape down the sides. Pour this mixture over the crust. Cover the pan with aluminum foil.
4. Pour the remaining 1 cup of water into the Instant Pot and insert a trivet. Using a foil sling or silicone helper handles, lower the pan onto the trivet.
5. Lock the lid. Select the Manual mode and set the cooking time for 6 minutes at High Pressure.
6. When the timer beeps, perform a natural pressure release for 10 minutes, then release any remaining pressure. Carefully remove the lid.
7. Cool for 5 to 10 minutes before slicing and serving.

Simple Lemon Squares

Prep time: 20 minutes | Cook time: 30 minutes | Serves 6

Lemon Squares:
2 tablespoons flaxseed meal plus 6 tablespoons water
1¼ cup almond flour
3 tablespoons coconut flour
1 cup beet sugar

1 large lemon, zested and juiced
¼ cup butter, melted
2 cups almond milk
Cooking spray
1 cup water

Topping:
5 tablespoons beet sugar

1 lemon, zested and juiced

1. In a bowl, mix the flaxseed meal with water and allow to sit for 15 minutes to thicken.
2. In a separate bowl, combine the almond flour, coconut flour, beet sugar, and lemon zest until mixed. Whisk in lemon juice, butter, milk, and the flax egg.
3. Grease a springform pan lightly with cooking spray and pour the batter into the pan.
4. Pour the water into the Instant Pot and insert a trivet. Place the pan on the trivet.
5. Lock the lid. Select the Manual mode and set the cooking time for 20 minutes at High Pressure.
6. When the timer beeps, perform a natural pressure release for 10 minutes, then release any remaining pressure. Carefully remove the lid.
7. Remove the pan and pierce the top of the cake with a skewer.
8. Make the topping by whisking together the beet sugar, lemon juice, and zest. Sprinkle the mixture on top of the cake and cut into squares to serve.

Vanilla Plum Dumplings

Prep time: 10 minutes | Cook time: 10 minutes | Serves 6

1 can crescent rolls
1½ cup sliced plums
4 tablespoons butter
½ cup coconut sugar, plus additional for garnishing
½ teaspoon vanilla

extract
1 teaspoon cinnamon powder
A pinch nutmeg powder
¾ cup apple cider juice

1. Press the Sauté button to heat the Instant Pot.
2. Remove the crescent rolls from the can and roll them out flat on a lightly floured surface. Fold each plum slice in each crescent roll.
3. Add the butter to the pot and turn off the Instant Pot. Stir in the coconut sugar, vanilla extract, cinnamon powder, and nutmeg.
4. Place the stuffed pastry in the sugar sauce, side by side, and drizzle the apple cider juice on top.
5. Lock the lid. Select the Manual mode and set the cooking time for 10 minutes at High Pressure.
6. When the timer beeps, perform a natural pressure release for 10 minutes, then release any remaining pressure. Carefully remove the lid.
7. Let cool for 5 minutes and then spoon the dessert with sauce into serving bowls. Serve sprinkled with additional coconut sugar.

Pumpkin Pie Cups

Prep time: 5 minutes | Cook time: 6 minutes | Serves 4

1 cup canned pumpkin purée
1 cup almond milk
6 tablespoons unrefined sugar or pure maple syrup, plus more for

sprinkling
¼ cup spelt flour or all-purpose flour
½ teaspoon pumpkin pie spice
Salt, to taste
2 cups water

1. Stir together the pumpkin purée, milk, 6 tablespoons of sugar, flour, pumpkin pie spice, and salt in a medium bowl until well incorporated.
2. Pour the mixture into 4 ramekins and top with a sprinkle of sugar.
3. Pour the water into the Instant Pot and insert a trivet. Place the ramekins onto the trivet, stacking them if needed (3 on the bottom, 1 on top).
4. Lock the lid. Select the Manual mode and set the cooking time for 6 minutes at High Pressure.
5. When the timer beeps, perform a quick pressure release. Carefully remove the lid.
6. Allow to cool for 10 minutes before serving.

Yogurt Pudding with Macadamia

Prep time: 10 minutes | Cook time: 15 minutes | Serves 4

2 cups almond milk
1½ cups coconut yogurt
1 teaspoon cocoa powder

1 teaspoon cardamom powder
1 cup water
¼ cup macadamia nuts, chopped

1. Lightly grease 4 medium ramekins with cooking spray. Set aside.
2. In a bowl, combine the milk, yogurt, cocoa powder, and cardamom powder. Pour mixture into ramekins and cover with foil.
3. Pour the water into the pot, fit in a trivet, and place ramekins on top.
4. Seal the lid, select Manual mode and set cooking time for 15 minutes on High Pressure.

5. When timer beeps, perform a natural pressure release for 15 minutes, then release any remaining pressure.
6. Unlock the lid, remove ramekins, take off foil, and let cool slightly. Top with nuts and serve immediately.

Navy Bean Biscuits with Walnuts

Prep time: 10 minutes | Cook time: 12 minutes | Serves 8

6 ounces (170 g) navy beans, cooked
1 cup wheat flour
3 teaspoons brown sugar
2 tablespoons coconut oil
1 teaspoon vanilla extract

½ cup flax meal flour
¾ teaspoon salt
½ teaspoon ground cinnamon
¼ cup chopped walnuts
1 cup water

1. Mash the navy beans with a fork or blend them in a blender.
2. Transfer the beans to a mixing bowl, along with the wheat flour, vanilla extract, brown sugar, coconut oil, flax meal flour, salt, and ground cinnamon. Stir the mixture with a spoon until smooth.
3. Fold in the chopped walnuts and knead the dough.
4. Make the log from the dough and cut it into 8 even pieces.
5. Make the balls from the dough pieces.
6. Pour the water into the Instant Pot and insert a trivet. Line the trivet with parchment. Place dough balls on the trivet.
7. Secure the lid. Select the Manual mode and set the cooking time for 12 minutes at High Pressure.
8. Once cooking is complete, do a quick pressure release. Carefully open the lid.
9. Let cool to room temperature and refrigerate until chilled before serving.

Appendix 1:Measurement Conversion Chart

VOLUME EQUIVALENTS(DRY)

US STANDARD	METRIC (APPROXIMATE)
1/8 teaspoon	0.5 mL
1/4 teaspoon	1 mL
1/2 teaspoon	2 mL
3/4 teaspoon	4 mL
1 teaspoon	5 mL
1 tablespoon	15 mL
1/4 cup	59 mL
1/2 cup	118 mL
3/4 cup	177 mL
1 cup	235 mL
2 cups	475 mL
3 cups	700 mL
4 cups	1 L

VOLUME EQUIVALENTS(LIQUID)

US STANDARD	US STANDARD (OUNCES)	METRIC (APPROXIMATE)
2 tablespoons	1 fl.oz.	30 mL
1/4 cup	2 fl.oz.	60 mL
1/2 cup	4 fl.oz.	120 mL
1 cup	8 fl.oz.	240 mL
1 1/2 cup	12 fl.oz.	355 mL
2 cups or 1 pint	16 fl.oz.	475 mL
4 cups or 1 quart	32 fl.oz.	1 L
1 gallon	128 fl.oz.	4 L

TEMPERATURES EQUIVALENTS

FAHRENHEIT(F)	CELSIUS(C) (APPROXIMATE)
225 °F	107 °C
250 °F	120 °C
275 °F	135 °C
300 °F	150 °C
325 °F	160 °C
350 °F	180 °C
375 °F	190 °C
400 °F	205 °C
425 °F	220 °C
450 °F	235 °C
475 °F	245 °C
500 °F	260 °C

WEIGHT EQUIVALENTS

US STANDARD	METRIC (APPROXIMATE)
1 ounce	28 g
2 ounces	57 g
5 ounces	142 g
10 ounces	284 g
15 ounces	425 g
16 ounces (1 pound)	455 g
1.5 pounds	680 g
2 pounds	907 g

Appendix 2:Recipe Index

References

10 Tips: Healthy Eating for Vegetarians. (n.d.). Choose MyPlate. https://www.choosemyplate.gov/ten-tips-healthy-eating-for-vegetarians

Chidsey, K. (n.d.). Tried and True Instant Pot Recipes and Tips. A Mind "Full" Mom. https://amindfullmom.com/real-food-3/instant-pot/

Ciera, Lauren, & Melinda. (2020, September). 5 Best Instant Pots - Sept. 2020. BestReviews. https://bestreviews.com/best-instant-pots

Funk, J. O. (2013, September). The Veggie Table: 8 Sneaky Foods Vegetarians Should Avoid. Food Network. https://www.foodnetwork.com/healthyeats/2010/04/8-foods-vegetarians-should-avoid

Types of Vegetarianism. (n.d.). VEGETARIAN NATION. https://vegetarian-nation.com/resources/common-questions/types-levels-vegetarian/

Vegetarian Times Editors. (2007, June 15). 16 Reasons You Should Go Veg. Vegetarian Times. https://www.vegetariantimes.com/health-and-nutrition/why-go-veg-learn-about-becoming-a-vegetarian

Made in the USA
Middletown, DE
14 June 2023

32504765R00106